NEW BEING (1967), by Jose De Creeft (1884-1982), Spanish born American artist. The Wichita State University Endowment Association Art Collection, Edwin A. Ulrich Museum of Art.

CONTINENTAL, LATIN-AMERICAN AND FRANCOPHONE WOMEN WRITERS

Selected Papers from the Wichita State University Conference on Foreign Literature, 1984-1985

Edited by
Eunice Myers
Ginette Adamson

UNIVERSITY
PRESS OF
AMERICA

LANHAM • NEW YORK • LONDON

Copyright © 1987 by

University Press of America,® Inc.

4720 Boston Way
Lanham, MD 20706

3 Henrietta Street
London WC2E 8LU England

All rights reserved

Printed in the United States of America

British Cataloging in Publication Information Available

ISBN (Cloth): 0-8191-6290-6

All University Press of America books are produced on acid-free
paper which exceeds the minimum standards set by the National
Historical Publication and Records Commission.

TO THE MEMORY OF SIMONE DE BEAUVOIR, 1908-1986

CONTINENTAL, LATIN-AMERICAN AND FRANCOPHONE WOMEN WRITERS
Selected Papers from The Wichita State University
Conference on Foreign Literature, 1984-1985

EDITORS
Eunice Myers
Ginette Adamson

EDITORIAL ADVISORY BOARD

Carl Adamson, The Wichita State University (German)

Wilson Baldridge, The Wichita State University (French)

Claudine Fisher, Portland State University (French)

Elías Miguel Muñoz, The Wichita State University (Spanish)

Janet Pérez, Texas Tech University (Spanish)

Gisela Ritchie, The Wichita State University (German)

Michael Vincent, The Wichita State University (French)

ACKNOWLEDGEMENTS

We wish to express our appreciation to a number of people who made the conference and this publication possible. First of all to the participants, for sharing their abundant ideas with us, to our keynote speaker, Madeleine Monette and the Délégation du Québec who added to the international content of the conference. We also thank the Editorial Board.

Our gratitude goes also to our colleagues in the Department of Modern and Classical Languages and Literatures, especially Anthony Cárdenas, Christine Gaudry-Hudson and John Koppenhaver, who helped proofread these essays; to Deans Phillip Thomas and Martin Reif of the College of Liberal Arts and Sciences for their financial help and encouragement; to other Wichita State University faculty who contributed their time to the success of our conference. Special thanks go to Roberta Mildfelt and her team, whose efficiency in typing and helping us meet deadlines cannot be surpassed.

The photograph of <u>New Being</u>, by José de Creeft, was kindly provided by the Edwin A. Ulrich Museum of Art. The sculpture belongs to the museum's extensive collection of outdoor art at The Wichita State University.

The following contributors will retain copyright privileges: Roseanna Dufault, Harriet Margolis, Elias Miguel Muñoz, Amy Kaminsky, and Emelda Ramos.

The editors gratefully acknowledge permission from the following to quote from their works:

    Hélène Cixous
    Rosario Ferré
    Olga Savary
    Lucía Guerra

TABLE OF CONTENTS

Ginette Adamson
    Introduction xi

Sally Kitch
    French Feminist Theories and the Gender of the Text 1

Marie-France Hilgar
    Literary Currents in the Works of Juliette Adam 13

Claudine Fisher
    Hélène Cixous' Window of Daring Through
    Clarice Lispector's Voice 21

Janine Ricouart
    La violence dans la mère durassienne 29

Ruth Carver Capasso
    The Solitary Woman and Friendship in
    Madame de Lafayette's Zaide 39

Paul Benhamou
    Pauline Julien et Angèle Arsenault:
    Chansons de libération 45

Robert E. Ziegler
    The Suicide of "La Comédienne"
    in Rachilde's La Jongleuse 55

Roseanna Dufault
    Personal and Political Childhood in Québec:
    Analogies for Identity 63

Anne Duhamel Ketchum
    Defining an Ethics from a Later Short Story by Colette ... 71

Mary Greenwood-Johnson
    The "Different" Cinema of Marguerite Duras 79

Ida H. Washington
    Isak Dinesen and Dorothy Canfield:
    The Importance of a Helping Hand 87

Frank W. Young
    Elfriede Jelinek--Profile of an Austrian Feminist 97

Hanna Lewis
    The Woman's Novel Parodied: Fanny Lewald's Diogena 107

Harriet E. Margolis
    The Ideal Marriage:
    Woman as Other in Three Lewald Novels 119

Thomas C. Fox
    Sexist Literary History?
    The Case of Louise von François 129

Elías Miguel Muñoz
    La mujer y la historia en Más allá de las máscaras
    de Lucía Guerra 139

Amy Kaminsky
    Gender and Exile in Cristina Peri Rossi 149

Rodrigo Solera
    Tres escritoras de Costa Rica y su aporte a las
    letras nacionales 161

Emelda Ramos
    Hacia una narrativa femenina
    en la literatura dominicana 167

Suzanne Gross Reed
    Notes on Hans Christian Andersen Tales in Ana María
    Matute's Primera memoria 177

Carmen Vega Carney
    "Cuando las mujeres quieren a los hombres"
    Manifiesto textual de una generación 183

Joyce Carlson-Leavitt
    "Eroticism in Olga Savary's Repertorio Selvagem:
    The Struggle for Full Freedom 195

INTRODUCTION

Why a conference on Continental, Latin-American and Francophone women writers, and not just all women authors? First of all, other channels exist already for the others. If we were to include English for instance, the format of the conference would have gained in scope but not in depth. Secondly, on the practical side, this project emerged from a department of Foreign Languages and not of English. Many contributors, however, come from English departments and especially from Women's Studies because the nature of their orientation leads them to more interdisciplinary subjects. The Department of Modern and Classical Languages and Literatures is grateful to the contributors from these Departments and encourages others to join us in the future. The fourth annual conference will take place April 9-11, 1987. The present publication represents samples of the first two, held in 1984 and 1985.

The interdisciplinary orientation of our conference, as the reader will discover, is evidenced in the variety of articles published in this volume. What the reader will not experience is the stimulating discussions which took place at the end of each session, due greatly to the presence of an interdisciplinary audience. The diversity of the audience, as well as the variety of approaches taken in these papers, prove that this conference is unique and confirm its relevance. This collection of "selected papers" will show to what extent literature written by foreign women writers can provoke heated intellectual debate covering a wide range of subjects, from traditional literary themes to the most audacious textual approach. We hope that the excitement and enthusiasm we found in our audience will be shared by the readers of this volume.

The literary works studied herein were written by women from diverse cultural heritages: some differing dramatically. Yet, they pursue a common goal: an expression of the self through the power of language. For example Hélène Cixous, a product of Algerian and French cultures, finds in the Brazilian Clarice Lispector's writing the precise image she seeks.

The contributors to this publication are as diverse as the topics chosen by them. Some of the studies are pioneering efforts in the U.S.: Ramos' article introduces women writers from the Dominican Republic (Ramos is herself a writer of fiction); Solera discusses three Costa Rican women's contribution to their nation's literature. Both newly discovered writers and those universally recognized in the literary world are discussed. The articles are distributed as follows: eight on French, two on Québecois, six on Latin-American, one on Spanish, and five on German and Austrian literatures.

We find interesting comparative studies amoung the essays included here: Hélène Cixous to Clarice Lispector, Hans Christian Andersen's influence on Matute, Lewald's Diogena as a parody of other "women's writing," Isak Dinesen and Dorothy Canfield.

Besides fiction, poetry and song, theory finds its place in this volume: Hélène Cixous' celebration of the female body as the text itself, Julia Kristeva's thesis on "le sémiotique" versus "le symbolique," and Monique Wittig's views on the role of language presented in Sally Kitch's essay. Amy Kaminsky, emphasizing the differing attitudes of men and women enduring exile, deals with the theory of the gender of the text.

Women's history is explored by Elías Miguel Muñoz who shows how Lucía Guerra presents women and history from a feminine point of view rather than a patriarchal one. Thomas C. Fox also studies sexism and literary history in Louise von François' work.

Mary Greenwood-Johnson's paper on Marguerite Duras demonstrates women's creativity in the cinema. The recent women's film festival, which took place in France in 1986, confirms the relevance of this form of women's art, especially in the case of Marguerite Duras who presents the film as a work which can be both read and viewed.

The militancy of women's writing in Latin-America, Québec, France, Germany, and Austria, resounds in most of the papers. Claudine Fisher points out that women are concerned with more than their personal lives, for they are also politically involved; Cixous concern for love, pleasure, and poetical esthetic is complemented by her political concerns. "The love of the Orange is political too," asserts Cixous herself. Duras concurs: "Quand on fait du cinéma différent il est forcément politique."

Marie France Hilgar's paper discusses Juliette Adam's contribution to raising the consciousness of women who, she believed, should emancipate themselves, thus becoming men's companions rather than their slaves. Adam's example of looking at things with both her eyes and body illustrates precisely the fusion of emotions and intellect sought by many women writers today.

Janine Ricouart offers the reader an analysis of violence in Marguerite Duras's mothers, which implies a new look at the erstwhile passive female image. The mother-child relationship based on love and violence is, according to Ricouart, a way for Duras to force us to re-think the status of women in society.

To the readers and literary critics who have idealized Colette's characters as "music hall dancers and gigolos in the Gay Paris before World War I," Anne Duhamel Ketchum demonstrates that the characters portray many other aspects of women's lives from childhood to motherhood, especially those influenced social and political corruption and male domination.

Paul Benhamou explains how Pauline Julien's songs in Québec serve also as champ d'exploration for women to demystify "la femme par la femme." Benhamou suggests that this is a revolutionary act for the time, because Pauline Julien implies that women exist outside the male phantasmagoric world.

Roseanna Dufault's theory about Québécois women writers' social and political engagement is applicable to all the women's works presented in these articles. Dufault asserts that from the nineteenth century to the 1970's, "women writers have crystallized collective concerns from a distinctly feminine perspective. We have seen an evolution from helpless resignation, through the questioning of awakened consciousness, to the position of strength, permitting a positive creative movement forward."

The editors hope that these varied thematic studies and analytic approaches will awaken the reader's interest in exploring yet other areas of women's writing.

Ginette Adamson

FRENCH FEMINIST THEORIES AND THE GENDER OF THE TEXT

Sally Kitch
The Wichita State University

A few weeks ago, a respected visitor to our campus made the statement in a seminar about feminist literature that writing is male. Amid shudders of horror, the mostly female audience rebelled. "But women write all the time," said one woman, "the real problem is getting published." "That's a male chauvinist point of view," cried another. From the perspective of these women, whose approach to the question of women's literature was from within that literature itself, from within their own familiarity with that literature, this man's statement was patently absurd. How could he assert that writing is male when there is so much writing by women to contradict him?

Coming from his perspective, however, the statement made and makes sense. As a professor of French literature, this visitor also knows that women have written profusely, and profoundly, and that in fact they have often dominated the genre of the novel. But in recent French intellectual theory, writing and women present a problematic--a puzzle--with importance, I think, even for pragmatic American readers and scholars of women's literature. What this speaker meant to say is simply that writing has, for various reasons, a symbolic identity with maleness. This identity makes us question the problems and possibilities for women who pick up the pen. It is that problematic of women and writing, predicated on the theory that language is imbued with maleness, that I would like to make the focus of this paper.

Part I--Why is writing problematic for women?

Even in American approaches to the relationship between gender and text, the association of literature with maleness is not unknown. Writers such as Norman Mailer have asserted that "a good novelist can do without everything but the remnant of his balls."[1] Less bluntly, W. H. Auden said much the same thing when he explained, "The Poet is the father who begets the poem which the language bears . . . as the husband, it is [the poet], not the language, who is responsible for the success of their marriage . . . " (Auden, <u>Poets at Work</u>, in Olsen 239). If Auden seems briefly to suggest that language, as the "bearer" of the poem might be female, he quickly disabuses us of that notion by explaining that language is merely the vehicle for the begetting, the incubator and not the creator of the text. Another example of literature's alleged maleness is contained in Harold Bloom's recent book which explores the Oedipal, father-son relationship between the writer and his text.

One reaction to such bravado might be simple resistance to the idea that women must relinquish the territory of literature to males just because they have had the nerve to stake it out and to keep women intimidated, uneducated and/or domesticated. Many women have reacted in just this way, among them Cynthia Ozick who declared in 1976 that "The term ´woman writer´ has no meaning, not intellectually, not morally, not historically. A writer is a writer" (Ozick at <u>Literary Women</u> symposium, Olsen 251).

Others who may have accepted gender-in-text, have questioned whether the gender of the author is necessarily equivalent to the gender of the text, or, following the assertion that writing is male, have wondered whether all texts might be male, whether they are written by men or women. That is, if language or writing is male, then perhaps anyone writing or using language may be de-castrated or masculinized, or become "status males" for the purpose of writing. Conversely, if there are gender differences in texts, would women accept all writing by all women as female? Would a text by Phyllis Schlafly be female? How about a text from the past, written by a woman with an un-raised consciousness?

Although I find such questions interestingly complicating of the problematic with which we began, it is my purpose to consider only that species of reaction to the notion of gender in the text which embraces the idea that texts are gendered and seeks to locate the source of gender both in the text and in the author of the text. (I must make an aside at this point. I will use the terms "male" and "female" to designate the appropriate gender in both author and text, rather than masculine or masculinist on the one hand and feminine and feminist on the other, because there is not time to define those various terms properly. To search for the precise term would provide another interesting complication to our problematic, however.) In other words, rather than denying gender differences in texts, a perfectly legitimate denial perhaps, the reaction I will be exploring demands that we acknowledge those differences, embrace, discover and define them.

First, however, I would like to consider the possible loci in literary texts for gender. That is, if we claim that some texts are male and some female, where might that gender be found? It seems to me that there are three possible loci--theme, form or style, and language.

THEME

The theme or content and subject of a piece of literature has been most readily acknowledged among American feminist critics as a locus of difference in male and female writing, although we must remember that the gender of the author and that of the text may or may not correspond. Unlike sexist critics, however, feminist critics celebrate gender differences in the text and honor such differences rather than use them as evidence of female inferiority and male superiority. Many feminist critics who use the thematic approach to gender agree that male texts tend to exclude female experience, to take male experience and attitudes as universal, to stereotype women, and to trivialize women's activities. Themes in women's texts have been identified variously as "personal, intuitive, sensuous," as rooted in female reproductive biology and/or sexuality, as more self-expressive and domestic, and less social and political than men's texts (Olsen 252-53).

FORM OR STYLE

The second locus of gender--form or style--has also been explored by American critics, some of whom have characterized male writing as demonstrating "bluntness, thrust, and force . . . abstraction, detachment" (Olsen 250). Such accounts are in accord with French critics who have declared male writing to be "linear, directed, logical."[2] Others of both nationalities have considered the possibility that some genres--such as drama and the novel--are necessarily male. Female form, according to such an approach, is more open, fluid and simultaneous, less "terminating" and linear (Makward 101).

LANGUAGE

In many feminist theories, the third category--language--locates gender in the actual words of a text, sometimes in addition to and in conjunction with form and theme and sometimes not. Maleness in language has been associated with the greater use of correct, formal terms, the universal "he," the treatment of woman as other, linear syntax as well as logic, and the use of male metaphors, including the phallus. Femaleness in language has been associated with non-linear syntax as well as logic, and with female metaphors, particularly those based on female body imagery. Some critics have suggested a female approach to the redesign of language, as in the case of Mary Daly who has both invented and redefined words. Her book, <u>Gyn/ecology</u> offers new and unusual meanings for its title; similarly, her redefinitions of "spinster" and "hag"--the first reclaiming the dignity of women as spinners and weavers, the second reclaiming an allegedly obsolete meaning, "woman reluctant to yield to wooing"--reveal the sexism inherent in the more familiar usages of such words.[3]

Part II--The French Feminist Contribution

French feminist theories tend to locate gender in the text itself, usually in the category of language, with some incursions into the category of form. But these theorists also relate the psychological gender of the writer to the gender of the text through a combination of two strains of recent French thought-- psychoanalysis and structuralism.

PSYCHOANALYSIS AND STRUCTURALISM

According to Jacques Lacan, the psychoanalyst often referred to as the French Freud, maleness can be found not so much in writing as in the nature of language and in the relation of language to the individual psyche. Lacan, like other Freudians, has accepted the keyness of the Oedipus in the development of human psychology and in the creation of gender. But unlike his American counterparts, Lacan's view of the Oedipus is less biological--less concerned with the physical possession of the penis--than it is linguistic. That is, the phallus is important not as flesh but as symbol of maleness both within and beyond the family domain. The phallus is the symbol of the lack which is at the center of human existence, and becomes a favored object either of possession or of desire. The phallus represents the Law of the Father--primarily the law against incest--imposed upon the child via the Language of the Father. Language in Lacanian thought, therefore, is equivalent to cultural laws imposed upon the individual through the metaphor of the phallus which establishes male dominance and which becomes the symbol not only of gender and family relationships but of desire in language.[4]

In this interpretation of the Oedipus can be seen the marriage of psychoanalysis and structuralism. Structuralist theory generally asserts that individuals are created by their culture and that culture becomes internalized in the individual as she or he learns language. Psychoanalysis thus can be seen as proposing the mechanism by which culture and the psyche merge. That is, the child learns the symbolism of the phallus, which is equivalent to the symbolism of the family and the society built upon familial laws, as he or she learns the structures and content of language. Language is designed to define and distribute rights and non-rights in relation to the phallus, a process which is evident in the child's taking of his/her father's name, learning of his/her place in the family constellation, and imaging gender in terms of the phallus--that is, the male is he who possesses the phallus, the female is she who desires the phallus.[5]

The news contained within Lacanian theory does not seem encouraging for women so far, but there is another aspect which feminists have embraced and expanded upon in interesting ways. Some have interpreted Lacanian thought to imply that language is male because it accompanies and symbolizes the increased influence and social role of the Father in relation to the child in Western childrearing practice. That is, language acquisition accompanies the Oedipus.[6] Because of these same childrearing practices, however, most Western children experience a pre-Oedipal period which is influenced primarily by the Mother or another female caretaker. The pre-Oedipal period in Lacanian theory is the time during which non-linguistic aspects of language--such as metonymy, metaphor, language play, humor, non-linguistic images, dream imagery, and so forth--are internalized by the child. Although the pre-Oedipal period also includes a phase of alienation, in which the child becomes aware of herself/himself as separate from the mother--what Lacan calls the Mirror Phase--this period is characterized by a sense of oneness with the maternal body, a sense of psychic integration rather than the overriding sense of alienation which marks the Oedipus phase and its resulting "symbolique." The pre-Oedipal period, or "imaginaire," may therefore be seen as either a time or a locus of femaleness within the human psyche (Lemaire, "Role" 82-87). Very importantly for our purposes, the imaginaire is also characterized by the association of certain aspects of language with the maternal body.

In my view, feminist theorists have understood the pre-Oedipal phase primarily as locus, as an enduring but repressed reservoir of non-masculinist language and non-linguistic imagery available throughout the individual's lifetime for release. The goal of these theorists has been the description and/or prescription of methods by which a conduit from that reservoir of femaleness might develop both into conscious uses of language and into a more feminized culture which would inevitably result.

Although I have identified a Lacanian view of the existence of pre-Oedipal imaginaire as basic to French feminist theories of the text, I must hasten to add that not all feminist theorists embrace or even acknowledge it.[7] But several do seem to write in reference or reaction to such a concept. I would like to present three examples of theorists who address, in differing ways, this female potential.

The first example is the approach of Hélène Cixous, who celebrates the existence of a reservoir of femaleness in the psyche. She advises women to write the female body, that is to reflect in language that symbiosis with the feminine usually repressed in post-Oedipal culture.[8] She argues that women have more access to the female psychic reservoir than men do because female essence is closer to the _imaginaire_. Women are less repressed physically than men, and the female body experiences a qualitatively different kind of sexual pleasure--which she calls _jouissance_--than does the male body. Though she does not call for a cessation of male-female sexual relations, Cixous prefers the greater variety offered by bisexuality.[9] The experience of _jouissance_, plus the connection, in "white ink" between mother and daughter, unlock the gates to the psychic reservoir of the female, and reveal the archaic or "birth-voice within."[10] The release of that voice forms the basis of a new female language to be written in the text. In _Vivre l´orange_ she describes this depth as "la terre intérieure de la vie, a cet état d´être, ce murissement qui prolonge l´entendue, la durée, la vie de la vie, au-delà de ses propre limites, qui fait pousser la vie de la vie, réelement, spirituellement, matériellement, en profondeur comme pousse le corps intérieur de la vie . . . où la vie d´une vie rejoint la Vie, la Grande Vie Mère" (61) (translation: "the inner earth of life, at that state of being, that ripeness that prolongs the expanse, the duration, the life of life, beyond its own limits, that makes the life of life grow, really, spiritually, materially, deep down as the inner body of life grows . . . where the life of a life rejoins Life, the Great Mother-Life"). Cixous labels texts which embody released female language as _sexts_--women´s texts that are outside culture, open, plural, and characterized by multiple meanings ("Castration" 36-40).

Julia Kristeva represents another approach. Like Simone de Beauvoir, Christine Fauré and others, Kristeva does not accept the idea of the female as essence. Like the male, she is social category; made not born. Further, she argues that all we can know of woman is what we have learned through phallic language, which only tells us what woman is not--"la femme, ce n´est jamais ça."[11] In this she echoes Lacan, who has said, "[la femme], elle ne se dit pas" (Makward 101). Kristeva asserts gender differences only so that woman will not be subsumed by the universal "man," but she regards the reservoir of femaleness in the psyche as accessible to both males and females. She labels that reservoir _le sémiotique_ in contrast with the post-Oedipal male language which, like Lacan, she calls _le symbolique_.

The writing Kristeva encourages is that which allows _le sémiotique_ to erupt into _le symbolique_, to disrupt the grammar laws and paternal metaphors of phallagocentrism. She does not want to limit this possibility to women, however, because she worries that a distinctly female language will further marginalize women. Differences we currently see in male and female language, she believes, only reflect differences in what has been repressed in the two sexes. Both sexes are capable of releasing that repressed language in the text.[12]

Kristeva characterizes writing as a duality, as embodying both phenotext--the language of communication--and genotext--non-linguistic elements of language such as metaphor, rhythm, play, and the interaction of the "I" (the subject) with the laws of language. The genotext is the source of language and cultural revolution. It contains the struggle of the individual against social control, challenges history, and allows writer and reader to merge with the maternal body--a possibility not present in le symbolique.[13]

Kristeva believes that the novel form can embody this genotext, particularly in the dialogue which mediates between speech and writing and conveys the interaction of the speaking subject with the social context. A novel which successfully portrays this aspect of le sémiotique she calls a polylogue (Kristeva, Desire 168-180).

The third approach I would like to consider is that of Monique Wittig, author of Les Guerillères and known for an approach, which contrasts with Cixous' l'écriture féminine, called questions féministes. Wittig agrees with Kristeva that femaleness is not an essence. She believes, rather, that women are a class, and that all categories, such as man, woman, history or culture, are ideological and not natural. Her texts reflect the class approach in their consideration of women only in the plural--elles rather than elle. As a class conscious of itself, Wittig's women are not exclusively sexual beings. Rather they are women who will, like Mary Daly's "virgins," define themselves without male frames of reference. To Wittig, lesbians are what women might have been had they developed unconcerned with male discourse, context or approval. Femaleness in Wittig's writing is the creation of new political realities based on class-consciousness and new sexual structures in which women are subjects rather than objects.[14] Her language is designed not to elevate the metaphor of the female body but to change the metaphoric bases on which human communities are formed--the mirror reflection rather than the notion of opposites, the collective rather than the individual, love rather than war. Although she rejects the psychoanalytic message that any configuration of the human psyche is inevitable, she does seem to embrace its structuralist bias, reinforced by Marxism, that pre-existing structures and material reality contribute to the creation of individual consciousness. Her work suggests that new social and linguistic realities can therefore create new consciousness.

Part III--Exploration of Texts

With this background in mind, I would like to examine some brief excerpts from fiction which might illustrate these points.

I have chosen the approach of Cixous because it demonstrates what is perhaps most easily demonstrable, the relationship of gender and figurative language, including all forms of associative and synonymous meanings. I see figurative language as a key to the question of gender in the text because of its essential role, both in the process of writing and in the uniqueness, interest, and even genius of a particular text. Such language also seems to be the intersection, in writing, between creator and creation.

In conducting this experiment with gendered text, I wanted to locate a similar metaphor in the works of two writers, one male and the other female. For the male author and/or text I have chosen James Joyce, primarily because of the way he explores the human consciousness through language in his work, but also because both Cixous and Kristeva have cited his work as significant in their own approaches to language. Joyce's work is perhaps the most likely of male texts to exemplify the release of the repressed female in a male writer (as Kristeva might have it), or to illustrate the intransigence of maleness even in the face of experimentation with consciousness via language (as Cixous might predict). The figure in both texts is fruit--specifically the orange.

From James Joyce's <u>Ulysses</u>:

He [Bloom] walked back along Dorset Street, reading gravely. Agendath Netaim: planter's company. To purchase vast sandy tracts from Turkish government and plant with eucalyptus trees. Excellent for shade, fuel and construction. Orangegroves and immense melonfields north of Jaffa. You pay eight marks and they plant a dunam of land for you with olives, oranges, almonds or citrons. Olives cheaper: oranges need artificial irrigation. Every year you get a sending of the crop. . . .
   He looked at the cattle, blurred in silver heat. Silvered powdered olivetrees. . . . Oranges in tissue paper packed in crates. Citrons too. Wonder is poor Citron still alive in Saint Kevin's parade. And Mastiansky with the old cither. Pleasant evenings we had then. Molly in Citron's basket chair. Nice to hold, cool waxen fruit, hold in the hand, lift it to the nostrils and smell the perfume. Like that, heavy, sweet, wild perfume. Always the same, year after year. They fetched high prices too Moisel told me. Arbutus place: Pleasants

street: pleasant old times. Must be without a flaw, he said. Coming all that way: Spain Gibraltar, Mediterranean, the Levant. Crates lined up on the quayside at Jaffa, chap ticking them off in a book, navvies handling them in soiled dungarees. There's whatdoyoucallhim out of. How do you? Doesn't see. Chap you know just to salute bit of a bore. His back is like that Norwegian captain's. Wonder if I'll meet him today. Watering cart. To provoke the rain. On earth as it is in heaven.[15]

From Hélène Cixous' <u>Vivre l'orange</u>:

"What have you in common with women? When your hand no longer even knows anymore how to find a near and patient and realizable orange, at rest in the bowl?" Mute I fled the orange, my writing fled the secret voice of the orange, I withdrew from the shame of being unable to receive the benediction of the fruit giving itself peacefully, for my hand was too lonely, and in such loneliness, my hand no longer had the strength to believe in the orange. . . . my writing was separated from the orange, didn't write the orange, didn't go to it, didn't call it, didn't carry the juice to my lips. . . . Certain voices have [the] power [to]. . . put the orange back into the deserted hands of my writing . . . our childhoods have the natural science of the orange. . . . I dedicate the orange's existence, as it has been given to me by a woman, according to the entire and infinite bringing-together of the thing, including . . . air and . . . earth, . . . the sense relations that every orange keeps alive and circulates, . . . life, death, women, forms, volumes, movement, matter, . . . ways of metamorphoses, invisible links between fruits and bodies . . . perfumes . . . catastrophes, all . . . the thoughts . . . woman can nourish, starting out from a given orange; including all of its names, the silent name . . . the name as proper to it as god's name to god; its family name; and its maiden name. . . . Not forgetting the orange is one thing. Recalling the orange is another thing. Rejoining it is another. . . . (14, 16, 18)

The Joyce excerpt appears early in the novel and portrays Bloom walking through Dublin and imagining the Orient, the East, just as Ulysses dreams of the bounty and lures of Ithaca.[16] In this passage, Bloom sees a sign (which should read "Agudath Netaim," according to William Tindall) over an importer's shop (in Ellmann, 152n). The imported fruit which he sees and imagines includes oranges, which in turn suggest agricultural methods and conditions, other signs of human-induced fertility in the desert-- cattle, olives, citrons--and the difficulty of exporting such products over long distances (Tindall, in Ellmann). The names of the fruits remind him of events and people in his life. The qualities of the fruit--"nice to hold, cool waxen . . . hold in the hand . . . smell, sweet perfume"--are juxtaposed to a vision of his wife Molly in a basket chair. Presumably, she is also plump, round, nice to touch, and sweet-smelling. I see Joyce's oranges as part of a string of associations and displacements, a part of a metaphoric chain whose links move away from orangeness to a world of commerce, industry and relationships between himself and other people. In this way, Joyce may, therefore, be drawing upon the sémiotique in a male way, not only by seeing the female body (Molly) as external to himself and allying himself erotically with it, but also in having to move in a linear, associative way from each of his images to the other. The process of metaphor takes him away from his own psyche, perhaps so he will not see the femaleness within it, and objectifies the female so that she can be handled in his mind as commerce is handled.

Cixous also makes a variety of associations with the orange, but hers explore the inner qualities of the fruit as sign of the depths of her own inner being. She associates orangeness and femaleness, which because of her gender is an association of the fruit with herself. The qualities of orangeness--"goodness, fullness," juiciness--suggest inner essences of "life, death, women, . . . matter . . . metamorphoses" rather than events or social structure. When other people appear, such as Clarice in later passages, they too are identified with and not distinguised from the narrator. Cixous senses rather than knows the orange, identifies with it rather than from it, sees herself as metonymous with orangeness rather than as metaphor-maker whose language moves her away from the fruit. She writes as the fruit, sees the fruit as subject, as herself at her most engaged and authentic.

Although these two excerpts are not meant to represent male and female texts in any general way, they do perhaps suggest a means for the consideration of gender in text. Using these excerpts as examples, I find an intriguing distinction. For Cixous, the associations with the orange are organic and involved, reflecting, perhaps, a willingness of the female author to identify with the image-making portion of the psyche acquired during the Pre-Oedipal phase. For Joyce, the associations are external, objectified and metaphoric—in Lacan's sense of term as the substitutive linking of signifiers characteristic of the symbolique (Lemaire, "Philosophy" 190-210).

Both writers are stimulated by the figurative possibilities of the orange, of course, and that fact suggests that they have perhaps shared the internalization of the fruit as image. The difference in their use of the image may offer a clue to the differences in linguistic associations of the two people and may, further, provide insight into the role of gender in the creation of those associations.

NOTES

[1] Norman Mailer, Advertisement for Myself, 1959, quoted in Tillie Olsen, Silences (New York: Delta/Seymour Lawrence Edition, 1965) 238.

[2] Christiane Makward, "To Be or not to Be . . . A Feminist Speaker," trans. Marlene Barsoum, Alice Jardine, Hester Eisenstein, in The Future of Difference, eds. Hester Eisenstein and Alice Jardine (Boston: G. K. Hall, 1980) 100.

[3] Mary Daly, Gyn/Ecology (Boston: Beacon Press, 1978) 9-15.

[4] These ideas are articulated in Jacques Lacan, Ecrits: A Selection, ed. Alan Sheridan (London: Tavistock Publications, 1977) passim; see also Lacan, "Symbol and Language," trans. Anthony Wilden, in The Language of the Self, ed. Wilden (Baltimore: The Johns Hopkins Press, 1968) 40-43.

[5] See Anika Lemaire, "The Philosophy of Language in Jacques Lacan," in her Jacques Lacan, trans. David Macey (London: Routledge and Kegan Paul, 1977) 58-60. See also Lacan, "The Function of Language in Psychoanalysis" 17-27, and Wilden, "Lacan and the Discourse of the Other" 186-187, 270, both in Wilden, Language.

[6] Anika Lemaire, "The Role of the Oedipus in Accession to the Symbolic," in Jacques Lacan 82-87; see also Wilden, "Lacan and Discourse," in Language 262-273.

[7] See especially Hélène Cixous, "Castration or Decapitation," Signs 7.1 (Autumn 1981): 41-48.

[8] Hélène Cixous, "Utopias," *New French Feminisms: An Anthology*, eds. Elaine Marks and Isabelle de Courtivron (Amherst: The University of Massachusetts Press, 1980) 245.

[9] Cixous, "Sorties" 93-97, and "The Laugh of the Medusa" 259-260, *New French Feminisms*. See also Cixous, "Castration," *Signs*: 36-54.

[10] Hélène Cixous, *Vivre l'orange* (Paris: Des Femmes, 1979) 16.

[11] Julia Kristeva, "La femme, ce n'est jamais ça," *New French Feminisms* 137.

[12] Elaine Marks, "Women and Literature in France," *Signs* 3.4 (Summer 1978): 832-842.

[13] Julia Kristeva, *Desire in Language: A Semiotic Approach to Literature and Art*, ed. Leon S. Roudiez, trans. Thomas Gora, Alice Jardine and Leon Roudiez (New York: Columbia University Press, 1980), Introduction.

[14] Hélène Wenzel, "The Text as Body/Politics: An Appreciation of Monique Wittig's Writings in Context," *Feminist Studies* 7.2 (Summer 1981): 264-287.

[15] James Joyce, *Ulysses* (1918; rpt. New York: Random House, 1934) 60.

[16] Richard Ellmann, *James Joyce* (New York: Oxford University Press, 1965) 372-373.

LITERARY CURRENTS IN THE WORKS OF JULIETTE ADAM

Marie-France Hilgar
University of Nevada, Las Vegas

1836 - 1936: Juliette Adam is not the only woman who lived to be almost a hundred, but not many centenarians can claim having known Lamartine and having known about Hitler, of having introduced to the public such authors as Paul Bourget and Julien Viaud, better known as Pierre Loti, and having welcomed to her salon politicians of all parties as well as the most eminent personalities in the letters and the arts. "It will be impossible to write the history of France since 1870 without writing hers," as Paul Acker wrote in 1912 in his Portraits de Femmes; he called her salon "the chapel of the third Republic."[1] In his Souvenirs de la vie littéraire, Antoine Albalat describes Juliette Adam as an extraordinary woman who gave to the world of French literary and patriotic propaganda all the strength of her intelligence and of her heart.[2] After having founded and directed her literary Nouvelle Revue for twenty years, she started Paroles françaises à l'étranger in which she expressed her enlightened political ideas.

To analyze Juliette Adam's career and influence would force us to study the role she played in politics, both at the national and international levels, and in literature with her Nouvelle Revue. We will limit ourselves however to one of her lesser known talents, that of author of novels and plays.

Juliette's first literary work appeared in 1858. It is a thin volume of poems interesting only because we find in it the themes which will dominate most of her career: God, faith, and woman. An article of hers had appeared two years earlier in Le Siècle of February 20, 1856, in which she ridiculed the wearing of crinolines which made women too large for the architecture around them. In September of 1858 she published her Idées anti-proudhoniennes sur l'amour, la femme et le mariage in which she attacks, of course, Proudhon and his ideas but also demands "la libre accession de tous, femmes ou hommes, aux fonctions auxquelles chacun est le plus propre," which is an early statement of equal opportunity, and among other things the right to divorce and the right to become "mairesse". Then with Le Mandarin, in 1860, Juliette continues and brings up to date Montesquieu's Lettres Persanes. Again she fights for the emancipation of women, so that instead of being treated as slaves, courtesans or dolls, they may be considered the companion, the confidant and the partner of man.

To her first volume of short stories published almost at the same time as Le Mandarin, Juliette gave the simple title of Mon Village. It is a charming, engaging, well written book in which she describes a village where equal rights are implemented. She avoids long discussions of a philosophical or ideological nature but shows what can be gained from collective solidarity, and provides the reader with sober but fascinating descriptions.

The Récits d'une paysanne in 1862 were a big success. Her style is as clear and simple as her stories which are lessons in morality: courageous and charitable people are rewarded. Juliette still believes, as she always will, in the rights and merits of women. Thérèse Leroux, the heroine of Germain, is psychologically strong enough to impose her views.

After having described her native region, Juliette the Picarde discovered the south of France and threw herself, body and soul, into the exploration of the still unknown Midi. Her new love gave birth to more volumes of short stories: Voyage autour du grand Pin in 1863, and Dans les Alpes, nouveaux récits in 1867.

Soon Juliette found that describing scenes of real life in short stories was too restraining, and she embarked on the writing of novels which were conceived and published rather rapidly; 1869: L'Education de Laure; 1870: Saine et Sauve; 1876: Jean et Pascal; 1877: Laide; 1879: Grecque; 1883: Païenne; 1889: Jalousie de Jeune fille, and some twenty-five years later: Chrétienne. When we read Juliette's novels and keep in mind the many interests which occupied her life, we discover that she developed in each one of her novels her main preoccupation at that particular time. Hers is more une oeuvre engagée than a work of art. Before 1870, she dreams of utopia, of equality; she believes in progress and science. These themes are found in L'Education de Laure which is devoted to the failure of spiritualism, and in Saine et Sauve which affirms the final triumph of a bourgeoisie that has ennobled itself through work and the interest it takes in the living conditions of the working classes. After Sedan, Juliette preaches patriotism and fidelity to the lost provinces in Jean et Pascal. With her Greek trilogy, the author proves that it is possible to speak of love, of different kinds of love, without stooping to the vulgarity and the gross details which naturalist authors enjoy so much. Then much later, the title of Chrétienne lets the reader guess the topic.

Juliette Adam's heroes are exceptional people, but they often lack the psychological complexity which is the essence of human beings. In Pascal Mamert, the hero of Jean et Pascal, we find nothing but a deep love for fatherland; Jehan, of L'Education de

Laure, is "spiritualiste à outrance," in favor of authority for everything and everywhere, enemy of the Revolution, hater of socialism. The goal of Juliette in this novel was to prove that spiritualism is no good and to proclaim her faith in a materialistic, socialistic and humanitarian socialism. Estelle de Villeneuve, in Saine et Sauve displays an unrestrained love for mundane life. Almost all of Juliette's principal characters show only one aspect of themselves. They lack reality. They are created to deliver the author's message which confers upon them a certain realism of actuality, but they are more sentimental than rational and express their feelings with the excesses of an outdated romanticism.

Juliette Lamber Adam is a contemporary of Zola, born in 1840, but her novels and plays seem to be at the antipodes of those of the naturalists. Her literary work is almost entirely an apotheosis of the earth and of life upon earth. She believes in the goodness of things and of people, in beauty, in elegance, and she loves to live with the Ancient Greeks. The religion of the Greeks appeared to her to be the finest, their life the most natural and the noblest, their art the most perfect. Nobody has seized upon the Greek dream with more fervor, enthusiasm. Juliette Adam has attached to this antique dream the most modern thoughts and feelings. She has given to artistic piety the appearance of a moral cult and of a faith that rules over life. Her least disputable originality is the very ardor at the time of her pagan faith. "What am I? I am a Pagan. That is what distinguishes me from other women," says the heroine of Païenne.

Juliette Adam's work is but the triumphant hymn of the most noble and joyous human feelings: the love of man and woman in Païenne, the love of country in Grecque, the love of beauty in Laide and everywhere the love of nature, and the worship of the Greek Gods; all the heroes of her Hellenistic novels and plays are practicing pagans. Intoxication of being and feeling, free life which is happy and noble at the same time, obedience to the natural inclinations tempered by a fondness for classical measure, reconciliation of matter and spirit, harmonious development of the complete person and the exercises of superior faculties to temper and purify the instincts of the flesh: such are the bases of Madame Adam's novels.

Her stories are quite simple. In Laide, Hélène, disfigured by a disease, is dying because she is ugly and is not loved by the painter Guy Romain. After an unsuccessful attempt at committing suicide, a new sickness restores her beauty and gives her Guy's love. In Grecque, Ida, exiled from Crete, prefers her country and her gods to her weak lover who dies crushed by the marble statue of his rival Apollo. As for Païenne, it is merely a long and burning love duet, without a story of external incidents, and even without an interior drama. The lovers have hardly an hour's doubt and spend their time making delightful discoveries in themselves and in one another.

Jules Lemaître talks of Madame Adam's neo-Hellenism and demonstrates that neither in the religion of her heroes, nor in their love of nature, nor in the mystical side of their feelings, nor even in the form she gave to their thought was there anything authentically Greek.[3] Juliette is a late romanticist who does not draw on erudition. She takes from antiquity what is convenient to her views, her temper and her topic, and creates her own idea of ancient Greece. Guy de Maupassant is the only one, it seems, who pointed out the anachronism of Madame Adams's Greek trilogy: "Païenne aurait paru voici trente ans, ou mieux, voici soixante ans, on l'aurait louée avec extase. Tout change, surtout la mode littéraire. . . ." The Parnassian poets had exhausted some thirty years earlier a temporary passion for Greek antiquity, and contemporary readers, generally speaking, did not understand Païenne, which is considered her masterpiece. They only saw its sensual aspect and neglected its mystical one which is just as important. Maupassant again says of the same novel that it has "une manière de dire les choses qui rappelle un peu les périphrases de l'abbé Delisle," and he adds, "Une des qualités de ce livre lui a nui. Ayant à exprimer des choses difficiles à dire, surtout pour une femme, l'auteur s'est efforcé d'être chaste dans son verbe. Il lui a donc fallu avoir recours à des tournures auxquelles nous ne sommes plus accoutumés."[4]

When discussing Juliette Adam's neo-Hellenism, or pseudo-Hellinism we must mention her Petit Théâtre. In 1880 the théâtre des Nations presented a play Juliette adapted from a modern Greek playwright named Basialadès. Galatée was performed once only, but so successfully that other foreign authors asked Juliette to adapt their works to the French stage. In order to entertain her many famous guests, especially in her homes of Gif and Antibes, Juliette started writing her own little plays. Most of them are lost, but we know that one was performed in front of Gambetta, a close friend of Juliette;[5] other ones were entitled La Fée, and Qui a vécu vivra. La Nouvelle Revue published Le Temps nouveau and Mourir. These two plays are found now in volume XVI of her complete works which also includes Coupable, Fleurs piquées, and Galatée.

In Mourir, which was played in Saint Petersburg, the chorus informs the public that the irate goddess Diana has been claiming, every year for twenty years, the lives of two young people. That particular year, two young lovers, Doris and Cios, have been designated. Delia, the girl's sister, who was made a priestess of

Diana against her will, decides to give up her life when she hears that Eusèbe, Cillos' brother, wants to die so that he will not be tempted to seduce the goddess' priestess. No longer will young people need to die every year, because the oracle's predictions have been accomplished: "Une prêtresse d'Artemis sera aimée avec chasteté; un homme jeune et beau offrira sa vie à la déesse pour ne pas la trahir et devenir sacrilège. Une prêtresse aimera cet homme le jour de sa mort et, pure comme lui, réclamera le bonheur du supplice à ses côtés."

Galatée shows the triumph of patriotic feelings and of brotherly love. The beautiful woman to whom Pygmalion has given life has failed to convince the one she loves, Rennos, to kill his brother Pygmalion. She is a rare example, in Juliette Adam's work, of a wicked woman, but she has an excuse: "Son âme n'étant point née des hommes, mais étant née du marbre, en a conservé la dureté."

Paganism, Hellenism, these words are equally fitting to designate the spirit of Juliette Adam's books. It does not mean however that nineteenth-century romanticism and naturalism are totally absent from her work, the most eminent merit of Juliette being her passion for fine landscapes and her power to describe them. Her pictures are brilliant and impressive. They are the warm and luminous landscapes of Southern France which she knew well: "The ravaged sides of Luberon display entrails of gold. The summits of its hills assume the wrinkled aspects of the skin of mastodons. One of the summits has the form of a monster. He seems to swim on the waves of the earth, to stoop and rise in the rolling movements of the globe, while the flaky clouds, resting on the monster, surround him with driven foam." Our author loves and describes only the landscapes of the south, the Provençal landscapes so similar to the sites of Greece.

Juliette Adam feels with a rare intensity the intoxication of forms, of light, of colors. Demi-gods and goddesses live in her deified landscapes. Her heroes and heroines are superb and lyrical creatures who share very special feelings toward nature:

> Loftier summits rear themselves upwards. . . .
> One finds oneself suddenly alone in spaces where the eye has no longer more than a dazzling and radiant vision, where the expanded intelligence becomes vague and has only perceptions of size, of light, of an immense circle. (Païenne)
>
> Hélène admires the universe and believes that she comprehends it. Yet, beneath what she

> sees, it seems to her that an unknown something attracts and beguiles her. What is this mystery of the real? Where is it hidden? In matter or in being? Are the secrets of appearances written on what manifests itself to the eyes, or are they shut up in the depths within us? (Laide)

Juliette Adam gives to the readers symbols of death and resurrection, of purification and of second life. Her pagan Melissandre writes these mysterious sentences:

> I wished to know the secret of things. My ideas were simple. They gravitated without effort towards the higher paths where one meets the gods. . . . I did not see them with my eyes alone, but with my whole being. . . . I penetrated the secret of the laws of exchange with nature, and mingled my individuality with the great whole. . . . I discovered the divine, human, and natural affinities of all force, all life. . . . (Païenne)

Juliette Adam described love as "a double current, mystic and sensual." To Pantheism and Romanticism she added the religious form given to the cult of woman, devout absorption in her contemplation, Petrarchism. The hero of Païenne, Tiburcius, expresses his feelings toward Melissandre in the following terms: "I have really possessed the happiness of the immortals. I have seen love bare itself, purify itself, become a religion, a worship and a prayer. For the first time I have experienced the delight of internal adoration" (Païenne).

Read Juliette Adam's novels. It is difficult to label her work with one word, be it realism or paganism or Hellenism. It does not express a philosophical system, a theory of the universe and of life, but rather of an intellectual and sentimental state. It is warm and living and it remains, at the very least, a rare effort of sympathetic imagination.

NOTES

[1] Paul Acker, <u>Portraits</u> <u>de</u> <u>femmes</u> (Paris: Dorbon-Aîné, 1912).

[2] Antoine Albalat, <u>Souvenirs</u> <u>de</u> <u>la</u> <u>vie</u> <u>littéraire</u> (Paris: Les éditions G. Grès et Cie, 1924).

[3] Jules Lemaître, <u>Les</u> <u>Contemporains</u> (Paris: H. Lecène et H. Oudin, 1886).

[4] Guy de Maupassant, "Bataille de livres," <u>Le</u> <u>Gaulois</u> (28 octobre 1883).

[5] Jules Bertaut, "Trois salons parisiens sous le même toit," <u>Candide</u> (16 octobre 1924)

HELENE CIXOUS' WINDOW OF DARING
THROUGH CLARICE LISPECTOR'S VOICE

Claudine Fisher
Portland State University

To Live the Orange, published by "Des femmes" in 1979, in bilingual edition, stands as Cixous' hymn to Clarice Lispector as a writer. "From far away, from outside of my history, a voice came to collect the last tear. To save the orange."[1]

The twelfth of October, 1978 (10), Hélène Cixous discovers Clarice Lispector, and is struck by this feminine voice who has "two courages": "That of going to the sources--that of returning, to herself, almost without self, without denying the going" (28). The courage demonstrated by Lispector, the Brazilian author, touches Cixous' soul, at a crucial moment when the latter despairs from ever finding in literature a voice which partakes of her philosophical joy. Cixous' writing expresses three essential necessities, among others: the search for a truth which reflects feminine concerns, a demanding approach to joyful simplicity, and a poetic ideal. This triangle which Cixous is creating, happens to be incarnated within the artistic endeavors of another contemporary woman, on the other side of the world, in another tongue, Portuguese. Surprise, as well as delight, awaken in the French writer, who perceives this coincidence as a sign of sisterly love through the medium of the written word. Her loneliness is lifted, a symbolic sharing takes place, to be gradually considered as the epitome of women's creativity. After the solitude and loneliness in the wandering for "ten years in the desert of books" (10), a mystical meeting of the minds occurs, mingling Lispector's voice and Cixous', echoing each other, in strength.

> She put the orange back into the deserted hands of my writing, and with her orange-colored accents she rubbed the eyes of my writing which were arid and covered with white films. And it was a childhood that came running back to pick up the live orange and immediately celebrate it. (14)

From the image of the desert of books, Cixous turns the metaphor upside down, to make the desert bloom with an orange-colored flower of signs: a sign of signs. The hand which writes blooms, the accents, melody of the voice and accents of the French punctuation, erase the aridity of the desert with all "white films," or specks in the eye. (Taie in French, speck and pillow-case of the white sheet of paper, voice of writing, thus as empty as the desert).

Naturally Clarice Lispector does not use the symbol of the orange. The orange is a particularly important Cixousian recurring element, which appears in her fiction as early as Portrait of the Sun of 1973. Lispector does use the apple, which Cixous transposes into her favorite symbol. She refuses the apple of Eve, loaded with the Christian myth of sin, and turns it into her own fruit "oranje."

> L'oranje est mon fruit de naissance et ma fleur prophétique. La première fois que j'ai coupé un mot c'était elle. (The Oran-I is my birth fruit and my prophetic flower. The first time I cut a word it was it/she.)[2]

The spelling of the orange in Portrait of the Sun sheds light on Cixous' interpretation of the fruit-flower. It is the town of Oran, in North Africa, where Cixous was born and it is the uttering of the self through the I of writing, and the eye/vision of the writer (thus the speck in the eye, cleared by the visionary freshness brought by Clarice, whose name will later be associated with light). The orange cut in two pieces, Oran-I, lets the juice flow, orangy liquid, blood and ink, and encompasses in its circle the memory of childhood:

> A peine l'ai-je ouverte qu'elle me mange: par son teint immémorial, par ce goût, le premier, par cette irrégulière sphéricité, elle m'englobe. Je vois orange, je rêve orange, je sens orange. C'est une façon de revenir aux premiers jours, y compris l'avant-premier. (Portrait 5) (Hardly have I opened it, that it eats me: by its immemorial complexion, by that taste, the first, that irregular sphericity, it contains me. I see orange, I dream orange, I feel orange. It is a way to come back to the first days, the day before the first included.)

The orange which evokes the memories of childhood is one of the first lessons to learn. By going back to the primeval garden and the school of the earth, the woman learns the lesson of nature in its complex simplicity. Thus, in To Live the Orange, Cixous comes back to the same motif developed in Portrait of the Sun, which is already the portrait of the orange and its corollary the sun, round orange mass of the shores of Algeria. It is then hardly surprising that a young woman from Algeria would sing the sun, and find in her counterpart on the sunny shores of Brazil, another woman singing the lesson of the earth. (Moreover, it is interesting to note that both women are from Jewish ancestry, whose families escaped Nazi Germany, and sing the land to which they were originally exiled.)

This orange, held in the hand, is the tangible proof of the existence of the intangible:

> I had the peace in my hands. I saw that the world that held the answer to the questions of my being was gold-red, a globe of light present here and tomorrow, red day descended from green night. (16)

The need to go to the sources is demonstrated by Cixous' and Lispector's writings, when the questions of the being are raised. It becomes the questioning of the world, and the birth-voice anterior to birth itself. It is the gesture of giving the orange, the art of patience and the state of peace.

The knowledge of the orange is not easy to acquire, as Cixous points out, and is difficult to transmit. Both movements of knowing and passing this knowledge to other women, need three stages. The first step deals with time and is related to patience and slowness. The second necessitates the memory of childhood in an unspoiled stage with its gifts from the heart, thus love and tenderness, which is able to understand the world in its orange-like essence. The third step calls for a good ear who can listen to "the music of the spheres," an ear which does not forget:

> The orange is a moment. Not forgetting the orange is one thing. Recalling the orange is another. Rejoining it is another. At least three times are needed to understand the infinite immensity of the moment. I have been living around an orange for three days. (18)

The art of the orange, as a beginning to women's awareness, relies on both memory and forgetfulness. It is seen by Cixous as the green garden which opposes men's metal-colored pursuits: the grey of the "cars, lorries and cannons" (20). The grey color clashes with the green and orange colors, symbolizing women's apprehension of the world. At that particular instant, the orange color is destroyed by the grey instrument of the French telephone, which interrupts the protagonist's vision in To Live the Orange. Reality strikes, snuffing the light:

> Coming out of the light of the moment to go
> into the color grey is a violent, strange,
> artless exercise, an obligation without
> directions. (22)

To Live the Orange poses the important question of feminist action, versus theoretical and poetic "action" through the act of creativity. Is the woman who presents her vision a dreamer, cut off from the woman's plight in modern society? Or is she the seer, able to put into words the very action of all women in modern times? Cixous' answer to this crucial point resounds unambiguous. The protagonist answers Renata's telephone call and to her anguished question "And Iran? You were forgetting?" (24), the italicized answer in the text explains: "the love of the orange is political too" (16). Cixous enhances this answer by a textual demonstration, as vivid, powerful and political as a demonstration in the street of Tehran by the Iranian women. Playing on the first vowel of Oran and Iran, both words gradually merging into one another, Hélène Cixous tackles the problem of the apple-orange, guilt and innocence. If Clarice Lispector's writing epitomizes innocence, it does not mean this innocence can be equated to unawareness and oblivion. On the contrary, the stage of innocence can only be acquired after agonizing suffering and awareness. The persona of the text differentiates the concepts:

> I am not innocent. . .
> I am not in ignorance of innocence. (26)
> No one has the innocence. (40)

In the green color of the apple devoid of ignorance and of the guilt fostered on all women through Eve's sin, which modern women should not espouse, Cixous creates a prenatal orange in the shape of the O, the egg, the ultimate zero, which encompasses all knowledge toward a desire for absolute innocence. "We do not forget that we forget" (96). So the Iranian women are not forgotten. They become the bronze-colored orange of the blood oranges and the roses of women with courage:

> Fifty thousand roses, less veiled than ever are
> manifesting themselves, in the center of
> Teherange, walk abreast more than unveiled,
> exposed, in the center of religions, refusing
> to let themselves be iranized. (96)

The city of Tehran, linking Iran, the Orient, Oran and Orange, knows the daring of the Iranian women who fight the oppression of the veil and of Iranian men's religion. They are the "amies," the friends, the women for whom the protagonist agonizes and sings as roses. The unveiling of the Iranian women is akin to Lispector's unveiling of life. In its double meaning, the French word "dévoile" stresses the unveiling and revealing or exposing, at the same time. The prefix de corresponding to the English un, becomes a source of semantic unveiling as in "de-facing," and "changing face," "unmasking" and "un-making up" (50). Clarice Lispector's écriture is being unveiled for the French writer, is being revealed. Clarice embodies light and revelation: "The face bent over. What happened I saw. Revealed to me. It was the revelation" (48). Clarice Lispector is not un-masked but de-faced, changed and not changed: "L'écriture se dévisageait" (50).

It is no surprise to notice that the translation by Ann Liddle and Sarah Cornell skips this Cixousian play-on-words. It is untranslatable. "Face" and "visage" are French synonyms, but the verb "dévisager" implies, in this case, the writing watching itself, staring at itself. Clarice Lispector's writing appears different from Cixous', and however, it is one and the same, the double of the same face or image, by the commonality of their vision. It is the gift offered freely by the writer to another reader and writer. "It was a mere nothing--that seized me absolutely. The Gift. At once taken" (52). This "mere nothing" happens to be the theme of Cixous and Lispector in the search for All, the 0 or zero and the knowledge of the universe.

A few words from La Passion selon G.H. by Clarice Lispector could be chosen at random, and the vision would definitely reveal itself as Cixousian. No wonder it was, literally, a wonder to Cixous:

> Now, to find the secret again, I would need to re-die. . . . For, at the very moment I struggle to know, my new ignorance which is the forgetting, has become sacred. . . . I will assume the horror till the metamorphosis accomplishes itself and till horror becomes light. . . . Though I had entered inside the room, it seemed I had entered inside nothing. Though inside, in a certain way I was always outside.[3]

One would only have to recall, one of Cixous' titles, Dedans, (1969) to discover the similarity of vision between the two fictions and the polarities of inside/outside, darkness/light, horror/metamorphosis.

To Live the Orange ends in the orgasmic joy familiar to Cixous' readers. The discovery of Clarice's window of audaciousness surprises and enthralls Cixous who ponders on the chance of the meeting of two texts, and its stroke of luck. An intertextuality of two fictions unaware of each other till 1978, draws under Cixous' pen another intertextuality through the Mallarmé poem A Throw of the Dice never will Abolish Chance:

> Through this window of daring. Things of beauty come to us only by surprise. To please us. Twice as beautiful for surprising us, for being surprised. When no one is there to take them. It seems to us when they spring forth towards us that they are the strokes of God: but when they come in we see by their smile that they are strokes of clarice. (110)

It is the supreme gift offered by the writers and expecially by women who have inside knowledge of the giving, as Cixous shows in Souffles (1985), where the word don (gift) is associated with vol (flight and theft) and makes the new-coined word dol, giving expression to the woman's profound inwardness.

To Live the Orange is not a book which speaks of Clarice Lispector. It is a book which speaks of her "inner music" and her meditation on the origins, through Cixous' prism. It enhances the "taste of her thought" and her "under writing" (62). That is why Clarice's story remains at the level of the nothing, whereas her metaphors thrive in Cixous' pages, and are perfectly woven into Cixous' own writing. Nothingness is transformed into a concrete reality of all abstractions. All the senses participate in this meditation feat. The lesson of "things" moves at the level of the "lesson of the apple" with the "acidulous taste of the word on the tongue" (64). Taste and tongue are united to shape the apple/appeal or call/recall brought by Clarice "the gentle, torrential woman-force," who is at times, spring and fountain of the earthly place, or "current of stars" and movement of the planets. She touches the heart and "the heart of our ears" (66) and, though faceless, reveals a multiplicity of luminous faces. She quenches the woman's thirst:

> A draught of her--gives us back the virtues of childhood: the smallness of body, the ignorance, the immoderate hungers, the thirsting impatience, the stampings of haste, the near-anger in the impatience to approach, to learn, the reelings at feeling the immensity of the infinite, the passions of thoughts wild with urgency before immensities, the heights, the depths, the quantities, the diversities. (68)

In the magic garden created by Cixous, Clarice is the gaze and the window opening up onto the real world of the unintelligible. The body as well as all the senses open up in front of the "carpet of the garden," green sheet of paper where flower-faces blossom "with bouquets of words" (70); oranges, roses, orchids, and crocus unceasingly shift symbols from women to words, to underscore the symphony of the true seeing: "To see and undersee and see-over until being able to cry: 'in truth, I have seen!'" (74). The true seeing demands rigor and the search for the abstract. However it never leaves the simple roots of the concrete sensations. It is in that sense that Lispector and Cixous can be called writers of the body. After a long philosophical approach, the everyday reality, in its simple beauty, re-creates a new birth of love. Between the poles of philosophy and simple truth for the body, one has to forget indifference and the "devitalized bodies" (78) of the death-life of modern society. Only then can the light from the window emerge, after the oblivion and "un-blinding" (78) of the self, and the art to "un-live" in search for "loving life before death" (90).

Cixous, like Lispector, rejects the death threats of our lives to sing the joy of love and life in the tradition of the mystics of old. "To read woman" is to learn the lesson given by Clarice, as the postface of To Live the Orange urges. Through Cixous' writing Lispector reaches a mythical level. She is the butterfly of the psyche, emblem of the soul in its desire to reach light, and rebirth. She is the voice of light and the specks of the iris, eye, seer and goddess Iris, orange lighting, white lily and the joy of laughter, the orange beam of the sun "around our window" (113) and "Aqua Viva."

"To read woman" is to be able to use the word "ours," as Cixous does with her gift of To Live the Orange.

NOTES

[1] Hélène Cixous, Vivre l'Orange/To Live the Orange (Paris: Editions Des femmes 1979).

[2] Hélène Cixous, Portrait du Soleil (Paris: Editions Denoël, 1973) 5. Where quotes are given in French, the translations are from our own hand.

[3] Clarice Lispector, La Passion selon G. H., trans. into French from Portuguese by Claude Farny (Paris: Editions Des femmes, 1978) 25, 27, 56. Where quotes are given in French, the translations are from our own hand.

LA VIOLENCE DANS LA MERE DURASSIENNE

Janine Ricouart
Miami University

La violence est un élément récurrent dans la littérature française. On la trouve par exemple dans Les Fleurs du Mal de Baudelaire, dans Les Chants de Maldoror de Lautréamont, ou dans le théâtre d'Arrabal. Le conflit entre le monde intérieur de la perception et le monde extérieur de la société provoque dans l'esprit de l'artiste une lutte continuelle qui aboutit à la création, à la folie ou au suicide. Traditionnellement, les femmes sont doublement aliénées: à la fois dans la société et dans la famille; reléguées aux fonctions familiales, elles concentrent donc leur énergie sur ce cercle restreint. La littérature féminine offre de nombreux exemples des conséquences dramatiques que les tensions familiales provoquent chez les femmes: ainsi, Virginia Woolf dans Mrs. Dalloway ou dans To the Lighthouse ou Sylvia Plath dans The Bell Jar. Pour ces deux femmes artistes, la folie et le suicide existent comme solution ultime face à la violence plus ou moins diffuse que l'on trouve dans le monde familial et social.

La violence physique ou psychologique existe également chez les personnages de Marguerite Duras. Elle s'exprime par le meurtre (Claire Lannes dans L'Amante anglaise), le suicide (Anne-Marie Stretter dans India Song), la folie (Lol V. Stein dans Le Ravissement de Lol V. Stein), ou les cris (la mère dans Un Barrage contre le Pacifique). Les cris ont d'ailleurs un statut particulier, car "les femmes savent que les cris existent, partout, toujours, au bord d'être criés mais qu'ils ne le sont pas, qu'ils le sont une fois sur des millions de fois. . . . Les femmes le savent, ça, à cause du silence dans lequel elles se tiennent depuis des millénaires."[1] Les héroïnes de Duras sont parfois violentes jusqu'au crime. Leur violence est souvent silencieuse, mais elle existe: elle transparaît dans les relations avec leurs amants, leur époux, ou leurs enfants. Une étude de la violence féminine, et plus particulièrement de la violence maternelle, remet en question l'image de la femme généralement considérée comme passive, et vise surtout à re-penser le statut de la femme dans la société. Il est important de remarquer que cette violence existe et de voir comment elle s'exprime et ce qu'elle signifie, afin de pouvoir reconnaître la variété de l'expression féminine et d'en reconstruire la richesse réelle, et non mythique ou fantasmatique.

La vision du "moi divisé" de R. D. Laing semble s'appliquer tout à fait aux personnages de Duras, car pour lui, la psychose, aussi bien chez l'homme que chez la femme, représente une réponse compréhensible et même saine à la société destructrice. Ainsi, la schizophrénie serait, selon Laing, une "stratégie spéciale qu'un individu invente afin de survivre dans une situation invivable."[2] Laing considérait en partie la psychose comme une révolte contre l'élément claustrophobique de la famille nucléaire traditionnelle. Cet élément peut s'appliquer à certaines familles durassiennes, où la violence maternelle, en particulier, prend plusieurs formes et concerne souvent la communication d'un amour très fort. Parfois, l'amour d'une mère étouffe son enfant; tous deux sont alors aliénés l'un par rapport à l'autre, dans un trop plein d'amour. Ainsi, dans <u>Des Journées entières dans les arbres</u> (1954),[3] la mère apparaît comme aliénée de son fils. Elle le battait quand il était enfant parce qu'il lui ressemblait et qu'il était paresseux:

> Quand j'ai vu que Jacques ne faisait toujours rien, je me suis dit que c'était cet instinct-- là que j'avais qui lui revenait. Alors, j'ai commencé à le battre, à le battre. Tous les jours. A dix-huit ans, je le battais encore. . . . J'ai persisté. Chaque jour, pendant cinq ans. (29)

Cette violence physique de la mère envers le fils semble s'opposer à la dépendance qui unit le fils à sa mère et à Marcelle, son xamie. La relation mère/fils est très complexe chez les personnages durassiens et dans ce texte, nous nous attacherons essentiellement au point de vue de la mère, afin de montrer comment la femme se sert de la violence dans sa relation avec ses enfants et ce que représente cette violence. La mère bat son fils parce qu'il lui ressemble mais peut-être aussi parce que l'amour qu'elle ressent pour lui lui fait peur. Par la violence physique, la mère communique donc l'intensité de son amour, mais en même temps, elle se déculpabilise face à son propre échec. Il est intéressant de noter la complicité du fils avec la mère qui vient d'évoquer le temps où elle le battait, car il s'en souvient en riant (<u>Des Journées</u> 29). Cette complicité se retrouve dans d'autres situations similaires; ainsi, dans <u>Un Barrage contre le Pacifique</u> (1950)[4]:

> D'habitude, Suzanne supportait mal qu'elle [la mère] la batte, mais ce soir, elle trouvait que c'était mieux que si la mère, après avoir pris la bague, s'était mise à table tranquillement, comme d'habitude. (139)

La violence physique constitue une forme d'expression dont la mère, plus que l'enfant, semble victime. En effet, dans ces deux cas, l'enfant est présenté comme celui ou celle qui reconnaît la nécessité pour la mère de donner des coups. L'enfant semble s'offrir en victime indispensable afin de pallier les frustrations de la mère:

> Ç'avait éclaté lorsque Suzanne était sortie de table. Elle s'était jetée sur elle et elle l'avait frappée avec les poings de tout ce qui lui restait de force. De toute la force de son droit, de toute celle, égale, de son doute. En la battant, elle avait parlé des barrages, de la banque, de sa maladie, de la toiture, des leçons de piano, du cadastre, de sa vieillesse, de sa fatigue, de sa mort. . . . Elle frappait encore, comme sous la poussée d'une nécessité qui ne la lâchait pas. (Un Barrage 136)

Ces coups sont nécessaires pour que la mère se libère de tout un passé d'espoirs déçus. Les enfants ont une connaissance profonde du désespoir de la mère, comme l'intervention d'un narrateur omniscient le révèle:

> On ne pouvait plus lui en vouloir. Elle avait aimé désespérément la vie et c'était son espérance infatigable, incurable, qui en avait fait ce qu'elle était devenue, une désespérée de l'espoir même. Cet espoir l'avait usée, détruite, nudifiée. (Un Barrage 142)

Dans Un Barrage, la mère n'a eu aucun contrôle sur sa vie, malgré de nombreux efforts. Elle a toujours lutté avec énergie pour essayer de changer les instances négatives de sa vie. En effet, comme la majorité des mères durassiennes, la mère de Suzanne et de Joseph (dans Un Barrage) est une femme qui élève seule ses enfants. Malgré cette solitude, elle trouve le courage de lutter contre les colons blancs qui l'exploitent. Cette lutte inégale l'épuise et la rend violente. Pourtant cette violence est ambiguë. D'un côté, elle n'est pas perçue comme un élément destructeur, mais bien comme un signe de vie, de combativité, que la mère lègue à ses enfants: c'est le cas de Joseph, qui décide de partir en raison justement de l'exploitation et de la misère que la mère a subies tout au long de sa vie: "Même s'ils devaient la faire souffrir, les projets de Joseph se tramaient en raison de ce qu'avait enduré la mère" (Un Barrage 284). Mais d'un autre côté, cette violence qui libère peut aussi étouffer:

> Elle [la mère] avait eu tellement de malheurs
> que c'en était devenue un monstre au charme
> puissant et que ses enfants risquaient, pour la
> consoler de ses malheurs, de ne plus jamais la
> quitter, de se plier à ses volontés, de se
> laisser dévorer à leur tour par elle. (Un
> Barrage 183)

Toutes les mères présentes dans les textes de Marguerite Duras ont en commun un amour violent et étouffant pour leur enfant. Sara, dans Les petits chevaux de Tarquinia (1953)[5], avoue cette intensité: "Depuis la minute où il est né je vis dans la folie" (28). Cet amour fou existe également chez Anne Desbaresdes dans Moderato Cantabile (1958)[6] qui confesse que son enfant la "dévore":

> Si vous saviez tout le bonheur qu'on leur veut,
> comme si c'était possible. Peut-être vaudrait-
> il mieux parfois que l'on nous en sépare. Je
> n'arrive pas à me faire une raison de cet
> enfant. (32)

Cet amour intense s'exprime souvent par des mouvements violents, brusques: "Anne Desbaresdes prit son enfant par les épaules, le serra à lui faire mal, cria presque" (14). Mais l'amour passionnel qu'Anne ressent pour son enfant est douloureux: "Anne Desbaresdes baissa la tête, ses yeux se fermèrent dans le douloureux sourire d'un enfantement sans fin" (17). Un tel amour est comme une fatalité à laquelle la mère ne peut pas échapper:

> La sonatine résonna encore, portée comme une
> plume par ce barbare, qu'il le voulût ou non,
> et elle s'abattit de nouveau sur sa mère, la
> condamna de nouveau à la damnation de son
> amour. Les portes de l'enfer se refermèrent.
> (Moderato 83)

En plus de la violence physique, on relève chez la mère durassienne une violence psychologique; par exemple dans Un Barrage contre le Pacifique, la mère "torture" psychologiquement ses enfants, en les forçant à lui obéir: "C'était son plaisir d'éprouver la patience de ses enfants. C'était sa douceur" (110). Une fois de plus, la voix narratrice donne aux enfants une connaissance spécifique des "raisons" de la mère pour les battre. La narratrice justifie ainsi les coups que la mère donne aux enfants. L'Eden Cinéma (1977)[7], qui constitue une reprise pour le théâtre de la même histoire qu'Un Barrage, met l'accent sur l'impact psychologique de la folie de la mère sur ses enfants, et notamment sur Suzanne. Celle-ci évoque son enfance à plusieurs reprises:

> La quitter. La fuir. Cette folle. Cette démente.
> La fuir.
> Ce monstre dévastateur, la mère. (Eden 99)

La nécessité d'une rupture par rapport au cadre familial étouffant est évident dans tous les textes de Duras où la famille est mise en scène. Ainsi, dans Nathalie Granger (1977)[8], qui est le scénario d'un film, Isabelle, la mère de Nathalie, accomplit la séparation souhaitée par Anne Desbaresdes. Dans ce "récit," deux femmes, la mère et l'Amie, enfermées dans une maison, doivent régler le problème de Nathalie, renvoyée de l'école. Alors qu'Anne, dans Moderato, émettait le désir de laisser à quelqu'un le soin de s'occuper de son enfant, dans ce texte, Isabelle réalise cette séparation d'avec son enfant, en la mettant en pension: "Elle [la mère] a signé la séparation d'avec son enfant comme ils ont dit les autres, qu'il fallait faire" (N.G. 31). Cette séparation, consentie par la mère, est renforcée par l'Amie, qui lui conseille d'oublier sa fille, Nathalie. La didascalie qui suit ce conseil en donne ici le sens exact: "Sens: 'C'est ce qu'il faut faire: coupe le lien de la violence, sépare-toi de ton enfant. Sa violence est dirigée contre sa mère. Oublie que tu es la mère'" (47). L'aspect essentiel de la relation mère/fille est basée sur la violence et le silence: "La pose de la mère la regardant rappelle celle de l'enfant. Toutes deux isolées dans une violence de même nature, sauvage: celle de l'amour, celle du refus" (69). Finalement, la violence qui habite la mère et la fille s'exprime contre les objets; l'une comme l'autre déchirent du papier dans un mouvement de résistance: la mère déchire le journal, puis la facture de l'Electricité de France, puis le livret scolaire de sa fille (77). Nathalie, quant à elle, "déchire ses cahiers, elle fait des taches partout" (35). Tout comme sa mère, Nathalie s'attaque une seule fois aux objets devant la caméra:

> Tout à coup, de toutes ses forces, Nathalie lance sa poussette contre une grosse pierre, la lâche. La poussette se renverse, ses roues tournent à vide. Seule "violence" de Nathalie de tout le film: fureur subite, contre les "choses". (66)

Cependant, tout comme Anne Desbaresdes, qui est "dévorée" d'amour pour son enfant, l'amour passionné d'Isabelle pour sa fille est associé à la nourriture, ou plutôt au manque de nourriture: elle est "privée de cette enfant, dans la faim de cette enfant, enfermée" (N.G. 72). Elle a "un regard d'affamée, de concentrationnaire" (N.G. 73). La violence d'Isabelle par rapport aux objets évoque également une naissance: "Dans l'une de ces femmes, une sorte de parturition est en train de se faire" (N.G. 76). Tout comme Anne Desbaresdes, qui a "le douloureux sourire d'un enfantement sans fin" (Moderato 17), Isabelle Granger vit le départ de son enfant comme une nouvelle naissance, et donc comme une seconde séparation. Cette seconde séparation est nécessaire à l'autonomie de la mère et de l'enfant, bien que la mère soit ambiguë par rapport à son désir de "laisser aller".

Outre une violence psychologique et physique évidente au fil de la plupart des textes durassiens, il existe une violence plus obscure mais plus profonde, qui suscite l'introspection du rôle de la société moderne. En effet, si la femme a recours à la violence, Duras semble suggérer que c'est à cause des cadres sociaux. Dans les textes plus récents de Duras, la récurrence de l'absence du père est palliée par une seconde présence féminine auprès de l'enfant, ce qui permet notamment à la mère de vivre sa vie de façon plus indépendante. Ainsi, dans Nathalie Granger, la présence de l'Amie permet à Isabelle de laisser son enfant et de vivre sa douleur face à la deuxième séparation. De même, dans Dix heures et demie du soir en été, la présence de Claire, qui s'occupe de la fille de Maria, permet à cette dernière de vivre son désir pour Rodrigo Paestra, sans abandonner son enfant à la solitude.

Ce transfert du rôle maternel oblige le lecteur ou la lectrice à remettre en question l'importance du rôle de la maternité dans la vie d'une femme. Le stéréotype de l'instinct maternel veut que l'amour d'une mère soit sans condition. De plus, la maternité est souvent considérée comme le signe de la "vraie" féminité. Cependant, Adrienne Rich explique dans quelle mesure la maternité n'est qu'un aspect de l'identité féminine:

> La maternité, au sens de relation intense et réciproque avec un ou des enfants particuliers est une partie du processus féminin; ce n'est pas une identité permanente. . . . Le processus de "laisser aller"--qu'on nous reproche en cas d'échec--est pourtant un acte de révolte contre la racine de la culture patriarcale.[9]

Très souvent, la femme ne peut pas se réaliser elle-même à cause de la présence des enfants. Ainsi, la mère, dans Un Barrage contre le Pacifique, est avant tout un personnage révolté par l'exploitation que les Blancs pauvres et les indigènes subissent avec le colonialisme. Sa révolte constitue un aspect important de sa personnalité, et pourtant, elle ne pourra s'accomplir que lorsque ses deux enfants seront partis, comme elle l'écrit aux agents du cadastre:

> Quand je serai seule, quand mon fils sera parti, quand ma fille sera partie et que je serai seule et si découragée que plus rien ne m'importera, alors, peut-être qu'avant de mourir, j'aurai envie de voir vos trois cadavres se faire dévorer par les chiens errants. (294)

Il semble donc qu'elle ne puisse pas envisager une action personnelle tant qu'elle "fonctionne" comme mère. De même, Maria, Anne Desbaresdes ou Isabelle Granger doivent être sans leur enfant afin de se réaliser elles-mêmes, malgré--ou justement à cause de-- leur passion pour cet enfant.

Dans le cas de la mendiante, dans Le Vice-Consul,[10] la situation est plus complexe, dans la mesure où la mendiante est rejetée par sa mère parce qu'elle est enceinte en dehors du système social établi: "L'histoire de la jeune fille tient tout entière en ce parcours qui la conduit d'un lieu déjà perdu, Battambang, à un lieu où elle "reste" à jamais, Calcutta."[11]

Ce parcours est destructif pour la mendiante, qui atteint le silence, la stérilité et la folie à Calcutta. Sans famille et sans mari, elle n'est donc socialement ni femme, ni mère. Réduite au rang animal, seule la nourriture qui lui est offerte lui permet de survivre. La séparation d'avec la mère est brutale et difficile pour l'enfant, la mendiante de Calcutta. Elle a été chassée une première fois à la naissance et une deuxième fois lorsqu'elle est "tombée" enceinte. Elle veut rendre cet enfant volé à sa mère et se sauver, cette fois d'elle-même: "Dans ta stupéfaction, tu oublieras de me tuer, sale femme, cause de tout, je te rendrai cet enfant et toi tu le prendras, je le jetterai vers toi et moi je me sauverai pour toujours" (Vice-Consul 10). Ce transfert d'enfant souligne le désir irréalisable d'un retour à la mère. La jeune fille de Battambang devient la mendiante de Calcutta. Elle connaît la faim de sa mère qui l'a menacée de mettre du poison dans son riz si elle revenait. Le retour à la mère est donc impossible, interdit, à partir du moment où la jeune fille a renié la loi du père et rompu le système d'échanges auquel elle devait se soumettre. Au niveau du discours, la mendiante perd non seulement sa mère, mais aussi la possibilité de s'exprimer. Son histoire est en effet racontée par Peter Morgan, car elle a oublié sa langue "maternelle": "Sa route, elle est sûre, est celle de l'abandon définitif de sa mère" (V.C. 28). Tout ce dont elle se rappelle, c'est d'"un chant enfantin de

Battambang" (que lui chantait peut-être sa mère autrefois) (V.C. 28). Le cheminement de la mendiante, "jeune fille très maigre chassée qui va avoir un enfant" (V.C. 18), est un cheminement lent et douloureux qui l'éloigne de plus en plus de sa mère. La naissance de son enfant est présentée comme une séparation pénible, qui lui demande une force presque sur-humaine, dans la mesure où elle est épuisée par son errance et par la faim: "L'enfant doit être très près d'être fait, elle le sait, . . . ils se séparent, c'est cela, il est immobile presque tout le temps, prêt, n'attendant qu'à peine un peu plus de forces maintenant pour la quitter" (V.C. 24). La mendiante est au centre d'un mouvement perpétuel: d'une part, la naissance est perçue par l'enfant comme un rejet de la mère, et d'autre part, elle peut être perçue par la mère comme un abandon de l'enfant. Il existe donc à ce niveau deux positions tout aussi valides: celle de la mère privée de son enfant, et celle de l'enfant privé de sa mère. Cette tension créée à la naissance se reproduit au moment où la jeune fille de Battambang "tombe enceinte" à son tour. La mise au monde est présentée comme un acte de violence entre la mère et l'enfant, acte qui semble se reproduire continuellement dans la violence de l'amour de la mère pour son enfant. Cependant, quand la mendiante de Calcutta semble avoir tout perdu, sa mère, son enfant et sa raison, il lui reste la nourriture pour survivre. C'est le seul lien qui lui reste avec d'autres humains. Mais la nourriture devient aussi un élément de violence, dans la mesure où la mendiante dépend des colons blancs de Calcutta pour obtenir cette nourriture.

Bien que la violence de la mère durassienne se manifeste de différentes manières, nous ne la rencontrons jamais sous un jour monstrueux. Nous avons essentiellement considéré la violence physique et psychologique que la femme impose à son enfant dans un trop plein d'amour. Nous avons également vu que cette violence est l'expression d'un malaise à la fois social et personnel, et qu'elle implique la nécessité et l'urgence de la ré-évaluation du rôle maternel en société. En effet, il existe dans l'oeuvre durassienne une progression au niveau de l'image de la mère et une émergence du discours de la violence: entre la passivité d'Anne Desbaresdes qui souhaite que quelqu'un s'occupe de son fils, et la violence d'Isabelle Granger qui résiste à une séparation brutale. Les limites imposées à la femme par sa fonction sociale de mère en font parfois un être marginal. Sa colère face aux limitations qui lui sont imposées est souvent réprimée, puis retournée contre elle-même, et ensuite dirigée contre ses enfants. Cependant, Duras démontre dans ses textes l'importance d'une ré-évaluation du rôle de la femme; en effet, pour que les individus atteignent l'autonomie et l'indépendance, ce qui est tû ou réprimé doit devenir partie de notre discours et de notre réalité sociale. Comme Janus qui regarde de deux côtés en même temps, les femmes doivent analyser d'une part les discours patriarcaux, et d'autre part leur propre discours, afin de retrouver leur pouvoir dans l'autonomie et non dans la violence provoquée par la répression.

NOTES

[1] Interview du 11 avril 1981 par Françoise Faucher pour l'émission: "Femmes d'aujourd'hui" sur Radio-Canada. Textes réunis et présentés par Suzanne Lamy et André Roy dans Marguerite Duras à Montréal (Montréal: Editions Spirale, 1981) 50.

[2] R.D. Laing, The Politics of Experience (New York: Random House, 1967) 79. Les traductions sont les miennes.

[3] Marguerite Duras, Des Journées entières dans les arbres (Paris: Gallimard, 1954). (Des Journées dans le texte).

[4] Marguerite Duras, Un Barrage contre le Pacifique (Paris: Gallimard, 1950). (Un Barrage dans le texte.)

[5] Marguerite Duras, Les Petits chevaux de Tarquinia (Paris: Gallimard, 1953).

[6] Marguerite Duras, Moderato Cantabile (Paris: Gallimard, 1958). (Moderato dans le texte.)

[7] Marguerite Duras, L'Eden Cinéma (Paris: Mercure de France, 1977). (Eden dans le texte.)

[8] Marguerite Duras, Nathalie Granger (Paris: Gallimard, 1977). (N.G. dans le texte.)

[9] Adrienne Rich, Of Woman Born, Motherhood as Experience and Institution (1976; New York: Bantam Books, 1981) 18. (La traduction est la mienne):
"Motherhood, in the sense of an intense, reciprocal relationship with a particular child, or children, is one part of female process; it is not an identity for all time. . . . The process of "letting-go"--though we are charged with blame if we do not--is an act of revolt against the grain of patriarchal culture."

[10] Marguerite Duras, Le Vice-Consul (Paris: Gallimard, 1966). (V.C. dans le texte.)

[11] Marcelle Marini, Territoires du féminin avec Marguerite Duras (Paris: Editions de Minuit) 159.

THE SOLITARY WOMAN AND FRIENDSHIP
IN MADAME DE LAFAYETTE'S ZAÏDE

Ruth Carver Capasso
Harvard University

Madame de Lafayette wrote four novels and novella, each named after a central female figure. This manner of selecting a title was conventional for the period, yet in the case of Madame de Lafayette's work, the focus on a single woman's name is particularly appropriate, not only revealing an innovative concentration of the narrative on one principal action, but also reflecting a fundamental truth about her heroines.

The women of Madame de Lafayette's creation stand alone in a world of constraint and conflict, with their principal definition deriving from their relationships to men. Friendship, that rapport so prized by moralists such as Montaigne, La Rochefoucauld, and Madame de Sablé, is denied to them. Without confidante or equal, they are solitary, silent figures. A significant exception to this pattern occurs only in the novel Zaïde, where we find two young women associated by parentage, but even more by friendship.

Let me briefly recall those portions of the novel which depict their relationship. Written in 1671, seven years before her masterpiece, La Princesse de Clèves, Zaïde is set in medieval Spain. Consalve, the young hero, has left his home, disillusioned by the infidelity of a mistress and the betrayal of a friend. Having found shelter with a fellow recluse, he remains in retreat until a tempest leaves two castaway women on the shore near his hut. We learn that they call one another Félime and Zaïde, and appear to be noble. But because the women speak an unknown language, everything else is a mystery. Yet their manner on first seeing one another after the disaster immediately indicates that they are friends. It is significant that their mutual tenderness is the only certain indication of their relationship or characters given to Consalve or to the reader for over one hundred pages.

Consalve immediately falls in love with the more beautiful Zaïde, but is separated from her by the language barrier and by ensuing events. When they are finally reunited, he learns the two women's story from Félime.

Félime and Zaïde are cousins, but, even more, they are close friends, raised together since infancy. When the Arab prince Alamir arrives at their home in Cyprus, he is at first drawn to both women. Only Félime responds to him. Yet as her attraction intensifies into love, Alamir increasingly prefers Zaïde. Finally Félime is forced to realize that Alamir loves her cousin. Struggling with this sorrow, she continues to share a life with her friend and rival. Eventually Félime even confides her feelings to Zaïde, who offers at once to speak to Alamir in her favor, but Félime's pride forces her to reject this aid.

In time Félime learns that Alamir is hardly worthy of her love. Exploitative and unfaithful, he has already hurt several women, and has only become genuinely involved with Zaïde because she is the first woman to reject him. This knowledge does not alter Félime's passion.

Forced to leave their homes because of a war between the Spanish and the Moors, the two women are shipwrecked and meet Consalve. Taken from him by Zaïde's father, they meet again during the war, with the women as Consalve's prisoners and Alamir as his wounded captive. As Alamir lies dying, Zaïde, faithful to Consalve, refuses to see him. Only Félime goes, finally confessing her love before he dies. Twenty-four hours later Félime also dies, and the novel ends quickly with the marriage of Consalve and Zaïde.

From this brief summary it can be seen that Félime and Zaïde spend much time physically together. This in itself is unique to the works of Madame de Lafayette, for if (as is the case with the princesse de Clèves) the heroine is bound by social conventions and obligations, nevertheless she is always forced to fulfill these duties alone. The other women to whom she speaks are distant—part of the crowded, impersonal court—or superior in age or station—her mother, the Dauphine; no other "princesse" stands at her side. In contrast, Félime and Zaïde are repeatedly presented side by side. They live in the same house, walk together on the beach before Consalve's cabin, and are quite literally in the same boat for two major events: first is the meeting with Alamir, whose sloop follows their pleasure boat in a kind of ballet of pursuit and flight that reveals the first delicate differences in the two friends' reactions to the Arab; second is the shipwreck that delivers them to Consalve.

This physical intimacy is neither circumstantial nor imposed upon the women. When leaving their island, both choose to travel on the same vessel, although this means that Félime will be separated from her father, that Félime will be always with her rival. Their physical closeness reflects a genuine emotional bond. Through Consalve we were witness to the women's affectionate reunion after the shipwreck; an even greater testimony is given by Félime herself, whose narration of their history reveals no bitterness or jealousy. She freely acknowledges Zaïde's superior attractions: "J'avais deux années plus qu'elle; il y avait aussi quelque différence dans nos humeurs; la mienne penchait moins à la joie; il était aisé de le connaître en nous voyant, aussi bien que l'avantage que la beauté de Zaïde avait sur la mienne."[1]

But certainly the greatest proof of the emotional tie between the women is presented when Félime confesses her love for Alamir to Zaïde. She has hesitated for some time before speaking; it has occurred to her that admitting her attraction may make the man seem more desirable to her rival (171). In addition, pride and shame make the avowal more difficult. Finally, however, she overcomes these barriers and speaks; the result is not only a closer bond between the women, but actual relief for Félime: "je trouvai beaucoup de soulagement à lui avoir ouvert mon coeur et à me plaindre avec elle" (174).

Unlike any other work by Madame de Lafayette, Zaïde shows a possibility of communication and of sympathy between its characters. It is true that confession always plays a major role in her fictions, but it is only in Zaïde that this form of communication can be seen in a positive light. In every other work, the heroine is eventually forced to divulge a guilty passion, and the only available confessor is the husband or admirer, the one person most tormented by this revelation. Language becomes a weapon, whether it be wielded thoughtlessly or in desperation. In each case, the act brings no benefit to the woman; for the princesse de Clèves, of course, it is a crucial step in her final tragedy. Beyond Zaïde, the only significant example of a woman confiding in a female friend occurs in La Comtesse de Tende, but the perspective and results translate the episode into a proof of infidelity, not of amity. The comtesse de Tende hears the confidences of the princesse de Neufchatel, but makes none herself; the reason is simple: the countess is in love with the same man and remains his mistress even after his marriage to this woman supposedly her friend. Here confidence is betrayed and friendship quickly transforms into guilt, as the characters struggle in a net of desires and deception. Seen in this context, Félime's confession is unique. It is of no consequence for the narrative; unlike the avowals of the princesse de Clèves and of the princesse de Montpensier, Félime's words effect no change in behavior, they bring no jealousy or torment. Her confiding in her friend serves only one purpose: to underscore the warmth and value of this friendship.

And yet, this same episode which does so much to affirm the significance of friendship as an emotional support, at the same time illustrates the very real limits of this relationship in

Madame de Lafayette's conception. Félime's confession accomplishes nothing, not because Zaïde is unwilling to help her, but because she has no power to act. All of Zaïde's good will cannot make Alamir abandon his passion for her, just as tender companionship cannot compensate for the helpless love felt by Félime. Friendship, although presented as a true bond between the women and a source of comfort and strength, is ultimately overcome by the negative force of passion; characters act and choose according to their sexual love, not their friendship. The failure of friendship to operate on a psychological level to motivate anyone's actions removes it as a deciding factor in the drama, which becomes only a struggle of desire and rivalry.

The minor value attached to friendship becomes strikingly clear if we consider the way in which the theme is developed by Catherine Bernard in her novella, Eléonor d'Yvrée (1687). Eléonor loves the duc de Misnie and is loved by him. Their happiness is threatened, however, when Eléonor learns that her best friend, Matilde, also loves the duke. For a time this rivalry results in a painful separation of the friends, and they are only forced back together when, participating in a royal celebration, the two boats in which they are riding touch and bring them face to face. This deftly written scene symbolizes their emotional separation just as the boating passages of Madame de Lafayette figure her heroines' intimacy. Eléonor, finally forced to choose between love and friendship, sacrifices her own happiness and marries another man. It is clear the friendship is as much a factor in her drama as family honor is to Chimène in Le Cid. By comparison, in Zaïde, friendship has no dramatic, but only pathetic power.

Friendship is thus relegated to a permanently inferior status--much like Félime herself. Indeed, it is possible to consider Félime as a figure of friendship. While Zaïde immediately captures the exclusive admiration of Alamir and Consalve, other men, whose judgment we are led to value, speak up in praise of Félime. Alphonse, Consalve's companion in his retreat, gently chides him for failing to recognize Félime's attractions. Don Olmond, a nobleman instrumental in bringing about the final reunion of the characters, declares himself a particular friend of Félime, and it is because of their friendship that Félime is willing to recount her story. The very technique of according a narrative role to Félime invites the reader to sympathize with her, even as it underscores her status as observer, on the sidelines. Zaïde, the figure of love, is a remarkably silent and distant being, endowed with little more than beauty and conventional responses, facts which make her attraction for men seem all the more irrational and inevitable.

Madame de Lafayette has shown friendship to be inconsequential in the realm of love. This is not surprising in the context of contemporary literature which, following the writings of Montaigne, regularly contrasted friendship and love, with the moral preference given to friendship (according to La Rochefoucauld, "un véritable ami est le plus grand de tous les biens"[2]) and the greater power and fascination accorded to love—once again, La Rochefoucauld writes: "ce qui fait que la plupart des femmes sont peu touchées de l'amitié, c'est qu'elle est fade quand on a senti de l'amour" (Madame de Sablé 115).

Love makes friendship seem colorless, according to this disillusioned philosophy. In the novel of Madame de Lafayette, it works a still greater destruction. When Alamir is dying, Félime alone goes to comfort him. After his death, she returns to the room where Zaïde waits. In grief Félime bursts out in reproach for her inhumanity, and wonders how Zaïde could fail to love the man. Consalve appears, the man who fatally wounded Alamir in a duel, and Félime refuses to see him. She becomes ill, and hours later, when she is finally able to speak, her last words embrace friendship and death: "Ne me regrettez point . . . je n'aurais plus été digne de votre amitié et je n'aurais pu aimer une personne qui aurait causé la mort d'Alamir" (230). Love has killed not only Félime, but her friendship, the essence of her character. It has destroyed her ability to cherish another's happiness, to live in and for her friend.

Thus the vision of friendship, so delicately, so tentatively drawn, is in the end overshadowed by the power of passion. Madame de Lafayette continues to translate the stern moralist's conception of a world where each individual struggles alone with her need and desire. Friendship, community, sympathy have no power in the face of love which is, in the words of Madame de Sablé, "toujours le maître" (Madame de Sablé 246).

NOTES

[1]*Romans et Nouvelles* (Paris: Garnier, 1961) 165. All subsequent quotes are drawn from this edition and will be noted in the text in parentheses.

[2]*Réflexions ou sentences et maximes morales, suivi de Réflexions diverses et des Maximes de Madame de Sablé* (Paris: Gallimard, 1976) 155.

PAULINE JULIEN ET ANGELE ARSENAULT:
CHANSONS DE LIBERATION

Paul Benhamou
Purdue University

Si, comme l'a affirmé Bruno Roy dans un ouvrage récent sur la chanson québécoise, "les chansonniers québécois sont nés d'un besoin" de dire, de chanter la nouvelle réalité québécoise des années soixante,[1] nous pensons, pour notre part, que Pauline Julien et Angèle Arsenault ont surgi sur la scène québécoise comme une nécessité intrinsèque à l'affirmation de la femme du Québec d'aujourd'hui, de sa vraie nature et de son rôle dans une société en pleine évolution.

Les grands chansonniers québécois, Gilles Vigneault, Claude Léveillée, Jean-Pierre Ferland, Georges Dor, ont certes tenu un discours sur la femme, cela est indéniable, mais leur perspective est essentiellement masculine et traditionnelle lorsqu'ils chantent la femme: images stéréotypées de la femme, idéalisation anachronique, point de vue chauviniste ou tout simplement prétexte.

Un discours féminin sur la femme du Québec ne pouvait donc être tenu que par des femmes, cela est évident, et celui qui nous a paru le plus éloquent et le plus révélateur de l'éveil de la conscience féminine du Québec, est contenu dans les chansons de Pauline Julien et d'Angèle Arsenault. Ce discours n'est qu'une manifestation partielle et chantée de la remarquable pléthore d'oeuvres littéraires publiées par des Québécoises dans les dix derrières années. Il n'a rien de radicalement féministe dans la mesure où il ne poursuit pas les expériences littéraires des Louky Bersianik, Madeleine Gagnon ou Nicole Brossard (<u>écriture du corps</u>), et, en cela, il a l'avantage d'être accessible à un public très vaste et très divers par son langage d'abord: la chanson et parole, et aussi par ses moyens de diffusion: le disque, la cassette, la radio, la télévision. . . . Ce discours chanté au féminin, n'est associé à aucune organisation, à aucune idéologie; il est né parce qu'au Québec, comme partout ailleurs, les femmes ont été opprimées à tous les niveaux. Il est important de noter que la chanson québécoise au féminin qui fait l'objet de notre propos, n'est pas un phénomène qui a atteint l'ampleur et l'influence de sa contrepartie masculine, la chanson au Québec demeure encore une manifestation culturelle dominée par des hommes. L'oeuvre des chansonniers du Québec est sans nul doute "une manifestation populaire de la conscience collective québécoise," "le miroir d'un peuple," (Roy 34) comme on l'a souvent noté, mais elle n'en demeure pas moins une conscience au masculin, un miroir qui a laissé la femme dans l'ombre, et qui ne nous a transmis que l'ombre de la femme.

Si la chanson québécoise au masculin a établi l'existence du Québécois, la chanson au féminin vise à présent d'en définir l'essence; si la chanson au masculin était très souvent axée sur le pays, la chanson au féminin est sans frontières, universelle; si la chanson au masculin est le plus souvent centrée sur l'homme, la chanson au féminin concerne la femme et l'homme.

Nous pensons, en outre, que le phénomène de la chanson féminine, quoique minoritaire, constitue une évolution logique de la révolution du Québec et qu'il faut y prêter l'oreille et lui donner la parole.

Nous avons donc choisi quelques textes représentatifs de Pauline Julien (écrits par elle seule ou en collaboration avec d'autres femmes) et d'Angèle Arsenault, qui contiennent un authentique discours sur la femme.

Pauline Julien, qui est connue comme la "pasionaria" du Québec, s'est engagée très tôt dans la lutte pour la libération du Québec. Elle fut québécoise avant tout le monde. Car il fallait un fier courage en 1964, alors que le parti québécois n'existait pas, pour refuser de chanter devant la reine d'Angleterre, pour indiquer ainsi publiquement que les Francophones de la Nouvelle France ne se considéraient plus comme des sujets anglais. Elle a d'abord chanté les textes des autres (Levesque, Dor, Vigneault), avant de se mettre à écrire et à chanter au féminin.

Pauline Julien, la "sorcière" de la chanson québécoise, s'est lancée corps et âme dans la lutte pour la libération totale de la femme, elle parle aux femmes, les prend à témoins et les pousse à se libérer de leur long esclavage.

Elle a débuté dans cette nouvelle carrière en 1970 avec une composition révolutionnaire intitulée "Les Femmes," qui renverse toute la mythologie que l'homme a fabriquée sur la femme, une sorte de portrait négatif de la femme, produit de l'imagination et des rêves de l'homme. S'adressant aux créateurs de cette mythologie, elle dénonce la grande mystification de l'histoire:

>   Vous les fabriquez mères toutes aimables
>   Miroirs de justice, trônes de la sagesse
>   Vierges très prudentes, arches d'alliance. . . .
>   Vous les baptisez salut des infirmes
>   Reines des patriarches, roses mystiques
>   Mères du bon conseil, vierges clémentes. . . .

> Vous les exigez étoiles du matin
> Vases spirituels, mère sans tache
> Vierges vénérables, tours d'ivoire . . . [2]

Tous ces mythes masculins ont imposé une image de la femme, qui ignore la réalité de la femme, car, comme le dit Pauline Julien: "Vous rêvez Messieurs beaucoup." Cette démystification de la femme par la femme est un acte audacieux et en même temps révolutionnaire, car elle met en question une vision archaique et superstitieuse du monde et laisse entrevoir une femme qui existe indépendamment des fantasmes de l'homme:

> Mon Dieu que les femmes sont devenues exigeantes
> Elles ne pleurent plus, ne veulent même plus attendre
> En amour et partout, elles prennent ce qu'elles
>   demandent.

Cette écriture au féminin représente bien "l'acte de rupture" type, dont a parlé Paul Chamberland. Pauline Julien a pris la parole pour démystifier la femme, pour faire exploser les tabous qui l'étouffaient et pour revaloriser sa place dans la société. Mais cette rupture est loin d'établir un divorce définitif entre la femme et l'homme; au contraire, elle revalorise les rapports homme-femme et elle porte en elle la promesse du vrai bonheur. Ainsi, elle conclut "Les Femmes" en disant: "Mais demain, mon amour, nous serons plus heureux ensemble." Comme l'a noté Michèle Lalonde, cette entreprise constitue "une volonté d'humanisation des civilisations" qui ont opprimé la femme.[3]

Dans "Rassurez-vous Monsieur," Pauline Julien redéfinit le rôle de la femme au sein du couple, et, pour ce faire, elle commence par rejeter tous les rôles dans lesquels la société patriarcal avait emprisonné la femme et par refuser d'être ce qu'on l'avait forcée d'être. Cet acte de négation est en somme une affirmation de son existence et en même temps un défi au discours patriarcal sur la femme:

> Je ne serai plus
> Votre belle votre muse votre mère
> Votre fée votre femme votre objet votre sujet
> Votre ange votre rêve votre dame
> Votre déesse votre maîtresse[4]

Ce refus d'identification avec les valeurs et les normes qui rendirent les femmes prisonnières du système patriarcal, est, sans nul doute, traumatisant pour le groupe dominant qui les a inventées: l'homme se sent menacé de perdre ses privilèges et en même temps sa propre identité, d'où le "Rassurez-vous Monsieur" que Pauline lui adresse avec une ironie certaine.

Il n'y a cependant aucun désir de renverser les rôles, aucune agressivité chez la femme nouvelle, mais une très grande lucidité:

> Votre univers sera changé. . . .
> Ce ne sera pas la guerre
> Tout simplement d'autres manières. . . .

C'est littéralement la fin d'un monde que Pauline annonce ici et la naissance d'une femme nouvelle qui a "brisé l'infini servage" et qui "vivra pour elle et par elle," comme l'a prophétisé Rimbaud au siècle dernier.

L'homme, qui a jusqu'à présent tenu la femme captive, opprimée et colonisée en quelque sorte, ne pourra plus compter sur:

> Votre celle qui prépare
> Vos retours, vos départs
> Votre celle qui se tait
> pour que vous travailliez
> Votre celle qui attend
> pour que vous disposiez
> Votre celle qui cuisine
> et vous vous amusez
> Votre celle si douce
> parce que vous êtes pressé.

La femme qui s'est libérée, change non seulement sa vie, mais aussi celle de l'homme, et c'est cette transformation fondamentale que Pauline fait entrevoir à la fin de "Rassurez-vous Monsieur":

> C'est merveilleux monsieur
> Vous allez retrouver
> vos élans et vingt ans
> Pour un peu vous serez
> le père de vos enfants
> Et mieux encore pour moi
> Un bien meilleur amant.

Pauline Julien prend donc la parole pour libérer la femme québécoise d'un lourd passé de soumission, de complexes et de mythes, et en ce sens on peut dire que ses chansons sont subversives, profanatrices, iconoclastiques, et par conséquent poétiques.

"Qui chante, combat," ce proverbe de la sagesse populaire décrit à merveille les chansons au féminin de Pauline. Dans "Eille," elle encourage la majorité silencieuse, les femmes, à briser leur long silence, à se déterminer, à prendre la vie à pleines dents, à vivre sans peur:

> C'est assez de se laisser manger la laine sur le dos
> C'est assez de se taire
> C'est aujourd'hui qu'il faut chasser la peur
> qu'il faut s'emparer de la vie
> C'est aujourd'hui qu'il faut vivre. . . .

Comme Pauline Julien est proche de Madeleine Gagnon, cette autre femme de parole québécoise qui écrit dans "Mon corps dans l'écriture": "Si la femme se trouve aliénée dans la culture des hommes, qu'elle s'empare de la sienne et la dise."[5]

Et dans "Marie m'a dit" composé en collaboration avec Denise Boucher, c'est l'appel aux armes, à la rupture collective:

> Faudrait tout' partir ensemble
> Ou leur laisserait leur maison, leurs p'tits,
> leur vaisselle, leur prison
> Le temps qu'y apprennent à s'organiser y verrait ben
> Faudrait tout' partir ensemble
> Tu seule chu pas capable
> Faudrait tout' partir ensemble. . . .

Ces paroles que nous venons d'entendre, cet appel à la révolte collective trouvent un écho certain dans le chant du MLF <u>Debout les Femmes</u>, dont voici quelques extraits:

> Levons-nous femmes esclaves
> Et brisons nos entraves
> Debout! . . .
>
> Ensemble, on nous opprime les femmes
> Ensemble révoltons-nous
> Levons-nous. . . .
>
> Le temps de la colère, les femmes
> Notre temps est arrivé
> Connaissons notre force, les femmes
>
> Découvrons-nous par milliers
> Levons-nous femmes esclaves
> Et brisons nos entraves
> Debout! Debout!

Pauline Julien a pris la parole indépendamment de tout mouvement, pour parler de liberté et éveiller la conscience de la femme québécoise devant sa double exploitation. Sa parole n'est pas "oppressive," mais bien au contraire comme le suggère Annie Leclerc "une parole qui délie les langues."[6]

Elle est bien consciente de la difficulté de sa tâche: "Pourquoi est-il si long, long le chemin de la liberté?" se demande-t-elle dans "Eille," mais elle n'en demeure pas moins convaincue qu'une ère nouvelle a commencé pour l'homme et la femme au Québec:

>C'est par amour que nous changeons d'histoire
>C'est par amour que nous changeons l'histoire.[7]

Cette parole exigeante de Pauline Julien est un exemple éloquent du texte au féminin québécois qui tente d'accomplir ce que Michèle Lalonde a appelé "une révolution globale" qui donnera naissance à "une société originale avec pleins pouvoirs politiques et une égale liberté pour nos filles et nos fils."[8]

Nous avons choisi une autre "femme de parole" qui jouit d'une très grande popularité au Québec, bien qu'elle soit née dans l'Ile du Prince Edouard; je veux parler de l'incomparable Angèle Arsenault, qui a composé de nombreux textes au féminin.

Nous trouvons dans ses textes une volonté inébranlable de prendre en charge sa propre libération et une révolte contre le système patriarcal opprimant qui a dénié à la femme la liberté et la dignité de la personne humaine.

>Je veux toute toute toute la vivre ma vie
>Je ne veux pas l'emprisonner
>J'la veux toute toute toute pas juste p'tites gouttes
>Je veux toute toute toute la vivre ma vie . . .[9]

chante-t-elle dans une chanson à grand succès, qui est devenue une sorte de chant national de la femme québécoise d'aujourd'hui qui rejette tous les rôles traditionnels qui lui avaient été imposés par l'homme.

>Laissez-moi couper tous les liens . . .
>Laissez-moi trouver mon chemin . . .
>Laissez-moi tranquille, laissez-moi, laissez-moi,
>Mais laissez-moi exister . . .

Cette volonté d'assumer sa propre vie envers et contre tous, ce cri existentiel de désespoir qu'elle lance ici, montre bien la difficulté d'être elle-même dans une société dominée par l'homme. "Je trouve important de dénoncer le système de notre société qui empêche la personne d'être elle-même en lui fixant des prototypes bien établis," a-t-elle déclaré au cours d'une interview récente.[10] Comme dans les chansons de Pauline, le chemin de la libération passe d'abord par un processus de démystification des "prototypes établis" par le système, pour s'ouvrir ensuite sur la vision d'une société nouvelle où la femme est libre et où elle est un être humain à part entière.

Ainsi, dans "Je suis démaquillée,"[11] Angèle Arsenault oppose la femme du passé, créature artificielle du système à celle du présent qui s'est libérée de tous les masques, et devient la femme "naturelle":

>   Je me suis démasquée. . . .
>   Je me suis réveillée. . . .
>   Je me suis libérée. . . .

Angèle Arsenault ne le cache pas, elle parle aux femmes, veut les secouer de leur long esclavage et les encourager à suivre son propre exemple. Avec des mots simples mais directs et efficaces, elle dénonce le système aliénant du passé:

>   J'étais préfabriquée
>   J'étais toute inventée
>   J'étais utilisée
>   J'étais colonisée

à la réalité du présent:

>   Je suis réalité
>   Je suis d'la parenté
>   Je suis simplicité
>   Je suis démystifiée.

Le passage du "je" au "nous" dans les deux dernières strophes de cette chanson témoigne bien de la solidarité d'Angèle Arsenault avec toutes les femmes.

Signalons aussi que, comme chez Pauline Julien, il n'y a aucune répudiation de l'homme chez elle car l'amour reste le moteur de la vie:

>   Nous sommes de l'an 2000
>   C'est la fin de l'exil
>   Nous sommes égalité
>   Nous sommes la liberté
>   Nous sommes déterminées
>   Nous sommes prêtes à aimer.

Après avoir fait tomber tous les masques qui dénaturaient la femme, Angèle entreprend la tâche de redéfinir la femme ainsi que ses rapports avec l'homme. Dans la chanson intitulée "Je suis la femme," la femme se voit et s'accepte telle qu'elle est, au lieu être telle qu'on voudrait qu'elle soit:

> Jusqu'à l'âge de trente ans j'étais endormie
> Et voilà que maintenant le soleil luit. . . .
> Je me regarde dans le miroir je recommence ma vie
> Je me regarde dans le miroir et je me prends comme je suis
> Je me regarde dans le miroir et je souris à la vie. . . .[12]

Voilà donc la nouvelle femme indépendante, libre de vivre sa vie, d'assumer sa personnalité qu'Angèle Arsenault entrevoit et propose comme modèle aux autres femmes.

Quant aux rapports entre l'homme et la femme, ils resteront toujours une comédie d'erreurs tant que les deux partenaires se regarderont à travers des notions de virilité et de féminité héritées de la préhistoire de l'humanité.

Dans "Un jour une femme," Angèle Arsenault dramatise ces faux rapports, leur superficialité, voire leur absurdité: un homme rencontre une femme et tout arrive mécaniquement: l'amour, le mariage, la maison et les enfants, c'est le système qui le veut! Résultat, cette union de deux êtres humains qui ignorent le plus souvent leur vraie nature, aboutit au divorce. Mais Angèle Arsenault, qui est une optimiste par "parti-pris," nous offre dans cette même chanson la vision d'un bonheur possible dans un proche avenir:

> Un jour la femme
> Et l'homme pourront se comprendre
> Bientôt j'espère
> Qu'ils pourront enfin vivre ensemble
> Comme de vrais amoureux
> Faits pour être heureux
> Ils pourront se parler
> Ils pourront se donner
> Sans peur ni jalousie
> Ils ouvriront leur coeur
> Et petit à petit
> Ils arriveront au bonheur.[13]

Quand Angèle Arsenault chante, elle s'adresse aux femmes de tous les pays et les pousse à se redécouvrir, à briser les moules dans lesquels elles ont été fabriquées, exploitées, colonisées; elle leur donne des "coups de coeur" pourqu'elles aient le courage d'être elles-mêmes et de vivre leur vie à part entière. "Je veux lutter contre la société de consommation, contre la publicité frauduleuse qui présente la femme comme une Barby, belle, mince, bien maquillée et qui ne fait même pas pipi," a-t-elle déclaré au cours d'une interview avec Pascal Normand (179). Ses chansons transmettent ce message, et les femmes du Québec ont entendu ce message qui parle de liberté et delibération.

Angèle Arsenault, comme Pauline Julien, fait une révolution dans l'imagination de ses auditrices: elle fait entrevoir une femme libre, égale à l'homme, indépendante, sûre d'elle-même, heureuse et amoureuse. Et s'il faut en croire Hegel, lorsqu'on révolutionne l'imagination, la réalité ne peut pas tenir bien longtemps! Le chemin de la liberté est certes bien long, comme le déplore Pauline Julien, mais "Je suis libre" et "Personne ne peut m'arrêter," proclame Angèle Arsenault avec conviction.

Pauline Julien et Angèle Arsenault, deux femmes de parole qui font entendre la voix de la femme nouvelle du Québec. Si, comme l'a écrit Benoîte Groult dans Ainsi soit-elle: "Il faut que les femmes crient. Et que les autres femmes et les hommes--aient envie d'entendre ce cri,"[14] nous pouvons affirmer que Pauline Julien et Angèle Arsenault ont "chanté" la femme avec conviction et que leur message a été entendu. Leur art, la chanson, est une page capitale de l'histoire littéraire du Québec, nous devrions dire, dans l'histoire du Québec, car au Québec "tout commence par des chansons." Les chansons de Pauline Julien et d'Angèle Arsenault constituent dans une certaine mesure une "contre-culture" au féminin, puisqu'elles contestent la culture dominante de l'homme. Leur contribution à la transformation de l'image de la femme provoquera-t-elle une crise d'identité chez l'homme du Québec? Je ne le crois pas. Leur discours peut être considéré non seulement comme une re-naissance, une re-connaissance, une affirmation du féminin, mais aussi comme une réconciliation du féminin et du masculin. L'espoir vient en chantant!

NOTES

[1] Bruno Roy, *Et cette Amérique chante en québécoise* (Ottawa: Leméac, 1978) 20.

[2] "Pauline Julien," présentation par Louis-Jean Calvet, *Poésie et chansons* 29 (1974): 67-68.

[3] "Anatomie du féminisme," in *Défense et illustration de la langue québécoise, suivie de prose et poèmes* (Paris: Editions Seghers/Laffont, 1979) 209.

[4] *Femmes de Paroles*, Kébec Disc 935.

[5] Hélène Cixous, Madeleine Gagnon, Annie Leclerc, *La Venue à l'écriture*, Collection 10/18 (Paris: Union Générale d'Editions, 1977) 90.

[6] Kébec Disc 935.

[7] "Urgence d'amour," Kébec Disc 935.

[8] "Anatomie du féminisme" 213.

[9] Angèle Arsenault, "Libre," SPPS Disques, PS 19903.

[10] Pascal Normand, *La Chanson Québécoise, miroir d'un peuple* (Montréal: Editions France-Amérique, 1981) 179.

[11] Angèle Arsenault, Kébec Disc 503.

[12] SPPS Disques, PS 19903.

[13] Kébec Disc 503.

[14] (Paris: Bernard Grasset, 1975) 228.

THE SUICIDE OF "LA COMEDIENNE" IN RACHILDE'S LA JONGLEUSE

Robert E. Ziegler
Montana College of Mineral Science and Technology

Swords and daggers, bayonets and scalpels: all the pointed instruments men use for invading others' bodies are appropriated by the women characters in the novels of Rachilde. In the evolution of "l'amour compliqué"[1] that Barrès sees emerging in these works, the men are stripped of masculinity and weapons. They become vulnerable and sexless while the women turn into predators and warriors. Indeed, one need only consult Praz's list of "Belles dames sans merci," figures like Huysmans' Madame de Chantelouve or Clara, the torture-loving nymphomaniac in Mirbeau's Le Jardin des supplices, to realize how frequently such characters appear in "fin-de-siècle" fiction. In this respect, Rachilde's works differ little from the writings of her contemporaries. Still, her novels which show the conjugation of aggressiveness and female sexuality deserve attention, not just because they examine from a woman's standpoint the same questions dealt with by her peers, but because they point out the result of such a view of domination, sex and love, show it leading to a kind of suicide, the extinction of all feelings for another and, finally, for oneself.

Born in 1860, Rachilde, née Marguerite Eymery, emerged as a prolific writer whose works appeared well into the present century. Friend to the notorious Jean Lorrain, candidate for the affections of Catulle Mendès, later wife of Alfred Vallette, editor of Le Mercure de France,[2] Rachilde took pains to cultivate the image of her eccentricity. Yet there can be no doubt it was in her fiction, not in her life, that she advanced her boldest thoughts, there that she explored as few had done before her "ces formes d'amour qui sentent la mort" (Barrès 6).

Monsieur Vénus, La Marquise de Sade, La Jongleuse: In these three novels by Rachilde, texts which Claude Dauphiné regards as "les véritables jalons de l'oeuvre,"[3] one can see at once the author's changing attitude toward the conflict between the sexes. From the experiment with transvestism, the chaste voluptuousness of Raoule de Vénérande, who keeps her pretty boyfriend in a sumptuous apartment and lavishes on him gifts of hashish, clothes and flowers, to Eliante Donalger, the juggler of knives who kills herself with one of them to preserve her passion's purity, one sees in Rachilde's works the emergence of a death-dedicated love, one that does more than fight against the dominion of "les phallocrates" but that submerges sexuality in a true "pulsion de mort."

It is primarily in La Jongleuse (1900), the last of these three novels, that the ultimately suicidal nature of these characters' pursuits, the consequence of love's repudiation, at last becomes apparent. Earlier in Monsieur Vénus, Raoule had mentioned that women looked on love divorced from its expression as the greatest aphrodisiac. The same holds true for Eliante, who sees love not as Eros, the binding of the two attracted partners in a union that transcends them, but as the enhancement of the individual who feels that love within her. There is no focusing of consciousness on that which one desires and an attendant sense of emptiness until one merges with it. Love does not entail a yearning for its object. For Eliante it is not a future- or goal-oriented feeling, but is rather more inclusive. "Je suis réellement amoureuse de tout ce qui est beau, bon, me paraît un absolu . . .," she says. "Mais ce n'est pas le but, le plaisir; c'est une manière d'être."[4] Instead of joining with the being on whom attention narrows, the loving person takes in everything, enjoys an environmental fullness. "J'ai le dégoût de l'union," she says. "Je n'y découvre aucune plénitude voluptueuse. Pour que ma chair s'émeuve et conçoive l'infini de plaisir, je n'ai pas besoin de chercher un sexe à l'objet de mon amour" (La Jongleuse 49-50).

From this standpoint the love she feels for Léon Reille, the man who would possess her, is but one increment of the total emotional charge that ties her to the world. For Eliante, the more indiscriminate the love, the greater is the range of objects to which it may attach. Thus the alabaster vase she bought in Tunis can affect her with its symmetry, its human shape and beauty, can bring her to a climax as much as can a lover whose inconstancy she fears. As Léon watches her be overcome by flattering her urn--"ce fut plutôt une risée plissant l'onde mystérieuse de sa robe de soie--et elle eut un petit râle de joie imperceptible, le souffle même du spasme" (La Jongleuse 50-51)--he reacts with outraged disbelief at this assault on his male ego. "Il fut ébloui, ravi, indigne. --C'est scandaleux! Là... devant moi... sans moi? Non, c'est abominable! Il se jeta sur elle, ivre d'une colère folle. --Comédienne! Abominable comédienne!" (La Jongleuse 51). But of course the truth of Eliante's orgasm is really no pretense, no performance meant to embarrass him and wound his vanity. Yet he is right in calling her an actress, not because the reactions she expresses are simulated, false, but because Eliante is usually more intent on acting out her feelings than sharing them with him and risking their dilution: "je vous ai donné ce que je peux montrer d'amour à un homme," as she pointedly remarks (La Jongleuse 51).

In this cult of love where Eliante is priestess, it is unimportant what triggers the emotion, the words and acts through which it is expressed. Eliante's amphora, her collection of erotic Chinese carvings, even her idealized impression of Léon, function simultaneously as many things. They are the sensual/esthetic forms that arouse the love she values, they are that through which her love must pass to be further sublimated and that which, through their shape, their words or the figures they depict, confirms the beliefs she holds most dear. For this reason what Eliante brings to her sanctuary-bedroom must act as object of devotion, medium and testimonial all at once. Léon imagines it is his person that stirs this love inside her and that at length she must respond with the surrender of her body. He has failed to realize that once Eliante identifies him as a disciple of love's god, it no longer matters whether he is there with her or not. His effect on her has been assimilated into her religion of the beautiful, so that his continued presence is merely a redundance. As a performer, Eliante is her own most valued audience; what she is in love with is the chance to elaborate on her own self-created myth. Eliante, more than Raoule de Vénérande and Mary Barbe in La Marquise de Sade, is completely self-sufficient. Apart from her perverted husband, who had died some time before, she uses men as reiterations of her own views on love.

One way to understand more clearly the evolution of Rachilde's heroines is by examining the meaning of the knife/sword/dagger imagery that occurs in many of her texts. In La Jongleuse, the function of these figures is even more important, since the title of the book alludes to juggling with knives, one of which kills Eliante as she lets it plunge into her chest. With its deadly point, its ability to pierce, the danger that the knife holds out is often reinforced, but in the early pages of the book, the woman is referred to as a weapon that is usually kept sheathed, concealed inside "sa robe noire, cette gaine satinée presque métallique" (La Jongleuse 26). The clothed body of the woman is like her gloved hand--"la femme étira le bout de ses gants, ce qui lui ajoutait des griffes pointues" (La Jongleuse 31-32)--in that the lethal power both represent is latent. Still Léon Reille looks on Eliante and hopes that underneath, inside its envelope, he will find an instrument of pleasure, not destruction.

On one occasion, he learns from Eliante how she had learned in Java the art of juggling with daggers, a skill she put to use for performing at the teas she held for her niece Missie and her friends. These performances meant more to her than mere parlor room amusements: they allowed her to define herself before an audience comprised of men as well as girls. As she stood exposed in her maillot before male onlookers entranced "devant la forme non déguisée" (La Jongleuse 142), she would catch and then release again the knives so rapidly, that in motion they created an invisible but cutting wall that separated her from others. A dialectic of interdiction and desire, the act consisted of an implied seduction, invitation or offering of self and a withdrawal, denial or retraction of the promise. Thus Léon saw her "séparée de sa famille, de la société, du monde entier . . . par l'énigme de sa comédie perpétuelle" (La Jongleuse 143). In addition, Eliante's performances are narcissistic ones, not designed to entertain admirers, but to please and flatter her with her power to attract, her ability to magnetize the love, the look and the attention of her audience. Everything becomes a knife, a point, a blade: the whetting of the appetite, the hunger of the men transfixed by watching Eliante, their pointed gaze, and the cold inflexibility of "la jongleuse," "lame d'acier trempée aux feux des passions" (La Jongleuse 144), who is tempered against the emergence of emotions that might weaken her. Eliante loves no one, nothing but her philosophy of love. So to protect herself against the awakening of undesired feelings, she redirects her energy away from people who might touch her into an assessment of her reaction to them, excluding them as causes in favor of effects. Earlier the aggressiveness of Mary Barbe had made her look outside for victims. Only with a realization that the object of her hate might be an aspect of herself could her anger be internalized and the path to suicide from self-involvement be eventually described. This is the course that Eliante will follow, one based on denying any hold that others have on her, on withdrawing affect from those who make her feel, and investing it instead in an awareness of those feelings. Steel blade, "dédaigneuse de sang et de chair, n'usant plus que son propre fourreau noir" (La Jongleuse 144), she does not assume the male penetrating role, but over time destroys herself through a simple lack of contact with another but herself.

Through the accentuation of her ornamental beauty, her virtue and devotion to her niece, Eliante in many ways resembles "les créatures relatives" of whom Françoise Basch has written.[5] Yet she does not couple her attractiveness with docility, or obedience to men. Rather she manipulates them for amusement, juggles them like knives. She lives to feel their glances that are sharpened by desire. She exposes herself to them but is never in real danger. Yet she does fear growing older and not feeling others' looks, fears relinquishing the status of "prêtresse d'Eros" and being forced to take the role of "mendiante d'amour" (La Jongleuse 212-215). As much as she would like to see herself as an independent woman, not a creation or composite of men's opinions of her, it is only by attracting their admiration that she feels herself alive. At the same time she must detach herself from others, owe them nothing lest the autonomy she covets be all but forfeited. "On n'est libre qu'en tuant tout le monde . . .," she says (<u>La Jongleuse</u> 102). Freed from obligation, from the need to interact, she must also forego love as the means to be complete. First she is the dagger and its sheath, then the wound it opens up and finally the knife and her own dead body in which her weapon is embedded.

All the characters in Rachilde try to overcome the ascendancy of men: Raoule through an esthetic neutering of her boyfriend Jacques Silvert; Mary Barbe through attacks with hairpins, poison gases; and Eliante through a sleight of hand dissociation of sexuality and love. Still, concealed beneath their declaration of "la haine de la force mâle" (Barrès 19), is less a belief in women's self-acceptance than a flight from the spontaneous, the unpredictable and free. They are drawn to what is mechanical, highly structured, and recoil from emotions that make them give up self-control. Their ambition is to follow Raoule de Vénérande in making men wax robots that cannot challenge them to grow. What they deny is that women are reactors, their range of choices limited by their need to answer men, so they insist on leading, taking the initiative themselves. As the man is made an object, becomes "un être insexué," the threat he posed is neutralized. Thus Rachilde's women characters define their strategies, their goals in terms of an absence of constraint. They destroy what repels or frightens them, but do not know, cannot attain, what it is they truly want. Once Raoule makes Jacques Silvert her property or "thing," once Mary Barbe does away with the men that she despises, the objectives that were negative are effectively achieved. The tyrants are thrown down; the masters are destroyed and the woman's self as object is liquidated, too. Disconnected from the men who impose on her a role, Eliante is relieved of her old "en-soi" existence and can say to Léon Reille: "Je suis déjà morte" (<u>La Jongleuse</u> 100). But if there is no future to create free of their lovers' domination, their lives will not be purposeful, nor their identities self-defined. They flee the image-prisons they were sent to by their men, kill off the factitious selves they felt had stifled them. Yet they run the risk of finding underneath an empty center where no real self is hidden. Léon Reille wonders whether the "comédienne"'s many masks may in fact be covering the absence of a face. And so when he believes she has finally acquiesced, he learns the woman he has conquered was never really there. Through a last trick, Eliante makes use of Missie as a stand-in in her bed, so when Léon awakes in the arms of the wrong woman, he sees Eliante juggling for the last time with her "cinq glaives de douleur" (<u>La Jongleuse</u> 253), sees her about to become a victim of her most beloved performance. In death, for Eliante, there is no revelation, no disclosure of who she really is. "La femme glissa en arrière. Un flot pourpre noya le masque pâle . . . son dernier fard . . ." (La Jongleuse 255).

    At the end these "Belles dames sans merci" show less mercy toward themselves. They begin by captivating men with their mystery and looks, bewitching and ensnaring them so they can make them into slaves. Their purpose in attracting them is, in fact, to give them nothing. The seduction is an unkept promise whose object is frustration. Yet the greater their self-loathing, the more violent their revenge. Mary Barbe will make men bleed to eradicate self-doubt, will commit sadistic acts from a lack of self-esteem. These characters are committed to eliminating men as well as that part of their own psyche that was willing to submit. But with the removal of the self that once had taken part, that had collaborated in their initial degradation, they find there is still no buried truth, no sense of authenticity. They don their attitudes like the masks of Eliante, masks directed at an audience that is meant to be misled. Yet without the onlookers to be duped, they die to their old roles. They have no knowledge of themselves or who they really want to be, so the obsolescence of their anger, their resentment and their shame leaves them directionless and empty, with lives that have no point. With no hate to motivate them, they have nothing more to do, except mourn a useless past which had left them so embittered, had turned them into monsters, half-crazed recluses, and which in time would lead to suicide, make them victims of themselves.

NOTES

[1] Maurice Barrès, Préface, <u>Monsieur Vénus</u>, by Rachilde (Paris: Flammarion, 1977) 19. All further references to this work appear in the text.

[2] Referring to Rachilde and <u>Monsieur Vénus</u>, Emilien Carassus ascribes these tendencies to " [une] descendance . . . baudelairienne," adding that "le goût de l'artificiel, la tendance satanique font savourer des péchés nouveaux qui paraissent le fruit d'une civilisation dont la corruption mesure le raffinement." (Emilien Carassus, <u>Le Snobisme et les lettres françaises: de Paul Bourget à Marcel Proust</u> Paris: Armand Colin, 1966 428.)

[3] Claude Dauphiné, Présentation, <u>La Jongleuse</u>, by Rachilde (Paris: Des Femmes, 1982) 10. All further references to this work appear in the text.

[4] Rachilde, <u>La Jongleuse</u> (Paris: Des Femmes, 1982) 83. All further references to this work appear in the text.

[5] Françoise Basch, <u>Les Femmes victoriennes: roman et société (1837-1867)</u> (Paris: Payot, 1979) 21.

PERSONAL AND POLITICAL CHILDHOOD IN QUEBEC:
ANALOGIES FOR IDENTITY

Roseanna Dufault
University of Colorado at Boulder

Childhood and adolescence, and the associated quest for personal identity and self-expression, frequently serve as analogies for the political, economic and cultural questions of Québec. In an article published by the political journal Parti Pris, Michel Van Schendel compares the nation of Québec to a child afflicted by an illness so severe that all its strength is sapped.[1] In the introduction to Québec: Hier et Aujourd'hui, a collection of documents assembled as an anthology of French Canadian thought, Laurier L. LaPierre also compares Québec to a youthful person struggling to attain maturity.[2] Happily, from the perspective of the 1980's, Québec has weathered its adolescence. As Ralph Sarkonak states in his preface to the recent issue of Yale French Studies devoted to Québécois literature, "Québec has, since the sixties, attained her cultural maturity, her âge de la parole."[3]

Similarly, Québécois novelists have sometimes expressed contemporary reactions to social and political conditions in Québec through their portrayals of childhood. Four women novelists in particular, Laure Conan, Gabrielle Roy, Louise Maheux-Forcier and Yvette Naubert, have, at various points in Québécois history, capsulized prevalent national attitudes toward political and economic domination by England, as well as their own reactions to the additional submission imposed on women by male-dominated social hierarchies, through their adult female protagonists who look back on childhood experiences.

Let us begin by considering Angéline de Montbrun, which was published in 1884 by Québec's first woman novelist, Laure Conan, and which has been acclaimed by critics as the most original creative work of its genre in nineteenth-century Québec.[4] Nostalgic reflections on childhood are tenderly portrayed in the final portion of this novel, which consists of Angéline's personal journal. Laure Conan's heroine looks back regretfully on her early years as a paradise irretrievably lost. As Angéline laments, "Beaux jours de mon enfance, qu'êtes-vous devenus?"[5] Angéline's father plays a central role in her peaceful, protected childhood universe. In exchange for Angéline's willing acceptance of his authority, he surrounds her with continuous care and attention. Monsieur de Montbrun personally supervises his daughter's early education before turning this responsibility over to the Ursuline sisters. Because of his great affection for her, he attempts to prolong Angéline's childhood by postponing her prospective marriage. Indeed, Monsieur de Montbrun insists that his eighteen-year-old daughter is still a child, adding, "je désire beaucoup qu'elle reste enfant aussi longtemps que possible" (Conan 21). Tragically, his intentions are thwarted by his own accidental death, Angéline's subsequent grief and disfigurement and her fiancé's waning affection. Cut off definitively from her childhood utopia, Angéline is unable to accept a less than perfect future with a husband bound to her by duty more than love. Instead, she embraces her only option, that of a pious, charitable life of solitude and resignation.

Angéline's experiences in many ways parallel those of French colonists who remained in Québec after it was yielded to the English in 1763. The colonial period of peace and prosperity, overseen by a king perceived as benign, was sealed off forever by this disaster. French Canadian society responded by closing in on itself in an effort to preserve its cultural integrity.[6] Laure Conan expresses through Angéline the general mood of nostalgia for former happier times and the resulting tendency toward isolation and resignation that characterized Québec through World War II. Further, Laure Conan reacts to the limited options open to women in nineteenth-century Québec by highlighting her heroine's courage in rejecting the prescribed role of dutiful wife and devoted mother while exploring her own identity as an outcast.

Secondly, Gabrielle Roy's semi-autobiographical novel Rue Deschambault, published in 1955, reflects the broadened perspectives gained from the war years, which, as Gérard Tougas has observed, "brought to an end the cultural isolation of French Canada."[7] Gabrielle Roy's novel brings to light the conflicts and concerns of a family attempting to accomodate traditional values to a modern and rapidly changing world. Unlike Laure Conan, Gabrielle Roy does not represent childhood as a uniformly blissful experience. Her heroine, Christine, a young schoolteacher and aspiring writer, looks back on at least as many moments of grief and disappointment as she recalls times of joy. Mirroring the awakened Québécois consciousness, Christine is sometimes critical of authority, although she never openly rebels. She has very little communication with her morose father, who, overcome by the pressures of his job, imposes his gloomy moods on the family. Christine wryly remarks, "La maison était beaucoup plus gaie quand mon père n'y était pas."[8] Christine deplores the subservient role of her ever self-effacing mother. She is troubled by her mother's attempts to justify her desire to travel to her intransigent husband, and by her obligation to extol her husband's virtues in order to be well received by the relatives she visits. As Christine observes, "J'ai vu combien une femme qui se réclame d'un mari est mieux vue dans la société qu'une femme toute seule. Cela me parut injuste" (118). Christine especially rejects her family's forced frugality. She recalls with disdain the nights her mother sat up late sewing after sending the children to bed early to save money on heating. She rebels by purchasing cheap costume jewelry and impractical shoes, and by vowing to become wealthy. As she phrases it, "Je désirai ardemment gagner de l'argent" (283). Unlike Angéline, who did not object to having her childhood extended, Christine is anxious to grow up. She resents overprotection from her parents, and she is frustrated when they tell her she is too young to understand their problems.

Gabrielle Roy's writing illuminates Québec's post-World War II assessment of itself as a relatively poor, backward nation needing to catch up to the twentieth century. A critical look at authority and at traditional values, as well as an increasing discontentment with formerly accepted feminine roles, promise hope for greater independence for the nation as well as for women, and foreshadow the dramatic changes of the 1960's.

One century after Laure Conan's Angéline de Montbrun, Louise Maheux-Forcier published L'Ile Joyeuse (1964) during the Quiet Revolution. In this novel, the heroine Isabelle is almost destroyed by her love relationship to a disturbed man she meets at music school. Memories of the summers she spent on a beautiful secluded island as a young girl ultimately save her from personal disaster. As a child, alone and free in natural surroundings, she came to know herself. She explored the sensations of the wind and sand in unconscious acts of self discovery. As she describes it, "Je jouais avec ma robe, lui donnant ma forme, en reserrant la taille et l'imprimant dans la poussière blonde pour m'y coucher ensuite dans mon propre moule."[9] She uses images that connote primordial femininity as well as physical and spiritual rebirth to convey her experience: "Je plongeais, exténuée, dans le ventre de la nature, les cheveux défaits, épars autour de moi comme mon âme" (20). Later, when as a young woman, she wishes to share the island and what it represents to her with her lover Stéphane, he mocks her and tries to destroy its meaning. As Isabelle describes it, "Il souriait de mon île et je croyais lire son enfance dans sa fureur de me prendre comme pour détruire en moi ce qui était détruit en lui" (57). In the hopeless complexities of this destructive relationship, Isabelle temporarily loses sight of the personal values and self-assurance she had gained from the island. As she states it, she had lost her own identity in an effort to please Stéphane, and she made the mistake of looking to others for answers instead of taking responsibility for her own happiness. As she expresses it, "Je vivais cent vies sauf la mienne! . . . J'avais pris racine en enfer et j'attendais encore du monde extérieur ma délivrance" (169). Fortunately, the memory of the childhood experiences on the island well up in Isabelle at the moment of her deepest despair. She exults, "Du fond de mon enfance, mon île était revenue pour m'envelopper de . . . mes rêves, mes vérités!" (170) She regains her lost identity and experiences a resurgence of creativity when her adult self becomes reintegrated with the self she had discovered in her early years. As she expresses it, "Seule, j'ai senti que je me dégageais du chaos et que je débouchais, une fois encore, sur l'infini, par la porte miraculeuse des poèmes" (171).

Like Christine, Isabelle would like to grow up quickly. She feels even more negatively about the oppression imposed on her by her parents and teachers because she is a child. She harbors "une sourde rancune contre l'état d'enfance" (25). Isabelle's relationship to her parents has deteriorated even further than that of Christine in Rue Deschambault. Communication with them, although sometimes desired, has become impossible. While Isabelle's father, like Christine's father, is almost always distant and silent, Isabelle admires him and wishes he could be her friend. Sadly, she never finds the words to open a meaningful conversation. Having missed an opportunity to confide in him, she muses, "C'est hier que j'aurais dû t'approcher. Je suis seule . . . Et tu es seul aussi" (89). Lacking the essential "vocabulaire de la confiance," Isabelle is also unable to communicate with her mother, whom she scorns. She eventually spurns her own attentive but dull fiancé for fear of one day resembling this fastidious woman. She tells him, "François, je ne t'épouserai jamais . . . j'aurais trop peur de ressembler à ma mère et que tu ressembles à mon père" (163). She eventually refuses to give herself up for any man, and she welcomes solitude as an opportunity for self-expression. Her decision to remain alone is comparable to that of Angéline, although twentieth-century mores allow Isabelle a much greater possibility of functioning in society as a creative individual.

Isabelle's evolution in L'Ile Joyeuse reflects Québécois cultural phenomena of the Quiet Revolution. Her complete inability to relate to her parents, her realization that she must rely entirely on herself for answers to life's problems and the fierce independence she develops after being lost to herself for a time are clearly analogous to collective Québécois attitudes during the 1960's. Although a few acts of terrorism were inspired by strong sentiments of nationalism and independence, many positive changes came about as a result of the Quiet Revolution, including educational reforms, the recognition of French as the sole official language of Québec, and the proliferation of literary and artistic expression. Most significant, however, is the clear break with religious and political authority.[10] Isabelle's personal victory over what she describes as hell and chaos can surely be interpreted as a metaphor for the positive changes which took place concurrently in Québec. Louise Maheux-Forcier's theme of looking to the past to seize one's unique identity and purpose seems to echo the Québécois decision to replace the epithet "La Belle Province" with "Je me souviens," indicating an eagerness to reconfirm ties to French culture and historical identity.

Finally, Yvette Naubert's heroine Françoise in <u>Les Pierrefendre</u> (1972) recalls a few happy moments from her childhood, such as being snowed in at Christmas at her grandmother's house in the country, the flavor of wild berries and her own innocent laughter, that come back to her on happy days.[11] However, she is also haunted by hideous faces of cruel men--her uncle, whose brutal punishment turned her cousin into a vindictive pyromaniac, and her grandparents' deaf-mute handyman who sexually assaulted her. In addition, as a child, Françoise was badly misunderstood by her parents, who were too preoccupied with their own feelings of alienation to be concerned with her. To her profound chagrin, her father once took sides with a nun who accused Françoise of being demon-possessed without even considering his daughter's version of the conflict. Because of her father's reaction, "l'accusation prend des proportions inattendues et Françoise ne sait plus comment se défendre." Shocked and confused, she asks, "Alors en qui avoir confiance? En quelle homme placer son espérance?" (234) On another occasion, her mother punished Françoise for returning home late from school. It never occurred to her that Françoise might need consolation for the bitter disappointment that caused her tardiness: "En effect, sa mère ajoute à la déception en imposant la séquestration dans la chambre. . . . Françoise rumine son humiliation. . . . Son coeur bat la chamade et une rancune gronde en elle contre la camarade qui l'a bernée et sa mère qui la punit" (99). Françoise is further ostracized by her cousins and other children at school because of her interest in music and books. As a result of her childhood difficulties, and particularly because of her lost faith in her father, Françoise chooses to marry an Englishman whose heart is cold and cruel. As the novel unfolds, Françoise is about to give birth to this man's child. The agony of childbirth extends until she is able to silence all the "echoes" from her past and separate herself from her husband, her parents, and even from her twin brother in unconscious anticipation of his sudden death, in order to embrace ultimately her own identity as a strong, creative, unique and free woman (309). In juxtaposition to Françoise's personal drama, Naubert develops a number of sub-plots which treat current Québécois concerns, such as English and American control of business, the effects of industrialization on the individual and the influx of immigrants competing for jobs. The central issue is clearly the need to establish economic parity without risking assimilation. Françoise's personal struggle to overcome the oppressive aspects of her childhood and to free herself from her heartless husband is symbolic of Québec's need to shake off the cobwebs and break free from outside domination. Yvette Naubert apparently predicts a favorable national outcome, since Françoise Pierrefendre eventually achieves considerable fame as a musician, and her fervent but confused nationalist twin, who was accidentally assassinated by a terrorist, lives on in her happy, attractive son. It is even suggested that Claude is literally a reincarnation of his uncle since he was born at the exact moment when François died (310).

As we have seen, during the century that has elapsed since the publication of the first few Québécois novels, women writers have crystallized collective concerns from a distinctly feminine perspective. We have seen an evolution from helpless resignation, through the questioning of awakened consciousness, to the establishment of a position of strength permitting a positive, creative movement forward. In each of the novels we have considered, self-knowledge and personal independence have been crucial issues echoing the continuing Québécois preoccupation with national identity. Childhood experiences as developed by these four women novelists, Laure Conan, Gabrielle Roy, Louise Maheux-Forcier and Yvette Naubert are surely analogous to Québec's own development as a nation.

NOTES

[1] Michel Van Schendel, "La Maladie Infantile du Québec," Les Québécois (Montréal: Parti Pris, 1971) 19.

[2] Laurier L. LaPierre, ed., Québec: Hier et Aujourd'hui (Toronto: Macmillan, 1967) 3.

[3] Ralph Sarkonak, "Editor's Preface," Yale French Studies 65 (1983): iii. We shall use the French spelling of "Québec" as well as the adjective "Québécois" throughout this article in order to emphasize, as does Sarkonak in his preface, "that the accent is on the difference just as the difference is (also) one of accent."

[4] Arsène Lauzière declares Angéline de Montbrun to be "le roman le plus littéraire du siècle" in her article "Le Roman (1860-1900)" which appears in Histoire de la Littérature Française du Québec, ed. Pierre de Grandpré (Montréal: Beauchemin, 1971) 1: 251.

[5] Laure Conan, Angéline de Montbrun (Montréal: Fides, 1980) 121.

[6] Ben-Zion Shek discusses this phenomenon in his study, Social Realism in the French Canadian Novel (Montréal: Harvest House, 1977) 46.

[7] Gérard Tougas, History of French-Canadian Literature, trans. Alta Lind Cook (Westport: Greenwood Press, 1976) 147.

[8] Gabrielle Roy, Rue Deschambault (Montréal: Stanké, 1980) 102. Further references to this novel will be indicated by page number within the text of the paper.

[9] Louise Maheux-Forcier, L'Ile Joyeuse (Ottawa: Cercle du Livre de France, 1964) 21. Further references to this novel will be indicated by page number within the text of the paper.

[10] The impact of the Révolution Tranquille is discussed by André Gaulin in his article, "Une Longue Naissance: Abrégé Historico-Littéraire du Québec," French Review 53 (May 1980): 792.

[11] Yvette Naubert, Les Pierrefendre (Ottawa: Cercle du Livre de France, 1972) 11. Further references to this novel will be indicated by page number within the text of the paper.

DEFINING AN ETHICS FROM A LATER SHORT STORY BY COLETTE

Anne Duhamel Ketchum
University of Colorado at Boulder

The work of Colette, encompassing more than half a century of French bourgeois life, brings more than the fragrant realm of gardens and the complicity of friendly pets; more than the racy pranks of tomboy Claudine or the love rebuffs of courtesans, music-hall dancers and gigolos, in the Gay Paris before World War I. Sensitive, like Proust, her contemporary, to the deep changes French society was undergoing during the first half of the century, Colette promoted a truly feminine ethics, a fact which is not always clearly perceived. An ethics that is not only for women, but one facing openly the needs and concerns of women in a rapidly changing society.

Because Colette chose her characters from the lowest strata of society--aging courtesans, spoiled children of the "flaming youth," and the then despised "show business" people and homosexuals--the general consensus is that she had few concerns other than advocating easy-going morals and emphasizing a most frenzied sexual liberation, above all for women. Not only is this, of course, an oversimplification, but it can lead to gross misconceptions. Our purpose here, however, is not to re-evaluate all of Colette's attitudes throughout her work; we propose instead to examine the positions she had arrived at in one short story, "The Tender-shoot," written when Colette had sufficiently weathered and pondered the past to give form to her own set of values. We will not try in the least to "rehabilitate" Colette as we feel, with Jean Cocteau, that "Colette does not need to be rehabilitated, for she is sterling."[1]

The Képi[2] is a collection of four short stories: the "Képi" itself, "The Tender-shoot," "The Green Wax" and "Armande." We are concerned only with the second one. The volume is the work of a seventy-year-old Colette, during the terrible year of 1943, in occupied Paris. She feels the greatest anxiety about her husband, Maurice Goudeket, who had been arrested by the Germans in 1941.

France is cut in two "zones" and governed by an eighty-five-year-old soldier. More than one and a half million Frenchmen are prisoners of war in Germany, and the entire cost of the German occupation is levied on the French.

The Pétain government, with its motto "work, family, fatherland," is openly challenging the views of the third Republic: Catholic instruction is offered again in French schools; "return to the land" is praised, in a Barresian attempt to help the nation recover its "true roots." A beaten France submits to the idea that she needs workers rather than scholars, and measures are taken by the Vichy government to limit the number of young university graduates, an unprecedented measure.

Yet liberty is more than ever on the mind of the French people, and central to major works being published: The Flies by Sartre, The Stranger by Camus, Poésie et Vérité by Eluard. In such bleak context, tales and legends from the past bring the enchantment of a lost paradise, helping to soothe the pain of an intolerable present. It is the magic of the past which she tries again to recapture during World War II in publishing Looking Backwards in 1941, The Képi in 1943 and Gigi in 1944.

The date of "The Tender-shoot" is very precise: May 1940, a time when the French, taken by surprise by the invader, were "all like animals without a sense of smell." Albin Chaveriat, around seventy, with the natural distinction of a true Basque, oddly never married. In his spare time, he enjoys roaming around the woods and the countryside with a shotgun slung on his shoulder; for there is nothing he would like better than to become a hunter. But somehow he always returns with nothing more than "a handkerchief full of mushrooms," picked on his way. In his teens he experienced one of those "adolescent friendships to which a normal boy is more faithful at heart than to a mistress" (200). What Chaveriat calls a "beautiful sentimental solidarity" between the two boys became so important to him as to overshadow all other relationships. This exclusivity of feelings between two young males is by no means rare; it is at the root of all associations and clubs reserved to men so common in England, for instance. They have their counterpart in all the "sociétés," "mutuelles," "amicales" and veterans´ associations so active in France. They attest to the strong links tying men together in western societies. Officially justified by the necessities of business, their total exclusion of women elicits the belief that all matters of importance--business or other--can be dealt with only between men, another way to imply that only relationships between men count for much.

Very few of Colette´s contemporaries had her insight regarding the crippling consequences an exclusive friendship between boys might have for later life, tarnishing all relations with the other sex. Consider the very common practice of ancillary sex and, more generally, of holding all women simply as sex objects, of which Chaveriat is clearly a good illustration.

His friend´s ultimate marriage was taken as "the first treason," and a terrible blow. Out of spite, he turns, at thirty, to eighteen-year-old beauties, delighted by their "sincere abruptness," their "beauty in the rough" (201). Soon he discovers, "terrified," his preference for those "champions of the risk" who approach danger with surprising serenity; this was a trait particularly attractive to Chaveriat who, in spite of his visions of conquest, actually was shunning danger. But he defends himself against the common opinion that any man approaching young girls is a coward: Chaveriat insists on the contrary, that it takes a "special kind of self-control to resist them" (201). Since the rest of the story shows how little he resists such temptations, Colette's conclusion is very clear.

It is in 1923 that a fifty-year-old Chaveriat is invited to the country house of a friend. There he discovers a lovely, ancient house which he compares to a woman, "in négligé," "with a great coat of Virginia creeper, rose in places, covering one shoulder" (204). His contemplation is interrupted by a devilish black goat chasing him downhill, followed by a girl of fifteen--a strawberry-blonde peasant child, with freckles.

Louisette is nothing but a symphony in russet and rose. Responding to such beguiling signals, an enchanted Chaveriat compares the Renoir-like girl, significantly enough, not to a painting by that master, but to one by Boucher, giving from the start a licentious dimension to his interest. He describes the little "country girl" as "plump" with a "flawless set of teeth," as though he were a horse-dealer examining a filly. The young girl stiffens, haughtily retreating to her "castle" as she calls the dismantled old house, guarded by two imposing stone lions sporting only "lambsnouts" (296).

Terms of hunting are used in "The Tender-shoot" in the preparation for the conquest, but all Chaveriat gives of himself is his money, to buy a cheap little coral necklace. On several occasions will he thus attempt to buy the girl he calls "the prettiest little servant in France." "Bait in hand," the next day Chaveriat "lies in ambush . . . waiting for the game." The story takes an unexpected turn when Louisette "red with anger" throws the necklace at his face, not out of fear of her mother, but of "what her mother might think." The abrupt change in tone coincides with the discovery on Louisette's property of a magnificent spring of water, quite unexpected in the arid area. Its appearance at this point in the text, along with the great thirst of Chaveriat for its water, deserves our attention: in previous works, Colette at times has evoked such spontaneous thirst for an irresistibly pure water. One such occasion can be found, for instance, in <u>Retreat from Love</u> (427) the last volume of the Claudine series. To regain her balance, a disenchanted Claudine has fled from Paris to the very same Franche-Comté where

"The Tender-shoot" takes place. Part of the volume is concerned with opposing the vanity of facile pleasures to the goodness of all things natural; as they are revealed to Claudine, she evokes a sudden, quasi-mystical thirst from her childhood, one of the most beautifully poetical passages of the book. "I am thirsty. But only for the water colored with an ordinary and colorful wine which Mélie poured for me, in the cool, slightly musty dining-room. Give me a drink, Mélie, quick!" (433).

A very determined girl, then, and a "wild pony," she shows her lover very little "affection." Chaveriat feels that "it was not asking too much to hope that, softened and satisfied, she would come to treat her unselfish lover as a friend." This comic yearning for affection from the old goat should be taken for what it is: The suspicion, and the fear, of being used as a stud, a mere sex object by a girl who indeed, "treated sensual pleasure as her lawful right" (219).

"Shocked" by Louisette's aloofness, Chaveriat reassures himself that her lack of feeling for him, the "mutism" of an "adorable idiot" are only marks of her "want of intelligence." But he cannot fool himself much longer. Finally, the truth dawns on him, for only a brief instant: "It seems . . . not to have been such a gay adventure as I thought" (224). "Louisette was nothing more than a girl I was relieving of her boredom. . . . At the time, I used to wonder, now and then, whether Louisette were not exploiting me like a lecherous man who's found a willing girl" (222, 224).

The reversal by Louisette of traditional roles completely upsets Chaveriat's comfortable male standards. In a game where he longs to impose his undisputed rule (the "hunter"), he finds in a fifteen-year-old goose, a master. We have understood, by now, that ever since "the first treason," when he reproached a young wife for taking away his best friend, Chaveriat deeply resents women. It is his need to assert his supremacy as a man and a master that makes him turn exclusively to immature, defenseless girls who can best satisfy his senses without presenting any threat to his ego.

Louisette, however, becomes his ruin. Growing up in a remote corner of the French countryside, far away from the maleficence of urban civilization, Louisette is a child of Nature. Early aware of the needs of her senses, she sets about, with simplicity, to gratify them. When her choice falls on Chaveriat, it expresses itself with passion and with a directness of purpose which startles him a bit when she unhesitantly surrenders her body. But nothing else. Her own life, her person remain totally private, and entirely in her control. The only opinion she clearly cares for is not Chaveriat's, but her mother's, a fact which puts him off a good deal. Behind her silence and what Chaveriat takes for simple-mindedness, Louisette is a strongwilled, self-possessed person; alone with her widowed mother, she has learned early enough the harsh fight for survival. She is concerned about maintaining her integrity as a person in a hostile world, and about building up her self-confidence and respect. She easily relinquishes her virginity, simply because it is not the important thing to preserve. But in all circumstances she retains her dignity, sets when and where they meet, and is in control of the situation at all times.

It is also in the name of female dignity that Louisette's mother, descending regally the stairs of their "castle" with the lamp of justice in her hand, swoops down on the lovers, and puts them to shame. To Chaveriat's attempt to drape himself in whatever pride he has left and to bluff his way out, Louisette puts an unexpected stop: "I forbid you to talk to my mother in that tone." This leaves no doubt as to who is now in command. The question of Louisette's mother, "Monsieur, may one know your age?", (231) shatters Chaveriat, definitely throwing him off balance: "I found myself making a series of idiotic gestures such as running my hand through my hair, pulling my leather belt down over my loins, and drawing myself up to my full height" (231). He lies about his age.

Louisette's spontaneous reaction brings about the totally unorthodox dénouement, though the only natural one: "Do you want me to go for him, Mother? Us two, we'll chase him, shall we?" (233) "I had shot out of the house," admits Chaveriat, "and the Devil himself could not have stopped me" (233). He flees, then, as fast as he can! Just as he feels out of danger, he is literally stoned by both angry women, standing on top of a wall, above him! He feels sure that they would have stoned him to death if he had not had the sense to pass to the attack. Then, "they too recovered their reason and the conscience of their female condition, for after hesitiating, they fled and disappeared" (235). For Chaveriat then, both women had lost their reason in attacking the seducer, and "the conscience of their female condition" dictated that they consent to being seduced, humiliated and otherwise submissive to the male master. Colette's statement here is very strong, and Chaveriat is presented by her as the epitome of phallocratism. The end of the story stresses even more Chaveriat's vileness with his resigned admission that, for him henceforth, remains "the practice of the chambermaid."

Colette had no hesitation in ridiculing and punishing him severely. Mother and daughter, then, have succeeded in giving the old lecherous man a masterful lesson. Praising in both women the old basic sense of measure of the French peasant, Colette allows them to give to an otherwise poetical tale a twist reminiscent of the medieval farces, of picaresque adventures, of Rabelais, Molière and Beaumarchais to name a few, making lavish use of ridicule to shame the aggressor, and even of violence to chastise him.

All her life, Colette has had a very high idea of womanhood. But through the years, this idea has evolved a great deal. She was brought up, in a rather traditional way, by an exceptional woman who remained her constant model. Coming to Paris upset all the fundamental values Colette had learned and which were no longer in play in the big, ruthless city. It was a tremendous shock, from which she never fully recovered.

But she took, first, all the indispensable measures: she divorced, fought to conquer independence and respect, and decided that she would write about "things pure." Frustrated with the utter difficulty for a divorced woman to make her place in the world, she rebelled, with The Vagabond, against the double standard, against male possessiveness. She discovered also the duplicity women resort to, in order to outsmart men's treacherous ways.

In a second stage, we find Colette looking for models she could emulate: they are Mitsou, Léa first, Julie de Carneilhan later. Searching desperately for some measure of integrity in the human world, she thinks she had found it in Chéri, ultimately to realize that she had only found it in Sido.

Late in her life, Colette remembers Sido's maternal vigilance. Both in "The Tender-shoot" and in "The Green Wax" of The Képi does Colette proclaim the need for young girls--that choice prey in a male world--for the protection of their mother. She praises valiant mothers, such as Louisette's, as the last defenders in our corrupt society of truly human values against men's constant aggressions.

But the greatest need of women reaches beyond the liberation of their senses. For Colette, it remains the awareness of their priceless value in a world which uses them, abuses them as another priced commodity, the better to deny them equality.

Colette's ideas of women have changed greatly through the years. From the heroic, self-sacrificing archetypes of the early works, her heroines have evolved into stronger, more secure women, supported by the idea of their value as the creators but also the defenders of life and all which makes it worth living, against mercantilism, crime and war.

NOTES

[1] All quotations in the text are translated by the author from the edition of the complete works of Colette (Paris: Flammarion, 1948). All page numbers refer to this edition. My adaptation from the French: "Colette n'a pas besoin d'être blanchie, car elle est blanche." Jean Cocteau, "Discours de Réception," in <u>Bulletin</u> <u>de</u> <u>l'Académie</u> <u>Royale</u> <u>de</u> <u>Belgique</u>, Brussels, October 1, 1955.

[2] A "képi" is the official head gear of officers in the French army.

THE "DIFFERENT" CINEMA OF MARGUERITE DURAS

Mary Greenwood-Johnson
University of Kansas

In November 1984, Marguerite Duras was awarded the Prix Goncourt for her novel L'Amant, a best-seller which has given her, at age seventy, a kind of pop culture status as a writer, and which crowns a literary career that began in 1943 with the publication of her first novel, Les Impudents. Paralleling Duras's career as a writer of novels, plays and texts, is that of Duras as filmmaker. One of few significant contemporary women cinéastes, she has written and directed eighteen films between 1966 and 1982, yet because hers is an avant-garde, intellectual cinema, it is doubtful that most Duras films will ever reach the public at large. Duras often refers to her cinema as "le cinéma différent," a "different" cinema; her films give rise to reviews such as the following, which appeared in the Nouvel Observateur in 1983, and which refers to one of her latest films, Dialogue of Rome: "Marguerite Duras est horripilante. On voudrait parfois hausser les épaules, traiter ses films par l'indifférence et qu'on n'en parle plus. Ce n'est pas si facile."[1] After briefly tracing Duras's cinematic career, I should like to examine those aspects of her films which constitute the specificity of her cinema, and which both fascinate and frustrate the followers of avant-garde filmmaking. I shall then concentrate more specifically on Agatha, a 1981 film and one which best exemplifies the recent tendencies in Durassian cinema.

Duras's first taste for film came in 1959, when Alain Renais asked her to write a scenario for his film on Hiroshima. Duras's text, a love story between a Japanese man and a French woman, set against the background of the atomic catastrophe at Hiroshima, has become one of her best-known writings. Yet only the scenario and dialogues are hers; the movie is Renais'; and Hiroshima mon amour is often not included in filmographies of Duras's work. Many of Duras's own novels of the 1950's inspired other prestigious filmmakers: René Clément directed Barrage contre le Pacifique; Jules Dassin directed Mélina Mercouri in Dix heures et demie du soir en été, and Peter Brook created a film version of Moderato Cantabile starring Jeanne Moreau and Jean-Paul Belmondo. Bitterly disappointed by what she felt to be a distortion of her texts by other directors, yet still unsure of herself as a director of film, Duras enlisted the help of Paul Seban as co-director in 1966, to create a film version of her play La Musica, with Delphine Seyrig in the role of Anne-Marie Roche. After her involvement in the political events of May '68, Duras returned to the cinema again in 1969 with a film version of her novel Détruire dit-elle. In 1971 her novel Abahn Sabana David became a film, Jaune le soleil, and in 1973, L'amour became La Femme du Gange. With the film version of her text India Song in 1975, Duras achieved a certain notoriety among the advocates of avant-garde cinema, and was awarded the Grand Prix de l'Académie for her films. In the 1970's, Duras all but abandoned literature for filmmaking. L'amour, written in 1971, was her last novel until the appearance in 1980 of the short, erotic text L'Homme assis dans le couloir. It is during this period, beginning with La Femme du Gange up to the present, that Duras develops the techniques that are to characterize her "different" cinema.

For Marguerite Duras, creating an alternative cinema is in itself a political act. Disenchanted after 1968 with her years as a militant in the Communist party, Duras nonetheless retained a dislike of certain aspects of capitalism, among them commercial filmmaking and its excessively large budget, which she feels produces films that lull the viewer into complacency, in which the viewer is a passive participant who goes to a movie to be distracted or to forget. Duras speaks proudly of the fact that her films are acts of political defiance against the system: "Ce cinéma-là s'inscrit comme un acte politique. Faire un film en quatorze jours dans des conditions pareilles, avec des gens qui vous aident pour rien . . . c'est vraiment combattre le système. . . . quand on fait du cinéma différent il est forcément politique."[2] Raised in relative poverty in Indochina, Duras takes pride in creating low-budget films, rails against the indecency of waste. Often her films are compilations of clippings from former films, coordinated with different sound tracks: her shorts, Les mains négatives and Césarée are abandoned frames from a preceding film, Le Navire Night, frames which include the statues of the Place de la Concorde, which Duras considered too figurative, too sumptuous for the "desert" she wished to evoke in Le Navire Night. The first half of the 1981 film L'homme atlantique is composed of frames left over from Agatha; in a slightly different vein, the 1976 film Son nom de Venise dans Calcutta désert uses the same sound track as India Song, but creates a new image track by using clippings and frames from India Song in which human characters are totally absent. Perhaps Duras's most shockingly militant departure from traditional cinema is that of her 1977 film Le Camion (The Truck). Originally Duras had imagined a film which would take place in the cabin of a truck; there would have been a conversation between the truck driver and a middle-aged woman hitchhiker whom he would have picked up. Instead, what is filmed is Duras reading and improvising in a closed room, with the actor Gérard Depardieu who was to have played the role of the truck driver, the text of the film that would have been. Thus the project of a film becomes the film itself, as Duras and Depardieu read the scenario, interrupted from time to time by shots of a blue truck racing across the working-class suburbs of Paris to the music of the "Variations" by Diabelli on a theme of Beethoven.

The "outrageous" experiment of Le Camion is unique to Duras's career as film director. The other significant cinematic innovations that increasingly characterize her films as she moves from the early 1970's to the 1980's are the use of the voices off technique, the primacy of sound over image, and the movement toward blackness and the destruction of the image itself. One can find a certain bipolarity in Duras's films of the past fifteen years. On the one hand, in certain of her more traditional, naturalistic films, sound track and image track are synchronized: her characters speak their lines, and move mysteriously in and out of the camera as if on a theatrical stage, as in Nathalie Gunther, or in Des Journées entières dans les arbres. But increasingly, beginning with La Femme du Gange in 1973, there is a quasi-disappearance of all characters in Duras's films, and those that continue to move in and out of the film frames become like silent phantoms. They do not speak during the film, and their dialogue is read by voices exterior to the story. India Song is Duras's most successful example of the voices off technique. Here, two women's and two men's voices, on a pre-recorded sound track, comment on the images that we see; like the chorus in Greek tragedy, they alternately describe or try to remember the story that visually takes place on the screen.

Undoubtedly the voices off technique is the most important element in Duras's cinematic evolution, for through it, Duras discovers the infinitely liberating power inherent in the disjunction between sound and image. Speaking in 1976 of Le Son de Venise dans Calcutta désert, Duras states: "Je vais vers une sorte de no mans land du cinéma, où il n'y aura plus de corrélation entre le son et l'image, vers une sorte de temps désertique du cinéma."[3] And from the disassociation of text and image, of the sound track and visual track, Duras passes to the next step in her cinematic development, that of the supremacy of the text over the image, a striking reversal of traditional filmmaking, in which the written scenario normally exists to serve the image. As Duras points out, "la parole dans le cinéma commercial fait avancer l'image, elle correspond souvent à une économie d'images. Si quelqu'un dit: je vais aller voir ma fiancée, ça économise une séquence."[4]

Duras is, above all, a writer, a writer who has chosen to make films; for her, the written text remains more open, more imaginative than its accompanying images; the act of writing itself is, for Duras, the essential element of her cinema: "Quand je fais du cinéma, j'écris, j'écris sur l'image, sur ce qu'elle devait représenter. . . . J'écris sur le sens qu'elle devrait avoir. Le choix de l'image qui se fait ensuite, c'est une conséquence de cet écrit. L'écrit du film--pour moi--c'est le cinéma."[5] All of Duras's films since Le Navire Night of 1978 are inscribed in this notion of the all-importance of the text. Among these, Agatha, created by Duras in 1981, stands out as one of the finest examples of Durassian cinematographic technique in recent years. Speaking in Montréal during a series of interviews about Agatha, Duras affirmed that for her, Agatha is such an important text that no image can add an additional quality to it: ". . . le texte dit tout. La totalité du potentiel cinématographique contient le texte, est dit par lui, par le texte. Le film est un accident, une sorte de conséquence sans grande importance."[6]

Duras filme, a video presentation which shows Duras and her crew at work filming Agatha incorporates interviews which reveal both Duras's ideas on filmmaking and the intensely autobiographical nature of this text. Agatha is a film about incest, about the love of a brother and sister, inspired, as Duras has explained on several occasions, by the overwhelming love she felt for her younger brother who died at age 27 during the war in Indochina. Agatha and her brother meet during the winter, in the abandoned Villa Agatha; Agatha tells her brother that she is leaving; together they recreate past memories of summers spent together at the Villa; they restate their love for each other. Duras speaks of this film as the only film she has ever made about happiness: because this is a love between brother and sister, this love will never end: "C'est un frère et une soeur qui s'aiment, et donc c'est un amour qui ne se terminera jamais. . . . Ils sont du même sang. . . . Ils sont donc inséparables, puisque c'est comme un même corps, c'est ça que j'appelle le bonheur et qui est recherché constamment et toujours à travers les tentatives de tous les amants. C'est un amour incestueux, donc inépuisable, et frappé de virginité . . . parce que maudit."[7]

For Duras, the cinematographic interest in this film is her paradoxical attempt to show what cannot be shown--in this case incest, which remains one of society's greatest taboos. Agatha, says Duras, is a summer film, a film of unbearable desire, shot in the cold, at Trouville on the North Atlantic coast. The haunting Durassian text, the dialogue between Agatha and her brother, is read by Duras and Yann Andrea, two voices off. As in India Song, the image track shows silent figures, which, phantom-like, assume moving or immobile postures in an abandoned villa. One supposes that the young woman, played by Bulle Ogier is Agatha, and that the young man, embodied by Yann Andrea, is her brother. Interior scenes of the villa alternate with frames of the sea, the sky, close-ups of seashells that fill the entire screen, deserted tennis courts, black frames of nothing at all; these images are punctuated musically from time to time, in an almost mathematically structured fashion, by the Brahms waltz mentioned in the text.

By giving the viewer less to see, minimal images of shells, sea and sand, Duras offers more to think and hear--the viewer must necessarily assume a more active role. As in so many Duras films, the voices off technique also creates a doubling between past and present, between what is real and what is fiction, between the incestuous incident of years past between brother and sister, and their memories of it. The voices off, bearers of the narration, liberate both image and actor. One finds too, that one's grasp of the spoken text in a Duras film is of a sensual rather than of an intellectual nature. Her writing pleases in the almost musical configuration of the text, in the immediate, narcissistic pleasure of its enunciation. Priority is given to the voice, the "substance sonore." Nathalie Heinich writes in the Cahiers du Cinéma, "chez Duras, le comprendre se réduit, à la limite, à l'entendre (ce qu'on traduirait, dans l'ordre des mythologies modernes, par la primauté du signifiant sur le signifié.)"[8]

From a film such as Agatha, with its minimal representation of images, Duras moves toward total destruction of the visual in her film L'Homme atlantique, made shortly after Agatha. The first half of the film consists of unused frames from Agatha, and the second half is thirty minutes of blackness. This still more radical departure from traditional cinema was prefigured in remarks Duras made in "Les Yeux verts" a year before. Speaking of her film Aurélia Steiner Vancouver, Duras wrote: "Si on ne m'avait pas donné les cinq millions pour le tourner, j'aurais fait un film noir, une bande optique noire. Je suis dans un rapport de meurtre avec le cinéma. J'ai commencé à en faire pour atteindre l'acquis créateur de la destruction du texte. Maintenant c'est l'image que je veux atteindre, réduire. J'en suis à envisager une image passe-partout, indéfiniment superposable à une série de textes, image qui n'aurait en soi aucun sens, qui ne serait ni belle ni laide, qui ne prendrait son sens que du texte qui passe sur elle. . . . avec le film noir, j'en serais donc arrivée à l'image idéale, à celle du meurtre avoué du cinéma."[9] In the second half of L'Homme atlantique, one sees what appears to be black on black--a black rectangle on a black background; the voice of Duras, reading her own text, becomes a monochord solo accompaniment; the blackness is as if inhabited, haunted, by the author's voice. At the first showing of this film, Duras had wanted to have the doors locked so that the faithful could celebrate this "black mass"--only the fire codes prevented her from doing so. To some critics, this final stage of non-representational cinema, of total destruction of the image, is an arrogant act of elitism on Duras's part. Yet one can find in this black screen a mirror offered to the imagination, suggesting the comparison with the page blanche confronting the writer at the moment of creation. Bettina Knapp writes of L'Homme atlantique: "With Duras the non-image fills the eye of a camera like the void prior to the Creation, or the alchemist's prima materia as he seeks to realize the potential of the world before him: the unrealized, untried, unfelt. A variety of sensations enter the mind's eye as Duras proceeds to fill the blackness with eternal waters. . . To stare into the naught is to perceive for Duras."[10]

Happily, Duras has not left the viewer in the darkness of L'Homme atlantique; in spite of the creative possibilities for the imagination inherent in blackness, Duras's most successful films are those in which text plays off against image. With Dialogue of Rome, conceived for Italian television in 1982, Duras returned to the techniques of Agatha: accompanying the visual track of images of Rome--traveling shots of the Piazza Navona by night, the Roman countryside, panoramas of the Via Appia, are the voices off once again of Duras and Yann Andrea, who exchange enigmatic statements of their own past, of former civilizations, who speak of the tragic love of Berenice, queen of Caesar, and Titus, commander of the Roman armies. As in India Song and in Le Camion, the Variations by Diabelli on a theme of Beethoven recur as a musical punctuation throughout the film. Once again, Duras has created a film based on the impossibility of representation--Rome is a city of pure memory, peopled with phantoms, statues and shadows. All one can hope to do is affix one's own memories or obsessions on images of this eternal city.

The "different" cinema of Marguerite Duras both fascinates and exasperates. It is an intelligent cinema, one that confesses its disdain for commercial films and for passive viewers. Duras has moved in her cinematic experimentation straight toward the suppression of the primacy of the visual, as if it were a false plenitude. By exploring the sensual power of voice over image, Duras has tested the limits of representation. The words spoken in Duras's films by the voices off, through their interplay of language and silence, in their slow, neutral tones, echoes and repetitions, are exploited for their evocative and allusive power, rather than for their ability to convey precise information or to establish a fictional world of space and time. To accept the cinema of Marguerite Duras, the viewer must be willing to invest himself, to make new associations between sound and image. The full title of Agatha is Agatha ou les lectures illimitées--Agatha or Unlimited Readings. For the viewer who is disponible, open to the type of cinema that Duras offers, there is a beauty, a freshness, an enchantment in this type of alternative cinema, a writer's cinema, that lends itself to innumerable readings.

NOTES

[1] Frédéric Vitous, "Les Voies du Capitole: *Dialogue de Rome* de Marguerite Duras," *Le Nouvel observateur*, 29 mai 1983: n. pag.

[2] Nicole Lise Bernheim, *Marguerite Duras tourne un film* (Paris: Editions Albatros, 1981) 112, 119.

[3] Claire Devarrieux, "La dernière idole parfaite," *Le Monde international* 1879 (1-7 Nov. 1984): 13.

[4] Marguerite Duras, "Les Yeux verts," *Cahiers du cinéma* 312 (June 1980) 84.

[5] "Les Yeux verts" 48.

[6] Suzanne Lamy and André Roy, eds., *Marguerite Duras à Montréal* (Québec: Editions Spirale, 1981) 18.

[7] *Marguerite Duras à Montréal* 19, 57.

[8] "Aurelia Steiner," *Cahiers du Cinéma* 307 (Jan. 1980): 45-47.

[9] "Les Yeux verts" 48.

[10] Rev. of *L'Homme atlantique*, by Marguerite Duras, *World Literature Today* 56 (Autumn 1982): 645.

ISAK DINESEN AND DOROTHY CANFIELD:
THE IMPORTANCE OF A HELPING HAND

Ida H. Washington
Southeastern Massachusetts University

A little known chapter in the life of the Danish author Karen (or Tania) Blixen, who wrote under the pen name Isak Dinesen, is the vital role played in the launching of her literary career by the American novelist Dorothy Canfield. Without Dorothy's active assistance it is doubtful if Dinesen's first book, <u>Seven Gothic Tales</u>, would have found a publisher, and this was at a time when the Danish writer was so discouraged that she was almost ready to abandon her plans to be a writer. The behind-the-scenes story is contained in unpublished letters in the collections of the University of Vermont and Columbia University.

The relationship between the Danish and American authors developed out of the brotherly assistance of Thomas Dinesen, as he tells in his biography of Tania (whom he called "Tanne"). There he reports:

> One day Tanne said: "Listen, Tommy, you've had quite a bit to do with that American authoress, Dorothy Canfield. Couldn't you send my manuscript to her? Perhaps she could help me." It was true, I had met Dorothy several times and had corresponded a bit with her. I sent her Tanne's work and she replied almost at once.[1]

The reason for Dorothy's prompt and cordial answer lay in her warm friendship with the young people's aunt, Mary Westenholz. Miss Westenholz had written to Dorothy years before, after reading her novels, a letter that showed such understanding that an active correspondence developed between the Danish reader and the American author and continued throughout their long lives. On one of her many trips to Europe, Dorothy went to Denmark to see Mary Westenholz and was met at the airport by her nephew. So when Dorothy received Tania Blixen's stories accompanied by Thomas Dinesen's letter in August 1932, she answered:

> Yes indeed I remember every detail of my short visit to Copenhagen a couple of summers ago, and can still see you as you came down the long wharf to meet our aeroplane when it came in from Lubeck. Any connection of my dear Mary

87

Westenholz would never be forgotten by me, you can be sure of that.[2]

The bond between the cultured Danish spinster and the American writer had started out on a strictly literary basis and had gradually grown into a personal friendship. Since Dorothy wrote on a rich background in European literature, some aspects of her novels could be better appreciated by a reader who shared this heritage and could see beneath the surface of her writing and appreciate the deeper structure and meaning. In Mary Westenholz she recognized such a reader and responded warmly to her criticism and comments. She therefore looked forward to the Danish visit as a chance to exchange literary views with an old friend. The nephew, Thomas Dinesen, sent to the airport to meet his elderly aunt's guest, was merely an accessory to this visit. Tania's quoted comment that Thomas had had "quite a bit to do with that American authoress" exaggerates their acquaintance at this time beyond its real dimensions. Dorothy was, however, glad to extend a helping hand to a niece of her old Danish friend. She read the tales and reported in the same letter:

> I have read your sister's stories with extreme pleasure and interest. I had not thought that anyone could possibly use a language not his own with the sureness, richness, ease and subtlety shown by your sister. They are quite strikingly fine in quality--although I feel, perhaps rather obscure and complicated as to the construction. But that obscurity is a charm for many people, (I am among them,) and I don't think it will be a drawback for those capable of delighting in the unusually fine quality of the writing and of the reflections contained in those really extraordinary tales.

Dorothy's own knowledge of the European and American literary markets and the difficulty of publishing purely "literary" material in the United States led her to be cautious in her predictions of finding a publisher. Some of her own stories, later proclaimed her best (e. g., "The Murder on Jefferson Street" and "The Knot Hole") had searched long for a publisher. She was, nevertheless, willing to make an attempt to find a publisher for Tania's manuscript. To Thomas she wrote:

> A friend of mine, who is one of the best New York publishers, was visiting us when the stories arrived, and hearing my exclamations about the quality of the writing, he began to read them, and has taken them back to New York

> with him to show them to his partner. He agrees with me that there is little possibility that any magazine could use them serially, (they are too long, and with too little of what is called "narrative interest" for that, we both think) but the book publication by an American publishing house is apt to be rather more profitable to an author than the British publication. Although of course in this miserable year of depression and failure everywhere, it is impossible to predict anything at all. At any rate, if he is interested I will have him write you direct about any proposition he feels able to make.[3]

This first attempt to interest an American publisher in the tales was not successful, and in December Dorothy sent them to her literary agent Paul Reynolds. With him Dorothy had a long-standing professional relationship. She respected his literary judgment and listened to his advice. In the letter accompanying the manuscripts she wrote:

> I'm sending down to you under separate cover some stories written by a Danish connection of mine. They seem to me most original, strange, interesting and rich in texture. Whether any publisher could be found for them is another matter. Would it be asking you too much to look at them and see what you think? If you agree with me that they are worth doing something with--trying, at least--will you see what some publishers think about them, and greatly oblige me? The author, the Baroness Blixen, would like to have them published in magazine form. If not that, in a volume.[4]

Paul Reynolds doubted whether he would be able to market the strange tales. Dorothy was, however, one of his best and most popular authors. While he was hardly eager to back the stories from Denmark, as the tone of the following letter shows, he agreed to "try" a few publishers:

> I have looked at the stories by Baroness Blixen and I do not think they could be published in any magazine. I do not know whether they can be published in book form but I shall try some publishers and see what they say.[5]

Reynolds' doubts were in tune with her own, so Dorothy thanked him for his efforts and assured him that she was really just trying to do a favor to a relative of a friend. This was in the middle of the depression years, and both realized that few publishers could take a chance on a work that was so uncertain of acceptance by the public. She wrote:

> I too don't think really that the Blixen stories could possibly be taken even by the most "literary" of our magazines. And I don't know whether any publisher would be interested in them. Don't put yourself to much trouble about them. The opinion of two or three readers should be sufficient indication, I think. Just pass them on to me when you get them, and we'll call it a day and many thanks. I think it would be well to try the most literary-minded of the publishers--for instance, Knopf--don't you?[6]

By the end of the year, at least one publisher had seen the stories and had turned them down. Revere Reynolds, who had joined his father's firm, sent Dorothy this report on December 30:

> You will remember that you sent us several short stories by Baroness Blixen. I am enclosing a letter from Houghton Mifflin Company about these stories which you may care to send the author.
> We are going to try the stories further but as I am sure you realize, we doubt very much if we can induce a publisher to publish them or if they will attract attention and sell to the public if a publisher should bring them out in book form. We do, however, think Baroness Blixen has very real ability.[7]

The letter from Houghton Mifflin, to which Revere Reynolds refers, is not available, but it was clearly a very soft-toned rejection. At this time Dorothy felt that her obligation to help her friend's niece was essentially fulfilled, and she replied to Revere:

> I think too that it is really doubtful whether any publisher in this day will find it possible to consider publishing those stories of the Baroness Blixen's. Won't you please try just one more house and then send them back to me-- with the letter from the publisher if you get

> such a nice one as this. It was exactly what I wanted to send the Baroness, as a proof that I am really trying and that the opinion is general about the possibility of publishing them now.[8]

This letter was followed by a more definite request to Paul Reynolds:

> Just send back those Baroness Blixen stories to me. We've definitely established the fact that everybody thinks them charming--and not publishable at the present time.[9]

By this time, moreover, Tania Blixen was becoming impatient in Denmark. She decided to abandon the attempt to find an American market and to try to publish the stories with a subsidy in England. On January 22, 1933, she wrote to Dorothy and asked to have the manuscripts returned. In this letter Tania reveals what the publication of the stories means to her and also speaks of an African novel she wants to write, but as a second book, after the stories are published.

> I want to write about East Africa, [she says], where I have had for seventeen years what I shall ever feel to be my real life. And in this life of mine I have had one real wild devouring passion, which is my love of the Natives of East Africa, --for their country as well, but most for the people. I can not write about it all yet, I must get at it more of a distance, it would be, now, like writing a book about a recently lost child. And if ever I write about Africa, it could not be helped that the book would contain much bitterness and complaint about the way in which the country and the people have been treated by the English, and in which they have let loose upon it our mechanical and mercenary civilization. It would not be meant as any sort of political propaganda, but would be just the cry of my heart, but it would come out as much as the bitterness against serfdom goes through Turgeniev's "Diary of a Sportsman,"--if I may be allowed to compare a book of mine to one of that great Poet. --And this I hardly dare to do in a first book. It would do better in every way if I could have obtained some sort of name as a writer beforehand. I want to do what I

> can about the publishing of my stories on this account. --For an African book, if ever I get it written, would mean something very different to me: --I have been writing so far rather on two cylinders, or upon a flute only, but in a book of Africa I should be running a stronger car, and bringing more of an orchestra, I think.[10]

The book "about East Africa," to which Tania refers here, did indeed appear later with the title <u>Out of Africa</u>, was enormously successful, and was still later made into a very popular film with the same title. It is a powerful book, for it was written not only with literary skill, but out of the depths of her heart and spirit. However, <u>Out of Africa</u> would, according to the above letter, never have been written if it were not for the strange course of events which followed the first unsuccessful attempts to find a publisher for the <u>Seven Gothic Tales</u>.

Dorothy retrieved the manuscripts from her literary agent and wrote a letter to Tania, praising the tales and expressing the hope that they would find a publisher in England.[11] The stories were at her house in Vermont waiting to be wrapped and sent to Denmark, when a summer neighbor, the publisher Robert Haas, dropped in to visit. In an interview many years later, Dorothy recalled the subsequent events:

> I brought out these, and I perfidiously did not tell him that I'd already tried them on several other publishers. I said, "Here is a batch of manuscripts sent to me by the nephew of my dear Mary Westenholz." . . . Bob Haas took it back to read, and he was as puzzled by them as everyone else had been, but he was interested in the personal side of it, and said, "I'll take it back and see what the other people at Random House think." And I assume that he didn't tell them any more than I had told him, that he had been stumped by them. And they had a singular experience there. Everybody at Random House--all the readers, and even all the salesmen--was crazy about them. They felt, just as I did, that they were something new and different in quality, and that their strangeness was something precious. So with great enthusiasm they were published by Random House.[12]

At the request of Robert Haas, Dorothy wrote an introduction for the volume in which she said much the same thing about the strange and exotic quality of the tales that she had in her letters. Her involvement with the Seven Gothic Tales did not end with their publication, however. Dorothy was a member of the original Board of Selection of the Book-of-the-Month Club where her opinion carried considerable weight. Selection of a book by the Club guaranteed a large circulation and practically assured financial success and recognition to the author. When the Seven Gothic Tales came before the Board, as Dorothy reported later:

> The other judges were carried away by the exotic flavor, and also encouraged by the fact that they had been accepted by Random House, and were very much liked. You know, it takes a little courage to bring out something so different from anything that had ever been done before. . . . It was sent out with considerable trepidation, and was received with tremendous critical acclaim.[13]

The Board of Selection of the Book-of-the-Month Club was made up of leading authors and critics. These read forthcoming books and chose one each month to recommend specially as "the book of the month." Board members were instructed to choose, not on the basis of what they thought the public might like, but only books they liked best themselves. With this group of sophisticated readers, the Seven Gothic Tales found great favor, but they sent out their choice with considerable hesitation. The favorable reception of the work was generally a surprise, even to those who had recommended it.

Isak Dinesen's autobiographical novel Out of Africa and several of her later works were subsequently published by Random House and also became Book-of-the-Month Club selections. Her correspondence with Dorothy Canfield continued cordial, and they exchanged letters from time to time until Dorothy's death in 1958.

The Danish author's relationships with others were not always so easy. Tania's aunt, Mary Westenholz, was furious for what she saw as a totally unethical use of her friendship with Dorothy Canfield for her niece's selfish goals. Mary Westenholz had not been consulted about sending Tania's manuscripts to Dorothy, and this action exacerbated long-standing tensions between aunt and niece. Both women were strong-willed, and Tania once remarked, "One of my main reasons for going to Africa was to escape the tyranny of this aunt."[14]

Tania also tried the patience of her American publisher Robert Haas. It may have been the heady effect of the success of her first book, or perhaps it was simply the natural aristocratic tendency of the author, which made her haughty and unreasonable with a publisher whose mission, as she saw it, was to serve her interests. She had sacrificed a great deal for the title of "Baroness" and she took the distinction it conferred very seriously. When Tania's niece visited America in 1950, Dorothy therefore wrote to Robert Haas quite hesitantly:

> We have with us now for a few days a lovely young Danish visitor, Ingeborg Dinesen. She is daughter to Thomas Dinesen, hence niece of Tania Dinesen Blixen. . . . Would you like to see her and show her some attention as the niece of the author of "Out of Africa"? Or are you so out of patience with Tania's airs and graces (well, "graces" is hardly the accurate word) that you don't care if you never are reminded of a Dinesen again? . . . I'll either direct her to a meeting with you or keep still about your existence. She apparently has never heard a word about her Aunt Tania's American publishers, so you'd be safe.[15]

When Robert Haas replied with a warm invitation to the niece to visit, Dorothy wrote to him, "I think it sweet of you to bother with this young person, whose only connection is through Tania Dinesen Blixen, whose attitude is so laughably objectionable, seems to me, when she writes you!"[16]

A few years later, in 1956, Robert Haas asked Dorothy to do what she could to make his dealings with the Danish author easier. In response she wrote a letter to Tania that fairly glowed with admiration and sent a copy to Haas with this accompanying explanation:

> You will note in it that whenever the path of comment led to the brink of anything but admiration, I stopped. I feel justified in doing this because I don't think that anything I could say would help you in the ticklish job of "managing" an author as temperamental as she is highly gifted. Your skill in that undertaking is great and equals the need. But do remember what goes without saying that if I can ever be of use to you along those lines, I'm yours to command as always.[17]

Despite the problems which came to her as a result of reaching out a hand to help a sister writer from across the seas, and her New England annoyance with Tania Blixen's manifestations of aristocratic temperament, Dorothy Canfield never regretted bringing the Danish author's work before the public. Twenty-four years later Dorothy still vividly recalled her first impressions of the Seven Gothic Tales and spoke of them with genuine admiration, saying, "They were very fine, highly colored like a new kind of fruit or a new kind of wine. . . . I'd never seen anything like them."[18]

NOTES

[1] Thomas Dinesen, My Sister, Isak Dinesen, trans. Joan Tate (London: Michael Joseph, 1975) 127.

[2] Dorothy Canfield Fisher to Thomas Dinesen, August 12, 1932. (Copy in the University of Vermont)

[3] Ibid.

[4] Dorothy Canfield Fisher to Paul Reynolds, December 5, 1932. (In Columbia University)

[5] Paul Reynolds to Dorothy Canfield Fisher, December 8, 1932. (Columbia)

[6] Dorothy Canfield Fisher to Paul Reynolds, dated received December 14, 1932. (Columbia)

[7] Revere Reynolds to Dorothy Canfiled Fisher, December 30, 1932. (Columbia)

[8] Dorothy Canfield Fisher to Revere Reynolds, January 2, 1933. (Columbia)

[9] Dorothy Canfield Fisher to Paul Reynolds, dated received January 21, 1933. (Columbia)

[10] Tania Blixen to Dorothy Canfield Fisher, January 22, 1933. (Vermont)

[11] Dorothy Canfield Fisher to Baroness Blixen, April 30, 1933. (Vermont)

[12]Louis M. Starr, 1956, interview for Columbia Oral History Collection 61-63. (Typescript in Vermont)

[13]Starr interview.

[14]Quoted in Judith Thurman, Isak Dinesen, The Life of a Storyteller (New York: St. Martin's Press, 1982) 58-59.

[15]Dorothy Canfield Fisher to Mr. and Mrs. Robert Haas, October 30, 1950. (Vermont)

[16]Dorothy Canfield Fisher to Robert Haas, November 1, 1950. (Vermont)

[17]Dorothy Canfield Fisher to Robert Haas, August 14, 1956. (Vermont)

[18]Louis M. Starr interview 61.

ELFRIEDE JELINEK—PROFILE OF AN AUSTRIAN FEMINIST

Frank W. Young
California State University

Recent productions of the play, Clara S., and the publication of her first hard cover novel, Die Klavierspielerin, have focused renewed attention on the person and work of Elfriede Jelinek, a now thirty-seven-year-old Austrian writer whose first novel was hailed as a brilliant contribution to German literature, but whose subsequent work was received with diminished and largely negative critical response.[1] Although reactions to her latest novel are divided, the number and seriousness of critical reactions to it in the press have the effect of establishing Jelinek as an author deserving of broader critical resonance.[2] In a 1979 special issue of Modern Austrian Literature devoted to Austrian women writers, Jelinek is mentioned as a figure about whom "the amount of scholarly attention . . . stands in no direct relationship to the amount of discussion among scholars and in the press."[3] This paper undertakes to acquaint an audience interested in contemporary continental literature with Elfriede Jelinek's principal works and literary development.

Born in 1946 in the Styrian industrial city of Mürzzuschlag, Jelinek grew up in Vienna where she studied theatre arts and art history at the University of Vienna and music (organ, piano and composition) at the Vienna Conservatory of Music. National recognition of her literary talent came in 1969 when the then twenty-two-year-old student received awards for poetry and prose at the Twentieth Austrian Festival of Youth and Culture.

The pieces which gained her this early recognition owe much to the work of the Wiener Gruppe (Viennese Group), a circle of avant-gardists (Friedrich Achleitner, H.C. Artmann, Konrad Bayer, Gerhard Rühm, Oswald Wiener) who collaborated between 1952 and 1964. Startling juxtapositions of words and images, eccentric neologisms and metaphors belie such traditional lyric titles as "erwartung" (expectation), "langer sommer" (long summer), or "der kuss" (the kiss).[4] It is writing for other writers, recondite and seemingly capricious.

The first major prose work, the radio novel, bukolit (bucolite), completed in 1968 but published only in 1979, is, as the name suggests, a lyric fantasy on erotic themes.[5] Dream-like sequences are constructed around such motivic nuclei as morning awakening, a country outing, and the pillaging of a village. Thematic unity is provided by the male aggression that occurs in every episode in more or less erotic guise. Women's behavior, including the willingness to hurt other women, reflects the brutality that seems to pervade men's lives. In bukolit Jelinek evokes a spiritual landscape that is the antithesis of bucolic: erotic energy does not engender life-affirming pleasure, but rather the desire to conquer. As the last scenes show, this desire, when it has exhausted itself, leaves nihilistic monsters to function as the parents and preceptors of society.

The publication of wir sind lockvögel baby! (we're decoys baby!) in 1970 established Jelinek's reputation beyond the borders of Austria. The novel is a phantasmagoria of contemporary commercial trivia constructed according to the experimental methods of the nouveau roman. Characters and motifs from comic books, television shows, science fiction, adventure films, pop music, advertisements, etc., are blended with metamorphic personae who become a medium for the presentation of fantastic episodes grotesquely mirroring violent, dehumanizing events of the late sixties. In form and content the novel reflects the iconoclastic spirit of the times and of the writers with whom Jelinek then associated. In a preface entitled "operation instructions," readers are exhorted to alter the book to their liking, just as they are encouraged to bring social change outside the law. She discourages from wasting their time reading the book both those who are already actively involved in "undermining the massive official organs of repressions," as well as those who "lack the will to employ violence" to this end.

The revolutionary intent of the author is clearly formulated in the penultimate paragraph of the novel: "We must take leave of our companions who have accompanied us so faithfully."[6] Such companions include, for example, Bat Man, the White Giant and other heroes created by the bourgeois establishment to convey intimations of an omniscient, benign governing order at work behind the all too human social institutions. Did or does the message of the book come across to the reader? No, for the same reason that her poetry was read by only a small circle of enthusiasts. Despite the aperçus into the connections between language and the social conventions of whole strata of society whose consciousness may be shaped by them, readers accustomed to more conventional exposition find the idea content too meager to reward the effort required to discover it.

Jelinek, too, must have recognized how limited were the possibilities of such constructivistic prose, because in the same year lockvögel appeared she wrote a kind of literary manifesto distancing herself from her prior work. She accuses herself of having produced "barren literature" and vows to write no longer for artists, writers and literary managers. "My literature," she exclaims, "must abandon its isolation . . . must become as explosive as napalm. . . . I must nurture COMMUNICATION with those groups to which I myself belong and who are in a position to prepare the revolutionary transformation of the foundations of this society."[7]

The turn from art for other artists to literature as a weapon in the struggle for societal change was accompanied by, or was perhaps the result of, a period of critical reflection and intense study. "endlose unschuldigkeit" (endless innocence), an essay published in 1970, acknowledges a debt to Roland Barthes, Marshall McLuhan and other analysts of contemporary Western culture.[8] It provides useful clues to understanding Jelinek's views and aesthetic methods up to the present.

"Innocence," in the sense of this essay, is the naïveté that permits an "economy of compensations" to maintain the masses in an "infantile society"; i.e., a society which discourages individuals from accepting responsibility for their own destinies. This innocence is "endless" because its preservation serves the interests of the capitalistic system that also controls the means to perpetuate it. Of these means, the mass media are the most powerful and effective. Through commercial entertainment, advertising, journalism, etc., views of the privileged classes are conveyed to the masses as inevitable, natural truths about human nature. These messages function as cultural myths supportive of the status quo. By means of readily available and affordable compensations--material goods, vicarious experience, approval through observance of moral conventions--latent or overt rebellion against the patriarchal order is diverted from the social structure to concretized, expendable surrogates of that order.

Among the fragments of journalistic reports, film and fiction episodes that Jelinek incorporates into the essay to illustrate how trivial myths transmit repressive values, there is one that unfolds plot-like throughout the entire text. It is the tale of a young woman who is abducted, held captive, and finally assaulted. As the essayist concludes her observations by discussing the role trivial myths and the media that purvey them play in preventing the emancipation of women, the victim in the fragmentary plot seizes, in a desperate act of self-liberation, her oppressor's revolver and empties its contents into his body.

<u>Michael: A Young Person's Guide to Infantile Society</u> (1972) was the first major piece of fiction to appear after the manifesto.[9] In its style and structure the novel is still indebted to the montage method of her earlier prose. Episodes from films, television shows, magazine articles alternate with plot fragments to create a kaleidoscope of images. In contrast to

lockvögel, however, the figures in this novel take on a fixed identity and continuity. They function as caricatures of social groups; e.g., the idle rich, aspiring proletarians, petty bourgeoisie. Plot lines emerge to reveal the mentality and actions of these groups. Michael illustrates how patterns of human relationships are transmitted via trivial myths; how consciousness is subtly formed by the media, television in particular; and how the privileged class benefits from the attitudes and behavior thus adopted by the unprivileged. The novel exposes the media as agents of a power elite used to manipulate mass behavior and prevent social change.

In Die Liebhaberinnen (The Lovers), published three years after Michael, Jelinek ventures onto the thin ice of realistic narration. Despite intentional artificiality of structure, satirical diction, and the reduction of characters to the level of demonstration models, Die Liebhaberinnen succeeds in personalizing the destructive force of trivial myths. In thirty-two alternating, chronologically ordered segments, Jelinek traces the lives of two women from the awakening of the need for independence through marriage and its consequences. Although the destinies of the lovers diverge--Brigitte's toward middle class security and emotional atrophy, Paula's to the life of a proletarian--both remain the victims of myths against whose normative influences they are defenseless. "They have no destiny," the narrator notes, "they are given a destiny."[10]

The fates of the lovers are determined by the olympians of business and industry whose lives provide the ideals they (the lovers) struggle to emulate, but who themselves remain aloof from these struggles. Women are the protagonists in this vision of a culture that condemns its youth to perpetual immaturity. Precisely because the humanity of wives and mothers is so often betrayed, women unconsciously become links in a chain of suffering that deforms the lives of their children.

As if to heighten the exemplary intent of the novel, Jelinek published in that same year (1975) a short character study entitled "paula bei der rezeption eines buches, das am lande spielt, und in dem sie die hauptrolle spielt" (Paula's thoughts while reading a book set in the country in which she plays the main role.)[11] The hypothetical reader of Jelinek's Liebhaberinnen--who is, of course, identical with its heroine-- identifies sentimentally with the fate of the main character. As does Paula of the novel, the reader Paula blames herself, in particular her failure to maintain a slim figure, for the breakup of her marriage and the loss of her children. In keeping with the myths daily reiterated by parents, co-workers, magazines, television--and wholly contrary to the sense of the book she is reading--Paula accepts guilt for the actions and circumstances of which she is the victim. Apart from despair at the willingness of the oppressed to embrace their oppressors, "paula bei der rezeption . . ." provides a sardonic commentary on the effectiveness of literature as a weapon in social struggle.

The period following the appearance of <u>Die Liebhaberinnen</u> was one of great creative diversity: Jelinek translated Thomas Pynchon's novel, <u>Gravity's Rainbow</u> (published 1980); she wrote a filmscript and several radio plays; her first play was staged; she published a children's story, a short story and her first major piece of literary criticism. "kein licht am ende des tunnels" (no light at the end of the tunnel), a lengthy essay on the work of Thomas Pynchon (1976) reveals Jelinek's fine analytical capacities and her ethical commitment to reconciling the senselessness and cruelty of human affairs, as they are so convincingly portrayed by Pynchon, with a Marxist interpretation of history.[12] Pynchon's work represents for Jelinek a superb literary achievement rooted in, and therefore necessarily limited by, its author's individualistic, middle-class views.

The period of preoccupation with Pynchon marks a major shift in Jelinek's artistic approach. Stylistic changes, such as the adoption of conventional orthography and increasing reliance upon traditional syntax and structure, reflect a fundamental turn from the technique of collage and caricature to perspective and portraiture, from the creation of models to interpret "reality" to the interpretation of real models. Of the four major works that have appeared since 1979, one is based upon an actual event, two incorporate historical real or fictional personalities from Western European high culture, and the fourth presents a case study combining individual and cultural psychology.

Jelinek's first stage play, <u>Was geschah, nachdem Nora ihren Mann verlassen hatte oder Stützen der Gesellschaften</u> (What Happened After Nora Left her Husband or The Pillars of Societies), attracted considerable interest at its premiere in 1979, especially among feminists.[13] Ibsen's heroine is portrayed by turns as an effusive, just emancipated, upper-class housewife seeking to find herself in the world of work; a mistress of an industrial magnate; a compliant sexual pawn in her paramour's machinations against her former husband; a would-be revolutionary out of personal disappointment; and, finally, as a shopkeeper remarried to the man she helped ruin. Nora's fleeting insight into the fascistic hierarchy that controls her own and others' destinies comes late and is soon compensated by the promise of a life of comfort. The pillars of societies are the sturdy attitudes and values of the working masses, particularly of the women who enjoy fewer benefits than men in relation to the burden they share.

Die Ausgesperrten (The Excluded), a novel published the following year, is based upon the sensational 1965 case of a Viennese high school honor student who killed and dismembered his parents and sister.[14] The quartet of youths whose interrelationships propel the story are a microcosm of Viennese society in the period of recovery from the Second World War. Rainer and Anna Witkowski, the "excluded," are the twin children of a pauperized former member of the SS who vents his rage at the loss of power and status by forcing the mother of his children to be the subject of pornographic photography. The siblings display contempt for their better off classmates, for the life style and possessions they crave but cannot have. Their intellectual and artistic accomplishments, criminal adventures, sado-masochistic behaviors are all analogues of power born of impotence. The freedom both claim to seek outside the established order is a relic of bourgeois, romantic glorification of individualism. After losing his influence over an aristocratic girl classmate to a blue collar companion, Rainer is unable to bear the thought of life apart from the artificial hierarchy of the school. In his grisly act of liberation he paradoxically affirms the values and the social order that have destroyed him.

The stage play, Clara S., and the novel, Die Klavierspielerin, pursue the respective direction set by Nora and Die Ausgesperrten. The historical canvas in Clara S. spans the period from around 1830 through 1940. Salient events in Clara Schumann's life provide the framework for a demonstration of the repression of women. Her father, the pianist and composer Friedrich Wiek, her husband, composer Robert Schumann, and the celebrated author, nationalist and womanizer, Gabriele D'Annunzio, appear in scenes linked by film clips of Mussolini to tyrannize, exploit and cheat Clara of self-fulfillment. In the name of Robert Schumann's genius Clara extinguishes her own creativity to serve the artistic, psychological, physical and economic needs of her insatiable, now insane, husband. When he refuses to concede her right to musical self-expression--and, by implication, the right of any woman to artistic maturity--Clara strangles him to death.

Owing to its negative portrayal of the role of music (and of art in general) in the play, Jelinek subtitled Clara S. "a musical tragedy." This description is perhaps more appropriate for her most widely read novel, Die Klavierspielerin (The Pianist) published in 1983.[15] It is an ambitious and compelling book that succeeds well in capturing a desperate reality behind the concert halls and the Kärntnerstrasse. Here it is not a man or men who tyrannize the protagonist, but rather her own mother, ultimately she herself. The need to dominate is the driving motive of the novel. Music provides a means of attaining status and the medium of exercising power over others. As Erika had been tyrannized by her music teachers, so does she in turn tyrannize her students, all in the name of high culture, identification with which can elevate one (or one's family) above the masses. In the name of this supreme value the young Erika was cut off from association with others and her maturation repressed. As the piano teacher ages and experiences neither satisfaction in the recreation of music nor in her role as teacher or daughter, nature begins to avenge itself. Consistent with the patterns of male behavior, Erika seeks gratification in voyeurism. When a young man, a piano student, evinces romantic interest in her, Erika determines to control each move. Out of the young man's repugnance at her attempt to involve him in a sado-masochistic scenario, a spark of something approaching genuine love briefly illuminates her dreary emotional life. The wanton invitation, however, destroys the student's respect for her authority as a musician. No longer protected by the nimbus of cultural superiority, Erika's fantasy becomes savage reality.

In her poetry, prose and dramas Elfriede Jelinek depicts human relationships in a contemporary, class conscious, patriarchal Western European culture. Hers is a harsh reality molded by economic Darwinism and unredeemed by love in any form. Erotic love for men appears as eruptive gratification less of the sex drive than of the need to dominate others. Women learn to compensate for lack of sexual and emotional satisfaction by manipulating men's crippled sexuality to achieve possession, power, status. In the face of male ego- and phallocentrism, romantic love withers to sentimentality and maternal love becomes a surrogate for self-fulfillment. Women are alienated from self, from family, and from other women.

In a world in which human beings are lost to each other, one would hardly expect to encounter the love of God. Indeed, religious sentiments are as wholly absent from characters' experience as is the presence of the official church in their lives. Moral education takes place in the family where the "wisdom of the fathers" is implacably inculcated in the children. Friends and neighbors, the school, the workplace, and especially the media, see to it that rebellion against the existing value structure is publicly discredited or subverted. In terms of Freudian psychology, the gods insure that the son never kills the father; society remains infantile.

Jelinek shows how characters' aggressive and repressive behavior results from choices based on the values of the culture in which they live. These values are "man-made" and consciously propagated by a male power elite. To come to understand one's role in life, one's very feelings and aspirations as the product of purposeful manipulation for profit, and not as an expression of natural or divine law, is a necessary first step toward freeing oneself and one's fellow human being. Women and youth have been the most victimized segments of society. It is women, through the children they bear and rear, who offer hope of loosening the bonds of the patriarchal order. It is women and youth of whom Elfriede Jelinek has chosen to write.

Like Brecht, Jelinek confronts readers and listeners with the mutable circumstances that determine the destiny of the unprivileged majority in society. Unlike Brecht, Jelinek has won largely the enmity of literary critics who, while lauding her powers of observation and depiction, decry the vulgarity and artificiality of the world she creates. Her characters, it has been remarked, are two-dimensional figures whose actions and behaviors are obviously and arbitrarily governed by their creator; motives, motifs, and themes reflect the violent, sordid side of life; her diction is exaggerated and monotonous in its sarcasm and negativism. Jelinek would not, I think, take great exception to such characterizations. Indeed, she treats her characters with the kind of totalitarian contempt she sees accorded to the powerless in real life.

That her young protagonists instinctively crave and grope towards more humane relationships with others despite the obstacles to their realization is evidence of hope. Through the vehemence with which this hope is betrayed, Jelinek makes the reader or spectator share her anger at such needless destruction and at our own unwitting complicity in perpetuating it.

NOTES

[1] An incomplete bibliography of literature by and about Elfriede Jelinek through January 1981 may be found in Hans Christian Kosler, "Elfriede Jelinek," in Kritisches Lexikon zur deutschsprachigen Gegenwartsliteratur.

[2] Within four months of the novel's publication at least eighteen reviews appeared in major German language newspapers and magazines; e.g., Ria Endres, "Ein musikalisches Opfer," Der Spiegel 21 (May 23, 1983): 174-177; Benjamin Henrichs, "Mutterdämmerung," Die Zeit 29 (July 7, 1983): 29f; Lothar Baier, "Abgerichtet, sich selbst zu zerstören," Süddeutsche Zeitung (July 16, 1983).

[3] Donald G. Daviau, preface to Modern Austrian Literature 12.3-4 (1979).

[4] A collection of Jelinek's early poetry is available in ende: gedichte 1966-1968 (Schwifting: Schwiftinger Galerie-Verlag, 1980).

[5] bukolit: hörroman mit bildern von robert zepperl-sperl (Wien: Rhombus Verlag, 1979).

[6] wir sind lockvögel baby! (Reinbek bei Hamburg: Rowohlt, 1970) 256. Translations of titles and quotations are mine.

[7] Grenzverschiebung: Neue Tendenzen in der deutschen Literatur der 60er Jahre, edited by Renate Matthaei, 215 (Köln/Berlin: Kiepenheur un Witsch, 1970).

[8] "die endlose unschuldigkeit," in Trivialmythen, ed. Renate Matthaei (Frankfurt am Main: März-Verlag, 1970) 40-66). Reprint. Elfriede Jelinek, Die endlose Unschuldigkeit: Prosa -- Hörspiel -- Essay (Schwifting: Schwiftinger Galerie-Verlag, 1980).

[9] Michael: Ein Jugendbuch für die Infantilgesellschaft (Reinbek bei Hamburg: Rowohlt, 1972).

[10] Die Liebhaberinnen (Reinbek bei Hamburg: Rowohlt, 1975) 8.

[11] In Manuskripte 50 (1975): 49-51.

[12] "kein licht am ende des tunnels--nachrichten über thomas pynchon." In Manuskripte 52 (1976): 35-44.

[13] In Was geschah, nachdem Nora ihren Mann verlassen hatte? Acht Hörspiele von Elfriede Jelinek, Ursual Krechen, et al., ed. Helga Geyer-Ryan (München: dtv, 1982) 170-215.

[14] Die Ausgesperrten (Reinbek bei Hamburg: Rowohlt, 1980).

[15] Die Klavierspielerin (Reinbek bei Hamburg: Rowohlt, 1983).

THE WOMAN'S NOVEL PARODIED: FANNY LEWALD'S DIOGENA

Hanna B. Lewis
Sam Houston State University

The novels of George Sand had an impact upon the writings of almost all the women writers of her day. Her depiction of the psychology and the physiology of women and their relationship to men, the problems of marriage, and the question of what constituted true independence, called for some type of reaction, positive or negative, just as Goethe's Wilhelm Meisters Lehrjahre provoked the German Romantic writers to produce novels that imitated or tried to surpass the original. To a few critics, the women novelists seemed to proliferate excessively; one prejudiced German journalist wrote that "like Jews, you find them everywhere" (Prutz 252).[1]

Countess Ida von Hahn-Hahn (she married a first cousin, accounting for the double name) (1805-1880) was typical of the writers who imitated the style and content of George Sand's novels. The excessive drive for freedom, the initiation of action at any cost, the emancipation of the flesh, resulted in an egoism that approached the ridiculous. Her heroines are so aristocratic that they can hardly breathe common air and are always looking for the right man, "den Rechten." They are true princesses aware of any pea under the mattress. The heroine of Ilda Schönholm considers herself an aristocrat from head to foot, thanking God for this privilege, for only the aristocratic soul has true nobility, and keeps itself apart from the pollution of the common herd of people. Hahn's ladies think only of themselves, their feelings, their clothes, and their status. They speak in an elevated, effusive language that combines German, English, and French to display their erudition. Hahn-Hahn was actually a good writer; she had an excellent eye for detail and her character descriptions are frequently observant and accurate. But her general style made her a wonderfully easy subject to parody.

Fanny Lewald (1811-1889) was considered the leading woman novelist of her day by several critics (male and female), and her works are being reprinted today. So far, interest centers on her autobiography (always important in the feminist canon), her early novels about the problems of love and marriage, and the emancipatory writings of the 1860's and 1870's. However, the republication in 1985 of a book of her travel memoirs shows an expanding audience of contemporary readers, and her inclusion in most important anthologies of German feminist writers (especially those by Renate Möhrmann and Gisela Brinker-Gabler) indicates that

Lewald's literary and intellectual reputation is presently on the rise.

Lewald was widely translated in her lifetime; here in the United States, it is sometimes easier to get a book by her in English than in German, and both are as readily available from city and private lending libraries here as from university libraries. One paperback, published in Chicago in 1870, was available in German ($.20) and English ($.25),[2] with the page numbers corresponding exactly, so that housewives could teach themselves German. Her simple and colloquial style, unpretentious and easy to translate, makes her accessible to all levels of readers even today.

As a young woman, Lewald had been an admirer of Hahn-Hahn and naturally devoured Sand's novels also. She soon discovered that Sand's heroines loved honestly, though they were frequently destroyed by such a love, but, as she wrote:

> It was different with Countess Hahn. First of all, usually only countesses loved, and so, love was therefore considered an aristocratic prerogative; secondly, the countesses only wanted to love excessively, but could somehow never accomplish this. They really only existed to be loved. (Lebensgeschichte 307)[3]

In her fourth novel, Diogena (1847), published under the rather obvious pseudonym of Countess Iduna von H.-H., Lewald decided to attack Hahn-Hahn, firstly because the countess was an easy target, secondly because of pique, since Lewald's first secret love was now an admirer of the countess, and thirdly, as Lewald righteously stated decades later, she considered Hahn a basically good novelist, who needed some stylistic guidance.

It was almost inevitable that the two writers should clash, both because of their similarities and their differences. Both had converted from the faith of their childhood, both had been disappointed in love in their youth, both were influenced by George Sand. But the differences were even greater. Hahn, an aristocrat from a reactionary provincial family, poorly educated by governesses at home in the traditional manner of proper young ladies, was forced into an unhappy marriage of convenience for financial reasons. To exacerbate her misery, the only child born of this three-year union, which ended in divorce, was retarded.

Although Hahn showed much courage and initiative in her later life, traveling with her lover to such remote places as Istanbul, her perspective remained that of a young aristocratic woman, writing poetically as an avocation, detached from everyday life. Her former husband continued to support her generously, so she had no financial pressures. She was uninterested in social issues, other than those that affected her directly.

Lewald was archetypically bourgeois. The oldest child in a Jewish merchant family and her father's favorite, she benefited from his desire that all his children be well read and intellectually stimulated. Although she was not permitted to attend secondary school, a privilege limited to the sons of the family, no one doubted her intelligence or ability. She was too strong-willed to accept a marriage of convenience and when she married, it was a union of love after a ten-year extramarital relationship. By this time, she had also established herself as a best-selling author and was able to support her step-children and her ailing husband. It is therefore not surprising that she was contemptuous of women who must have the "right man" to provide for their material and romantic needs.

Hahn-Hahn never progressed beyond the scope of her early novels. Unable to cope with the political and social upheavals and the liberalism of the 1848 revolutionary period, shattered by the death of her long-time lover, she retired to a convent in 1850 and finally founded her own cloister. She wrote nothing else; she was a revolutionary manqué.

Lewald, on the other hand, after her father's death and the success of her early novels, including Diogena, began writing under her name, an action which had been previously impossible because of his disapproval. Although most feminist critics consider these early novels the best, the later novels and the journalistic writings about contemporary political and social issues are also of considerable significance. The incredible size of her oeuvre provides a rich feast for any reader. There is certainly enough valuable literature to balance the sometimes trivial and sentimental works, written only for the purpose of earning a living. And stylistically, she avoids the pedantic heaviness of many "great" German authors and achieves what could be considered a major criterion for any writer: readability. Her ideas for reform of the existing social system, her clear-eyed assessment of the political scene could be the product of the mind of a contemporary feminist. Obviously she had little sympathy for Hahn's extreme sensibility and limited point of view.

Diogena is a marvelously witty and entertaining novel, quite different from anything else Lewald ever wrote. It is her only humorous work; Lewald was a Prussian in every sense of the word, and although occasionally satirical, she took life very seriously. Diogena is named so because, as the Greek philosopher Diogenes was constantly looking for an honest man, she is eternally searching for the "right man": "den Rechten" (Der Rechte was the title of Hahn's most popular novel). Her family's coat of arms shows the Diogenean lantern, but it is the symbol, not of the search for truth, but for the right man, by generations of her female relatives. Lewald has wickedly given several of these ancestresses the names of characters from Hahn-Hahn's novels, including Ilda Schönholm and Der Rechte. As Diogena confesses to an attractive priest she encounters in a brief fling at being a nun:

> A heavy curse rests on my family. I am a descendant of Diogenes; I must seek a person as he did, a man in the ideal sense of the word, the right man. Untold women of our line have perished because of this, since only the heart and the soul are the divining rod with which you can find heart and soul, with which you can find the right man and--none of us has heart and soul. (Diogena 95)[4]

Naturally the nun's habit is vastly becoming to her, as is the jewelry and silks she wears when preparing to do her first and only dissection, assisted by an adoring professor, who is dazzled by her beauty. She has asked her current lover to obtain just the right kind of cadaver: "Couldn't you at least get me the corpse of a child from an aristocratic family? I would feel very uncomfortable operating on the body of a lower class person" (121).[5] Such sensibility had left her orphaned as an infant: her father was killed in a duel and her mother died, not of a broken heart, but of outrage, because the man, whose name she and her child had to bear, had fought with a bourgeois.

Diogena's narcissistic preoccupation with her own beauty, delicacy, and wardrobe is profusely expressed throughout the text. The smallness and whiteness of her extremities bears witness to her noble ancestry. A typical passage from Hahn's Der Rechte (1839)-- "His mother had narrow, fleshless, fine snowy hands, with slender fingers accustomed to command with disdainful movements, and were always cool" (Spiero 22)[6]--are echoed in Lewald, when Diogena's maid kneels at her feet, "half overcome by gratitude for the favor of my confidences, half overcome by the magic of my beauty. She kissed my fabulous little feet" (43).[7] Our heroine always refers to her own feet in this way. And in another passage, all these aspects are again emphasized:

> I was at that time at that adorable stage of feminine existence, in which the child suddenly becomes a woman, uniting all the grace of childhood with the magic of the woman. The rosy shawl, which enveloped me, revealed, as far as the water reflected my image, the flawless beauty of my aristocratic body. My goldenblond curls, adorned with brilliant reflections, hung down to my shoulders. The fine dark fringes of my heavy thick lashes veiled the black irises of my eyes, which though soft as velvet, concealed an all the more burning fire within. . . . (<u>Diogena</u> 24-25)[8]

One of the clichés of the romantic woman's novel was the escape to nature or the exotic world of the noble savage. Diogena and her princely admirer set out for the American West, naturally suitably attired:

> I looked like an Indian squaw, translated into a German aristocratic style, because even in the light painting of my body, consisting of thousands of small marvelously intertwined lanterns (her coats of arms), in my feather headdress, my arm and ankle bracelets and the moccasins fashioned for me by the foremost bootmaker in London, lay the totally charming nonchalance of a noble countess. (<u>Diogena</u> 157)[9]

She has also prepared herself by reading all of Cooper's and Sealsfield's novels to learn the habits of the Indians, studying the language of the Delaware and memorizing the conversations of Parthenia and the Indian Ingomar in Friedrich Halm's <u>Der Sohn der Wildnis</u> (1843). Needless to say, these assets do not prepare her adequately for life with her Indian chief, Coeur de Lion. He reluctantly accepts her offer of herself to him, although he points out to her that he could have any squaw he wants; she is a weakling, not getting any younger, and he will only keep her until he tires of her. Then he will graciously allow her to live and will buy himself younger women. Diogena is appalled at the difference between fact and fiction, but remains with him, trying to serve him for three days. On the fourth day, he discards her as completely useless. Her beauty has very quickly faded; her spirit and body are crushed by the hardships of savage life. Coeur de Lion casts her off scornfully:

> The white woman has aged in a few days and has sickened in the freedom of the forest. She is not worthy of the fresh air of the Great Spirit, not worthy of becoming the wife of the young warrior any more, who cannot feel desire for a sick wife. She cannot cook or carry weapons for him, she cries and would bear only miserable, sickly cowards. Let her go home to the cities of the wretched pale-faces, for whose men she is good enough, with her trembling hands and her tears. Coeur de Lion will buy himself a healthy young woman from his own tribe. The weak white woman is an abomination to him. (Diogena 173)[10]

Utterly destroyed, Diogena makes her way home, stopping only in China in a last attempt to find her perfect lover. She reasons that the Chinese are, after all, the closest thing to true aristocrats, since they have the smallest feet, the most "soigné" fingernails, the most magnificent beards, and not a trace of liberalism. Disappointed in the Far East, she ends her days in a sanitarium, with all her pretensions and delusions intact.

Diogena's concept of the nature of love is as confused as the rest of her ideas. As she explains to one of her countless aristocratic lovers:

> I know what love is by the faith in my heart, as the Christian has faith in the existence and the nature of eternal bliss. Love is the oneness of two; I stop existing and only become alive again in another. It is a regeneration, a dissolution in the beloved, whose whole being becomes entirely my own. One person alone does not penetrate the secret of existence, but two unite into one love, which penetrates it. They whirl upward toward the sun with the lark at daybreak, they hearken to the silent pulse of the earth in the dreamy night, they master the total range of feeling with a mighty magic wand, so that all the chords of human existence unite under their wills into a harmony of the spheres, the eternal text of which is the one word--Love. (Diogena 29)[11]

Many other effusions of this type permeate the book.

a few examples are given here to show this:

> "Aber das ist ein Horreur."
>
> "Alles bis auf den Comfort."
>
> "Wenn Ihnen alles indifferent ist . . ."
>
> "Die Deutschen sind so troublesome in diesen Angelegenheiten."
>
> "Wenn ich einen Remplaçant für Sie habe . . ."
>
> "Meine Mutter fühlte eine edle Aprehension . . ."
>
> "Lass uns Gott danken, dass wir zur Crême der Aristokratie gehören und diese Wonnestunde ohne arrière-pensée feiern und geniessen können."

Almost every page contains some examples of this usage, of which Hahn-Hahn was particularly guilty.

At the end of the novel, there is a change from a first person narrative by Diogena to one by the "author" of the book. In the sanitarium, Diogena is usually calm, but sometimes rages about the fact that she will never find "den Rechten." Her princely admirer hopes she can be cured, but the doctor is not so sanguine. "Madness caused by arrogance and egotism tends to be irreversible" (<u>Diogena</u> 180).[12]

Although Lewald was basically an admirer of George Sand, and certainly influenced by her to some extent, she lays a distinct blame for the condition of the nineteenth-century women's novel and the false aspirations of her sex at Sand's feet, just as Gustave Flaubert did in <u>Madame Bovary</u>. The doctor, speaking for Lewald explains:

> Her madness is the product of a cultural trend among the idle ladies of the aristocratic world, which could hardly have a different outcome. These silly blind adherents of the gifted George Sand, in a lack of understanding of what this great woman meant and intended, generally created a theory of feminine egotism, which has now reached a climax in German women's literature. The ladies all think themselves exceptional beings, incapable of loving anyone but themselves; considering themselves the center of the universe, they

demand, on the one hand, to be worshipped like the dissolute Roman emperors of old, and, on the other hand, deplore the fact that they cannot find a man worthy of their love. They don't understand their own egotism, and claim not to be understood; they're incapable of loving, and complain that no one fills the emptiness of their hearts and souls. (<u>Diogena</u> 178)[13]

George Sand was a revolutionary and Fanny Lewald was a reformer. Their ideas for changing the role of women in society were therefore quite different, although their goal was similar. Lewald practiced what she preached and none of her novels shows the flaws she parodies in <u>Diogena</u>. Her protagonists are usually middle-class merchants or artists, making their way upward in the world. Often they rise to the upper class because of hard work, intelligence, or talent. Her born aristocrats are frequently sympathetically depicted, but as major characters, they are often supplanted by or marry a bourgeois. At other times, her anger at their callous disregard of the feelings and rights of those below them on the social scale spills over into direct criticism. But only in <u>Diogena</u> does she use humor, directed at the aristocracy and the novelists, whose adulation of it she felt to be a danger to feminine self-perception and to literature in general.

NOTES

[1]"Die Frauen sind eine Macht in userer Literatur geworden; gleich den Juden begegnet man ihnen auf Schritt und Tritt."

[2]Fanny Lewald, <u>Stories and Novels</u> and Fanny Lewald, <u>Humoresken und Skizzen</u>, both published by Louis Schick, Chicago, 1885.

[3]"Bei der Gräfin Hahn war das aber anders. Erstens liebten in der Regel nur Gräfinnen, und die Liebe wurde dadurch gewissermassen zu einem aristokratischen Vorrecht erklärt, zweitens wollten die Gräfinnen immer nur sehr lieben, konnten es aber nie recht zu Stande bringen. Sie waren hauptsächlich für das Geliebtwerden auf der Welt."

[4]"Mein Vater! ein schwerer Fluch ruht auf meinem Geschlechte, hören Sie mich an. Ich stamme von Diogenes, ich muss einen Menschen suchen, wie er es that, einen Menschen, einen Mann in der vollen Idealität des Wortes, den rechten Mann. Unzählige Frauen unsers Geschlechtes sind daran zu Grunde gegangen, denn nur

das Herz und die Seele sind die Wünschelruthe, mit denen man Herz und Seele, mit denen man den Rechten findet und--wir Alle haben weder Herz noch Seele."

5"Könnten Sie mir nicht die Leiche irgend eines Kindes aus einem aristokratischen Hause verschaffen? Es liegt mir etwas Unbehagliches darin, an eine Leiche von niederm Stande zu operieren."

6"Seine Mutter hatte schmale, fleischlose, feine schneeige Hande mit schlanken, befehlenden Fingern, mit abwehrenden Bewegungen und waren immer kühl."

7". . . halb zu meinen Füssen hingezogen von dem Dankgefühl über die Gnade meiner Confidenz, halb überwaltigt von dem Zauber meiner fascinierenden Schönheit. Sie küsste meine fabelhaft kleinen Füsschen. . . ."

8"Ich war damals in jener reizenden Periode des weiblichen Daseins, in dem das Kind urplötzlich zum Weibe geworden, alle Grazie der Kindheit und allen Zauber des Weibes in sich vereinigt. Der Rosa-Tricot, der mich umhüllte, verrieth, so weit das Wasser mich preisgab, die makellose Schönheit meiner adeligen Gestalt. Meine goldblonden Locken hingen, wie mit brillanten Reflexen übersät, auf meinen breiten, mächtigen Augenlider, verschleierten die schwarze Iris meines Auges, die weich wie Sammet, doch so brennende Glut in sich verbarg."

9"Ich sah vollkommen wie eine indianische Squaw aus, ins Deutsch-Aristokratische übersetzt. Denn selbst in der leichten Bemalung meines Korpers, die aus lauter kleinen wunderlich verschlungenen Laternchen bestand, in dem Federschmuck meines Hauptes, in meinen Fuss- und Armspangen, wie in den Mokassins, welche der erste Schumachers Londons gearbeitet hatte, lag die ganze reizende Nonchalance einer nobeln Gräfin."

10"Das weisse Weib ist in wenigen Tagen alt geworden und krank in der Freiheit der Wälder. Es ist die frische Luft des grossen Geisters nicht werth, nicht mehr werth, das Weib des jungen Kriegers zu werden, der die kranke Frau nicht begehren kann. Sie kann nicht kochen und nicht die Waffen tragen, sie weint und würde elende, feige Memmen gebaren. Sie mag heimgehen zu den Städten der elenden Blassgesichter, für deren Männer sie gut genug ist, mit ihren zitternden Händen und ihren Thränen. Coeur de Lion wird sich ein gesundes, junges, schönes Weib seines Stammes kaufen. Die schwache, weisse Frau ist ihm ein Greuel."

11"Was die Liebe sei, dass weiss ich durch den Glauben meines Herzens so sicher, wie der Christ vermöge des Glaubens weiss, dass und was die ewige Seligkeit ist. Die Liebe ist das Einssein von Zweien; ich höre auf zu sein, um in einem anderen erst wieder zu werden. Es ist eine Regeneration, es ist ein Aufgehen in dem Geliebten, dessen ganzes Wesen dafür mein eigen wird, mein eigen ganz und gar. Ein Mensch allein durchdringt das Geheimnis des Daseins nicht: aber Zwei vereint zu einer Liebe, die durchdringen es. Die wirbeln sich empor mit der Lerche im Frühlicht der Sonne entgegen, die lauschen dem schweigenden Pulsschlag der Erde in träumerischer Nacht, die beherrschen mit mächtigen Zauberstab die ganze Skala der Gefühle, dass alle Accorde des menschlichen Daseins sich vor ihrem Willen zusammenfügen zu der wahren Sphärenharmonie, deren ewiger Text das eine Wort ist 'Liebe'."

[12]"Wahnsinn aus Hochmuth und Egoismus pflegte immer unheilbar zu sein."

[13]"Ihr Wahnsinn ist das Produkt einer Geistesrichtung unter den müssigen Frauen der vornehmen Welt, die kaum ein anderes Resultat zulässt. Unkluge Nachbeter der geistreichen George Sand haben in gänzlichem Misverstehen dessen, was diese grosse Frau meinte und bezweckte, eine Theorie der weiblichen Selbstsucht geschaffen, deren Höpenpunkte in der deutschen Frauenliteratur jetzt erreicht sind. Die Frauen bilden sich ein, Ausnahmwesen zu sein und unfähig, etwas anders zu lieben, als sich selbst; sich für den Mittelpunkt der Welt haltend, fordern sie einerseits, wie die verderbten römischen Kaiser, göttliche Anbetung, und klagen anderseits, dass sie keinen Mann fänden, den sie zu lieben vermöchten. Sie verstehen ihren Egoismus nicht, und behaupten, nicht verstanden zu werden; sie sind unfähig zu lieben, und jammern, dass Niemand die Leere ihres Herzens und ihrer Seele fülle."

WORKS CITED

Brinker-Gabler, Gisela. Introduction and Ed. *Fanny Lewald--Meine Lebensgeschichte.* Frankfurt am Main, 1981.

Brinker-Gabler, Gisela. "Fanny Lewald." *Frauen.* Ed. Hans Jürgen Schultz. Munich, 1981.

Kohlhagen, Norgard. *Nicht nur dem Manne Untertan: Frauen die die Welt Veränderten.* Frankfurt am Main, 1981.

Lewald, Fanny. *Diogena.* Leipzig, 1847.

Lewald, Fanny. *Meine Lebensgeschichte.* Berlin, 1871, v.3.

Möhrmann, Renate. *Die andere Frau. Emanzipationsänsatze deutscher Schriftstellerinnen im Vorfeld der Achtundvierzig Revolution.* Stuttgart, 1957.

Möhrmann, Renate. *Frauenemanzipation im deutschen Vormärz.* Stuttgart, 1978.

Möhrmann, Renate. *Die Frauenfrage in Deutschland.* Stuttgart, 1981.

Prutz, Robert. *Die deutsche Literatur der Gegenwart, 1848-1858.* Leipzig, 1895, v.2.

Spiero, Heinrich. *Geschichte der deutschen Frauenbewegung seit.* Leipzig, 1913.

Venske, Regula. "Disciplinierung des unregelmässig spekulierenden Verstandes: Zur Fanny Lewald-Rezeption." *Alternative* 25 (1982): 66-70.

THE IDEAL MARRIAGE:
WOMAN AS OTHER IN THREE LEWALD NOVELS

Harriet E. Margolis
Indiana University

In this paper I apply a twentieth-century paradigm to three novels by a nineteenth-century German bestseller, Fanny Lewald. The paradigm in question, derived from existential philosophy and Lacanian psychoanalysis, opposes self and other, often associating Woman with the role of Other. Whether the distinction between self and other is established through visual perception or linguistically based differences, this association of Woman with Other has contributed to a feminist narrative theory heavily influenced by related developments in film theory. Such an association is not unproblematical; according to one reading Woman as Other represents a powerful figure while another tradition argues against the subordination of Woman as Other to the determinant figure of Man as One. While Lewald's work predates this contemporary paradigm, it nevertheless speaks to various elements in <u>Clementine</u>, <u>Jenny</u>, and <u>Eine Lebensfrage</u>, her first published novels.[1]

Despite my German texts, my theoretical framework for discussing both visual perception and linguistically based differences is largely French in origin. I begin constructing my paradigm with reference to a psychoanalyst, Henri Wallon, who gives one definition of perception in which, "pour qu'il y ait perception, il faut que j'affirme la présence de l'objet. Affirmer la présence de l'objet c'est affirmer ma propre présence."[2] Sartre says that "we can not perceive the world and at the same time apprehend a look fastened upon us. . . . To perceive is to <u>look at</u>, and to apprehend a look is . . . to be conscious of <u>being looked at</u>."[3] Taken together, these two quotations suggest that, for other people, we come into existence, as other to them, through being looked at; and further, that our own sense of self is mediated by our perception of how others perceive us. Such a description presupposes a certain passivity on our part, tantamount to tacit acceptance of an image imposed on us by others; such passivity, however, the description implies, may be inescapable.

Through discussion of the well-known "mirror phase" of infant development, Wallon and Jacques Lacan both stress the visual perception of an external image of self in relation to other as crucial to the individual's sense of his/her identity. Lacan also stresses the importance of language, and for him the Other is implicated in language through the subject's incessant but fruitless search for truth, knowledge, and certainty in language. "When the subject addresses its demand outside itself to another," Jacqueline Rose explains, "this other becomes the fantasied place of just such a knowledge or certainty."[4] John Brenkman identifies this relationship as the mechanism which "supports all philosophical discourse since Plato": "The reference to a transcendental subject (serves) as the guarantee of truth, metaphysics having given different names to this subject--the One, God, Spirit, the transcendental ego"[5]--and, I would add, the Other, because of that confusion of usage which refers to the Other as powerful. Yet throughout his work Lacan argued against any notion of a transcendental ego. Thus Rose's explication continues that, although "the Other appears to hold the 'truth' of the subject and the power to make good its loss, . . . this is the ultimate fantasy. . . . The subject has to recognise that there is . . . no ultimate certainty or truth" (40).

In the binary opposition between man and woman this Other plays a particular role. Rose again:

> As negative to the man, woman becomes a total object of fantasy (or an object of total fantasy), elevated into the place of the Other and made to stand for its truth. Since the place of the Other is also the place of God, this is the ultimate form mystification. . . . The absolute 'Otherness' of the woman . . . serves to secure for the man his own self-knowledge and truth. (50)

The reference to woman as Other and object returns us to existentialism, for Simone de Beauvoir also uses these terms in The Second Sex.

> Humanity is male and man defines woman . . . as relative to him. . . . He is the Subject, . . . she is the Other. . . . The Other is posed as such by the One in defining himself as the One. But if the Other is not to regain the status of being the One, he must be submissive enough to accept this alien point of view. Whence comes this submission in the case of woman?[6]

A familiar question; it may be rephrased as a question of why people misrecognize themselves and their situations. Lewald's novels may be read as analyses of such miscognition.

As Renate Möhrmann shows in her invaluable book, Die andere Frau: Emanzipationsansätze deutscher Schriftstellerinnen im Vorfeld der Achtundvierziger-Revolution,¹ Lewald's early novels must be read both within the context of the male-authored literature immediately preceding the social upheavals of 1848 and within the pre-existing tradition of the German women's movement. For example, Lewald's critical investigation of the existing range of male/female relations and her opposition to the Konvenienzehen (marriages of convenience) which dominated middle and upper class German society can be found in the novels of such contemporaries as Ida Gräfin Hahn-Hahn as well. Although Lewald's concept of marriage rests on nothing more revolutionary to our senses than the dignity of individual choice based on sincere and voluntary commitment, her novels nevertheless involve a re-presenting and questioning of the patriarchal image of women and marriage which remained exceptional in a world that denied women educational opportunities, the right to a personality independent of father or husband, and the possibility of financial self-sufficiency through employment. Unlike her contemporaries, Lewald's economic, educational, social, and religious circumstances made her uniquely consistent throughout her life in writing about woman's need for self-definition. Jenny, for example, brings together woman and Jew, figures whose joint power as other challenges the validity of any image imposed from without.

Recognition involves perception, the affirmation of presence, according to Wallon. As a novelist, Lewald well knew that characters come to life only as they are perceived, whether by the narrator or by other characters. It is intriguing that crucial descriptions of her female protagonists often come through the eyes of their male friends and relatives. For example, in Clementine, although her sister and aunt have already been established as characters, it is Meining, Clementine's future husband, and Reich, her brother-in-law, who engage in the first lengthy discussion of her character (18-19). This is not to say that female characters would necessarily perceive women differently or that they might not also express male views. Clementine is in fact persuaded to foresake her principled stand against marrying because her aunt suggests a different interpretation of Clementine's personality which shakes the heroine's fundamental confidence in herself.

Whereas Clementine passively accepts the image imposed on her by others, Jenny finds this more difficult to do, perhaps because the images available to her fit so poorly. The narrator sees Jenny as naturally perfect, but male eyes, those of her first fiancé, Reinhard, see in her a lack. She is deficient precisely in the sort of religious fulfillment necessary for a woman's happiness and for her ability to make others happy (34). Much of the novel involves Jenny's various efforts first to alter herself in order to fit Reinhard's perception of her and then to tentatively suggest that he accept her as she is. Her attempts range from self-denial and an unconvinced conversion from Judaism to Christianity, to the general struggle to recreate herself according to his concept of what she should be.

Joseph, Jenny's cousin and a frustrated suitor, succinctly describes the crisis within Jenny as she searches for an intellectual truth compatible with the religious beliefs of her family and her lover:

> Und Du, grossgezogen in den Vorstellungen des jetzigen Judenthums, wirst nie aufhören, an Alles den Massstab der Vernunft anzulegen. Du hast gesehen, dass Deine Familie, gut und brav, den Gesetzen der Moral gefolgt ist, und doch die Gesetze, die das Judenthum charakterisieren, als blosses Ceremonialgesetz verwirft. Du bist erzogen in der Schule des Gedankens . . . , und Dir ist die Möglichkeit des Glaubens ohne Prüfung dadurch genommen. Du wirst hoffentlich ein Mensch werden nach dem Herzen Gottes, aber Du wirst niemals Christin sein noch Jüdin. (80)

Joseph speaks these words when Jenny's love for Reinhard is fresh and their steps toward marriage have just begun. Much later, even as she is about to convert, Jenny echoes Joseph's words in her own thoughts (202), and this inability to sacrifice her need for clarity and truth eventually leads to her break with Reinhard. Thus Jenny exemplifies the child of the Enlightenment, which does not escape Reinhard's mother's notice. The latter uses a standard Enlightenment image contrasting light and dark to criticize Jenny for preferring masculine to feminine circles of interest, saying her house would be one in which "Alles ist Licht! kein Halbdunkel, kein düsterer Schatten; aber auch kein stiller Raum, um den Schöpfer einen Altar zu bauen, kein traulich Plätzchen für schüchterne Liebe" (88).

Because Jenny does not fit the image of the perfect pastor's wife according to society (as represented here by her prospective husband and mother-in-law), her first engagement fails. A second engagement also fails because, as the daughter of a Jewish merchant, she does not fit social standards for a German nobleman's wife. Jenny's attraction for this nobleman rests, in fact, on the very qualities which disturbed her first fiancé. The novel implies that Jenny and Graf Walter, her second fiancé, if left to their own devices, could create a happy marriage, but that society would eventually make it a failure. In fact her fiancé dies in a duel revenging himself and Jenny for a slight to her honor.

Indeed the one happy marriage among all Jenny's young protagonists succeeds solely because the wife "lebte eigentlich nur in ihrem Manne und in ihren Kindern" (274). In Clementine the marriage between Clementine and Meining succeeds because the wife lives through her husband, and occasionally through the children of others. These portraits of marriages dependent upon the woman's renunciation and self-denial exemplify the socially accepted model; Lewald's true convictions show, however, in her outline of the relation between Graf Walter and Jenny and in the entire plot of Eine Lebensfrage. In this third novel marriages are made happy or unhappy not so much through the woman's ability to submerge herself in the fabric of her man's life, as her ability or inability to participate in his social and intellectual concerns. Minor as such a shift might seem on the surface, it reflects Lewald's lifelong commitment to the necessity for woman's education and equal opportunities for intellectual stimulation, for her ability to take part in "allem Grossen und Wichtigen" (Jenny 274).

As Clementine opens, the heroine falls in love with and then must adjust to the sudden departure of Robert Thalberg, the handsome and passionate lover who alone sparks her desire. She reacts to Robert's departure by working feverishly on her education and self-improvement "damit Robert, wenn er einst wiederkäme, sie nicht unter seinen Erwartungen fände" (6-7). Robert, on the other hand, speaks of his perception of others' desire for an object as creating a similar desire in himself for that object. The difference in these two reactions lies in the woman's recreation of herself according to her perception of the man's image of her, of what he would desire in her. Robert, a later episode shows, rather than changing himself to fit someone else's perceived desires, instead indulges his own desire for an object coveted by others. It is not by chance, either, that the object here in question is an actress; to be precise, a woman whose profession sets her apart and makes her other in so many ways. Not surprisingly, then, when Robert speaks from his male perspective of the love between himself and Clementine, he refers to her as "mein, mein anderes Ich" (219).

As the novel unfolds, however, Clementine marries Meining rather than Robert. It is not that she thus establishes an independent ego of her own, for in effect, Clementine renounces her own sexual fulfillment to continue life with father in the form of her marriage to Meining, a man old enough to be her father. Having identified fully with the patriarchy, she willingly and actively expresses agreement with Meining's opinions on the role of women, preferring the security of his approval to the challenging sexual uncertainties represented by the reappearance of her first love, Robert. If <u>Clementine</u> therefore offers us a mixed bag from the feminist point of view, let us bear in mind Möhrmann's suggestion that Lewald's first novel was perhaps a peace offering to her father, whose love and support did not fully encompass her role as lady novelist.

Even so, <u>Clementine</u> retains its feminist interest. If we consider Robert's view of Clementine as his "other self" in light of Rose's observation that woman becomes an object of male fantasy, we see a clear case of the opposition between man/subject and woman/object in operation. To some extent Clementine refuses this role of other granted to her by Robert, but it must also be said that Clementine is equally guilty of fantasizing, that, in fact, the whole novel can be read as a variation on the sort of female fantasy discussed by Tania Modleski or Janice Radway in their analyses of romances in the Harlequin vein.[8] Clementine acknowledges to herself that Robert's abandonment injured her pride (214); an element of self-gratification seems inevitable, then, in her rejection of his declaration of desperate and total love (228). She speaks of the subordination of egoism for virtue (251) in sacrificing her love for Robert to her duty to Meining, but a degree of egoism adheres to this 'virtuous' rejection of the man who once rejected her.

It must have been a sweet fantasy for Lewald since the author had herself once loved and been rejected by a man like Robert. Lewald, however, was an extremely practical woman, and even as she indulged the fantasy, she did not lose herself in it. In the first place, she introduced a strong element of irony with the exaggerated portrait of a socialite named Mariane Klenke, who seems to have her doubts about the unblemished sincerity of Clementine's virtuousness. Second, Clementine herself casts doubts on the perfection of her marriage. She realizes with frustration that Meining basically sees her as a child rather than as an adult, while she longs for a child of her own which her marriage will not provide.

Clementine reappears in <u>Jenny</u> in telling fashion. The nineteenth century, after all, saw the simultaneous rise of women's inactivity as an index of social status and the growth of hysteria as a commonplace among women's medical problems. At the summer resort where Jenny meets Graf Walter she also visits a reclusive friend of hers suffering from a nervous disorder. This friend is none other than Clementine, who finds herself ironically playing her aunt's role in encouraging Jenny to marry. While

Jenny says she would prefer to remain unmarried, Clementine speaks of the happiness women attain in living for others.

Lewald's third novel, Eine Lebensfrage, begins with one of its main figures already married. However, this poet, one Alfred von Reichenbach, is so unhappily married to his wife, Caroline, that he flees his country estate for the city with divorce on his mind. On the way, he coincidentally runs into Theresa, a love of his youth whom he forsook to honor his engagement to Caroline. Of course he and Theresa eventually will marry, but only after much anguish and attempted sacrifice to perceived duty on both sides. Their marriage will be successful, the novel implies, because Theresa has the ideal ability to submerge her own self in caring for others' needs and desires. The difference is that the others involved participate in major literary and legal events of the day; she has grown accustomed to intelligent involvement in their discussions where her opinion is respectfully considered.

Not everyone, however, recognizes Theresa's wonderful qualities. Strangers, for instance, often see her as "kalt," "stolz oder gar . . . unbedeutend," while those who know her recognize in her an "Ideal" (82). Lewald deliberately plays with such oppositions in Eine Lebensfrage. She sets up various female types in contrast to each other, e.g., blond and brunette, ingenue and mature woman, rich and poor, and especially, virtuous and disreputable women. This last contrast often plays on an inner, hence 'true' virtue, and society's acceptance of the outward show of virtue.

While Caroline is naturally opposed to Theresa in their rivalry for Alfred, as self-identified "virtuous wife" and mother, she is also set in opposition to the so-called whore of the piece, a French actress--a woman by definition of questionable morals-- named Sophie Harcourt who plays mistress to Theresa's brother, Julian. Lewald herself calls attention to the broad range of female types she presents in this novel, but with Sophie Harcourt her slow pan across the spectrum of feminine representation spotlights the image of woman as Other, for she specifically refers to Sophie as Other. This occurs during a scene in which Sophie woos her man through the charming variety of her self-representations. Forsaken by Julian, Sophie renounces the world to become a sister of charity. The last act of her old career is to disguise herself so that she can secretly tend Julian during one night of a grave illness before she takes up her new career as nurse to the world in general. Through the deliberate miscasting of Sophie as treacherous whore and Caroline as virtuous wife, Eine Lebensfrage disrupts the old stereotypes of good and bad women so familiar to us from nineteenth-century melodramas and twentieth-century films.

A progression in these three novels thus appears, which to some extent reflects the events of Lewald's own life. As she gradually broke away from her father's house to obtain independence financially and as a female living outside the family environment, the image of woman appearing in her novels also shifted. The discussion of women's rights and of a woman's role in marriage presented in these three novels makes it clear that Lewald never became a feminist in anything like our contemporary sense nor that of her own time. And yet her discomfort with woman's situation in her society is also quite clear, manifesting itself in her perception and presentation of her female characters, her posing them as existing only in relation to their male contacts. She might disagree with the politics of existentialism and psychoanalysis, certainly of current feminism, but she would hardly argue with their paradigm of woman as other in opposition to man as self and subject, for the same opposition characterizes her own work.

Last year I suggested that Lewald's Jenny retains its interest as a historical document, but that perhaps its contemporary relevance had not transferred well from the nineteenth to the twentieth century. Lewald herself has her characters in Eine Lebensfrage argue for a novel's relevance to contemporary issues as a criterion for its success. I focused last year on the Judenfrage, so that by Lewald's standards Jenny's success must have diminished with the passage of time. In contrast, this year I would argue against Lewald's judgment and in accord with Thomas Kuhn's thesis in The Structure of Scientific Revolutions that Lewald's work can and does take on new significance and relevance for us when viewed from the perspective of a new paradigm.[9] As a woman caught on the horns of a dilemma--espousing many patriarchal positions while recognizing many feminist concerns--Lewald displays the inherent tensions of such a situation in her work. And whatever else, as I said last year and quite possibly will say again next year, these novels retain their charm--which may ultimately be the most important criterion of all.

NOTES

[1] All references are to the following editions: *Clementine* (Leipzig: Brockhaus, 1843); *Jenny* (1843; Berlin: Janke, 1872); and *Eine Lebensfrage* (1845; Berlin: Janke, 1872).

[2] "L'acte perceptif et le cinéma," *Revue internationale de filmologie* 4.13 (1953): 99.

[3] *Being and Nothingness*, trans. Hazel E. Barnes (New York: Washington Square, 1975) 347.

[4] Juliet Mitchell and Jacqueline Rose, eds., *Feminine Sexuality: Jacques Lacan and the école freudienne*, trans. Jacqueline Rose (London: Macmillan, 1982) 32.

[5] "The Other and the One: Psychoanalysis, Reading, the Symposium," in *Literature and Psychoanalysis*, ed. Shoshana Felman (Baltimore, Md.: Johns Hopkins Univ. Press, 1977) 400 and 435.

[6] Trans. and ed. H. M. Parshley (New York: Vintage, 1974) xviii-xxi.

[7] Stuttgart: Metzler, 1977.

[8] Tania Modleski, *Loving with a Vengeance: Mass-Produced Fantasies for Women* (Hamden, Conn.: Archon, 1982); Janice Radway, *Reading the Romance: Women, Patriarchy, and Popular Literature* (Chapel Hill: University of North Carolina Press, 1984).

[9] Chicago: University of Chicago Press, 1970.

SEXIST LITERARY HISTORY? THE CASE OF LOUISE VON FRANÇOIS

Thomas C. Fox
Washington University

Until the waning of the Weimar Republic, many literary historians esteemed Louise von François (1817-1893) the equal of Marie von Ebner-Eschenbach or even Annette von Droste-Hülshoff; today, however, François and her finest novel, The Last von Reckenburg/Die letzte Reckenburgerin (1870), are largely unremembered, even by scholars determined to rediscover the contribution of women in the last century. In the following I trace the reception history of The Last von Reckenburg and examine--with special attention to the issue of gender bias-- reasons for the decline in that novel's reputation. The results contribute to the discussion raised by Elke Frederiksen, Renate Möhrmann, Gisela Brinker-Gabler, and other feminists as to whether, or to what extent, sexist ideology has fashioned German literary history.[1]

A select number of François's contemporaries valued her Reckenburg. Fritz Reuter kept it on his writing table and Marie von Ebner-Eschenbach declared she would have traded her entire oeuvre for the book.[2] In a review that brought François overnight fame, Gustav Freytag lauded the Reckenburg's form, language, psychology, and historical veracity; he termed the novel one of the finest in recent decades.[3] Karl Hillebrand, the noted critic, launched the Reckenburg auspiciously into literary history, judging it a model work in every respect. Hillebrand praised the novel's composition, language, and characterizations, concluding with the impressive remark that the book stood practically alone in German literature.[4] Conrad Ferdinand Meyer, who petitioned François for advice concerning the art of writing, prophesied confidently: "The Reckenburg will endure."[5]

François's subsequent reception has remained to some degree encomiastic. Richard M. Meyer asserted, for example, in 1900, that "The Last von Reckenburg will undoubtedly survive whenever one shakes the enormous number of German novels through the narrowest sieve; from the novels after Goethe hardly a dozen would share that fate."[6] Six years later Eduard Engel elevated the novel to a classic, adding:

> Among connoisseurs there was never a doubt that François belongs to the great, indeed to the greatest writers of the nineteenth century. Many very famous works of famous men have faded

in the last decades; the major work of François is still in ascendance.[7]

After the centennial celebration, in 1917, of François's birth, her reputation soared: during the Weimar Republic twenty-two editions or printings of The Last von Reckenburg appeared. At the end of the Republic, Paul Fechter correctly delineated François's place within German literary history when, after acclaiming the vital originality of her characters, he rated the Reckenburg "a novel such as had never up to that time been produced by a woman's hand--such as, in fact, had only seldom been produced by a man's."[8] In 1931 Arthur Eloesser also celebrated François's characters, as well as the composition and cultural-historical value of the Reckenburg, deeming it a book "with which she surpassed all the men around her."[9]

François's work continued to attract a small group of enthusiastic readers after the war. Emil Staiger, for example, highlighted her masterful use of language and proclaimed her the equal of Raabe or Storm.[10] In 1966 a new edition of The Last von Reckenburg, one in which the editor emphasizes François's verisimilar portrayal of class conflict, appeared in the German Democratic Republic: the fifty-eighth new printing or edition of the book since its appearance in 1870. Unlike the vast majority of novels written by nineteenth-century German women, The Last von Reckenburg has managed to maintain a stubbornly spirited publication history.

Clearly, however, the story has another side, for one easily ascertains that C.F. Meyer's prediction of Reckenburg endurance has proved rather too sanguine. Already in 1948 Sigrid Meinecke characterized her work on the author as a "rescue effort"; four years later Walter Reichle asserted that, in view of the general indifference surrounding François, it would be foolhardy to attempt to resuscitate her reputation.[11] In 1954 Emil Staiger, writing an introduction to François's second novel, Frau Erdmuthen's Twin Sons, felt compelled to explain:

> We dare to lay before today's readers the forgotten story of a half-forgotten author, with the conviction that even today there are connoisseurs enough to appreciate so unique and exquisite a gift. To be sure, a short introduction appears unavoidable. (Staiger 7)

Of the Reckenburg Staiger noted that the devoted student of literary history knows that it was once a famous novel, but few feel obliged to read it. When Staiger asserted, then, that François was but half-forgotten, he meant that specialists familiar with literary history might know her through her correspondence with Conrad Ferdinand Meyer or as a friend of Marie von Ebner-Eschenbach. Her works, however, were no longer read. Twenty years ago Lionel Thomas concluded an essay on François with the hope that his "short study will contribute to a reawakening of interest in her work and a re-assessment of her literary merit"; that has not occurred.[12] With the exception of an occasional mention in literary history, the silence surrounding François since the GDR edition of the Reckenburg has proved almost complete. Does this represent an example of gender bias in literary history or is it simply a matter of taste?

Of course many male, as well as female, authors have dropped out of literary history, often with good reason. Works by best-selling nineteenth-century German authors such as Georg Ebers and Johann Viktor Scheffel are little more than historical curiosities today, and few graduate students read the Nobel Prize Laureate Paul Heyse. Tastes change, and Fritz Martini may have summarized contemporary opinion when he judged the Reckenburg flawed by overly exaggerated polarities.[13]

We should, however, not discount the enthusiastic endorsements the novel has received from discerning readers ranging from C. F. Meyer to Emil Staiger; indeed, judged by most traditional axiological criteria, the Reckenburg acquits itself well. François employs, for example, alternating narrators and a complex time framework unusual for German novels of the 1860's, the period in which she wrote the book. Her narrators utilize adumbration, repetition, and symbolism in a sophisticated fashion, weaving an impressive text which resonates in its patterns of reference and cross-reference. Her experimentation and narrative play create one of the most innovative German novels of that decade. François furthermore displays an impressive control of language. Hardine von Reckenburg, the central narrator, writes an ironic, self-reflective prose, one shimmering faintly with a rococo sheen ideal for the late eighteenth and early nineteenth-century setting of the work. Critics, especially Staiger, invariably underscore the beauty of François's unique and finely-honed discourse.

Finally, modern readers will recognize, as the majority of earlier ones did not, the fashion in which the novel, while attempting to cleave to a conservative ideology, at the same time advances criticisms of woman's place. François undermines--probably unconsciously--her story and her ideology; she equips the novel with an optimistic conclusion which she simultaneously undercuts. The book hence attains a tension, an ambiguity, and a richness lacking in more overtly political novels by women writers from Ida Hahn-Hahn to Helene Böhlau or Gabriele Reuter. The difficulty François's masterwork has experienced can lie only partly in "objective" assessments of its value.

If we grant that, for axiological reasons, writers such as Ebers and Scheffel deserve their obscurity, while François does not, the fact remains that German literary history has also discriminated against male writers of quality; Jeffrey L. Sammons, for example, defends Alexis, Sealsfield, Raabe, Berthold Auerbach, and Spielhagen.[14] Nevertheless, it remains important that these writers were men, for literary history examined women writers within a different structure, utilizing a different language. This structure and language in turn reflected the disadvantageous position in society which works by women writers, and indeed women themselves, maintained.

François proved no exception here. After the initial furor created by Hillebrand's and Freytag's praise, nineteenth-century literary arbiters paid scant attention to François or her Reckenburg, and indeed, her champions, cited at the outset of this paper, have always constituted a small minority. Otto Lange allowed her a two-sentence, noncommittal entry, with several factual errors, in his literary history of 1875; writing in 1879, Robert Koenig allotted one sentence with a mistake.[15] Karl Barthel omitted François in 1879, as did Christian Oeser the same year and Wilhelm Pütz in 1881.[16] In 1883 Franz Hirsch, addressing "women's novels," covered François with a single sentence; he called the Reckenburg an important novel but did not discuss it.[17] Hermann Kluge made no mention of François in his 1892 literary history, and when she died in 1893 eulogists agreed unanimously that she had been forgotten in her lifetime.[18] As if to underscore this, her name does not appear in two literary histories published in 1894 by Adolf Stern and Friedrich Kirchner.[19] Friedrich Vogt and Max Koch ignored her in their standard and internationally respected version of literary history in 1904;[20] that, amidst similar omissions, prompted Eduard Engel to remonstrate two years later:

> We have much for which to recompense Louise von François. Literary history has generally relegated her to the swarm of novel-writing women. It has dismissed her with a sentence or a passing remark; indeed, it has left her out entirely. (Engel 977)

As we have seen, the popularity of The Last von Reckenburg expanded dramatically during the Weimar Republic. That popularity derived, however, neither from the growth of the women's movement nor from an increased appreciation of the novel's axiological merits; rather, it resulted from François's staunchly pro-

Prussian, anti-French stance. In a 1925 introduction Bruno Golz quotes approvingly François's ironic line from the Reckenburg: "What did it matter to us that German law was scorned, that German territory on the left bank and even on the right bank of the Rhine was plundered, devastated, and constantly conquered?"[21] Such sentences echoed with topical force during a period when, in 1923, French and Belgian troops marched into the Ruhr, or when, in 1925, allied troops continued to occupy the left bank of the Rhine as well as bridgeheads on the right. After Weimar, however, François's reputation has, with a few notable exceptions, declined. Sigrid Meinecke descried in 1948 a bias against François, whereas, she admitted, the origin of that bias remained unclear to her (Meinecke 6).

The language of literary history, like its structure, often evidenced gender-role stereotypes which, even when scholars intended praise, in fact trivialized women writers. Elisabeth Lorentzen wrote in 1902 of François: "Life did not grant her the blissful difficulties and worries of a happy little mother in the nursery"; Georg Ellinger compared her narrative mode to a mother talking with her children; in Die Frau, a leading paper of the women's movement, Else Fuchs-Hes admired François's "enjoyment of happy children's eyes and pure children's souls"; meanwhile, Walther Heynen speculated in Die Hilfe that François's writing would have lost some of its "hardness" had she been married.[22] Similar statements abound. In the 1950's, for example, Ernst Alker claimed insight into the wellspring of François's creativity: "The unmarried one, the childless one gave in her books the full richness of her motherliness. . . ."[23] Fritz Martini could still mention, in the 1970's, François's "womanly depth of feeling" (Martini 455).

Examining Droste-Hülshoff's not dissimilar reception, Gisela Brinker-Gabler and Elke Frederiksen have noted how diffuse such categories can become. Indeed, operating almost uniformly within the rigidly prescriptive categories of biological role clichés, critics have, in the past one hundred years, offered an impressive array of contradictory assessments concerning François's writing. Feuilletonists Eugen Lerch and Franz Deibel assured readers that her style appeared not at all "ladylike," while Elisabeth Lorentzen found it decidedly not "virginal"; Hans Enz, on the other hand, detected traces of "a spinster," as did Sigrid Meinecke and Til Urech.[24] Otto Roquette thought François's prose "vigorous and manly"; his nineteenth-century contemporary Julius Grosse noted of The Last von Reckenburg: "I have read the charming book and admit that it does not, in its style or its characterization, betray a woman's hand."[25] The noted twentieth-century Germanist, Reinhard Buchwald, disagreed, arguing that François wrote in a style "for which one finds hardly any other description than feminine. This writing . . . is in fact nothing other than the narrative technique of a--not even very young--unmarried woman, who is at the same time a unique and important person."[26] Such varying judgments demonstrate the inadequacy of biological role stereotypes as categories of literary criticism and help explain why François's work has been so difficult to locate on a scale defined by masculine values.

The panegyrics to a reified "manly" style are determined by societal context, in which "serious writing" remained the preserve of men. In 1911, the year the German emperor warned women to beware of feminism, the writer Paul Ernst noted apodictically in his afterword to the first Insel edition of the Reckenburg: "The educated reader has a prejudice against women's novels and his is certainly quite justified."[27] Ernst hastens to reassure his readers that to François the bias need not apply; his reasoning proceeds, however, not from axiological criteria but rather from ideological ones:

> The same events, observed, experienced, and depicted by a woman, appear differently than with men. And if one of the most important tasks of the novel is to give people of today a Weltanschauung, then one must always thankfully accept the correction of the male Weltanschauung by the woman--provided, to be sure, that she is a true woman. . . . Louise von François was a true woman of womanly perception. (Ernst 383)

Ernst hence begins in a promising and even exciting fashion, only to demonstrate that he remains firmly anchored in a worldview which insists women maintain a special place and which assigns them special qualities (womanly perception) while denying them others. Ernst presents the apotheosis of Frauendichtung as Helena Szépe has defined it: the admonition to women to write "like women."[28]

Karl Barthel revealed the ideological motivation of such thinking when he wrote in his literary history of 1879:

> Women's sphere is the home, the family. . . . If they, as writers, remain within the bounds of this calling and ability, then their writing will always count as an acceptable supplement to the writing of men; if they exceed these boundaries, then they fall without further ado into the category of emancipated women. (Barthel 923)

Barthel's crudely-stated set of dichotomous oppositions determined François's reception in the century. In 1906 Arthur Eloesser labeled her, with much approbation, a "real woman" (i.e., not emancipated), a phrase echoed by Paul Ernst's "true woman."[29] In the 1940's the Nazis still cited Ernst in their editions of François; in this respect, at least, his ideas on women coincided rather exactly with theirs.[30]

Conservatives uncomfortable with the women's movement celebrated François's lack of overt rebellion. Max Zollinger congratulated her in 1919 on avoiding partisan literature, the "evil spirit" of women's writing;[31] in 1925, at the height of Reckenburg popularity, Bruno Golz commented in an epilogue: "The ability of the author to lift a spinster beyond the shoals of bitterness, to transfigure her resignation without a trace of so-called women's liberation, celebrates in The Last von Reckenburg its highest triumph" (Golz 358). François, feuilletonists documented with some relief, did not write "political" books such as Gabriele Reuter's scandalous Of a Good Family/ Aus guter Familie; rather, everyone agreed, François wrote (almost) as well "as a man" while remaining "a true woman." As a result, The Last von Reckenburg could be consigned to the genre of the woman's novel, against which, as Paul Ernst discerned, the educated reader maintained a "justified" prejudice. Despite occasional praise by isolated admirers, the educators of readers have not investigated the Reckenburg seriously as a work of art. For that reason, more than any other, we have forgotten it today.

Ironically, while in the first half of the century François's reticence to agitate openly for women's rights brought her accolades from critics opposed to the women's movement, that same reluctance contributes to her continuing oblivion today. To be sure, her life and work seem hardly calculated, on the surface, at any rate, to excite the imaginations of contemporary feminists looking for prophets or allies. Unlike Louise Aston, Louise von François did not leave a husband, practice sexual freedom, or mount the barricades; she did not found a newspaper in the manner of Mathilde Franziska Anneke or Louise Otto. Living the lonely, spartan existence of a recluse in the small city of Weissenfels, François was far removed from spokeswomen, such as Hedwig Dohm, for the radical bourgeois women's movement of the later nineteenth century; the daughter of a bourgeois and a noble parent, the author of stories in which there are no workers, she remained yet further from the proletarian women's movement of Clara Zetkin. François believed, or tried to believe, many traditional, indeed reactionary, assumptions concerning a woman's place. Reflecting what Sandra M. Gilbert and Susan Gubar have termed the "anxiety of authorship," François reportedly told Paul Szczepanski of Daheim that she would have preferred knitting stockings to writing novels.[32] But she did write one fine novel, arguably the finest by a German-language woman writer of the nineteenth century. It deserves more attention than it has received.

NOTES

[1] See Gisela Brinker-Gabler, "Die Schriftstellerin in der deutschen Wissenschaft: Aspekte ihrer Rezeption von 1835-1910," Unterrichtspraxis 9 (1976): 15-28. Elke Frederiksen, "Deutsche Autorinnen im 19. Jahrhundert," Colloquia Germanica 14 (1981): 97-113. Renate Möhrmann, Die andere Frau (Stuttgart: Metzler, 1977).

[2] The anecdote concerning Ebner-Eschenbach is told by Otto Hartwig, "Zur Erinnerung an Louise von François," Deutsche Rundschau 77 (1893): 461. The anecdote regarding Reuter is from Hans Enz, Louise von François, Diss. Zurich 1918 (Zurich: Rascher) 146.

[3] Gustav Freytag, Vermischte Aufsätze (Leipzip: Hirzel, 1901) 139.

[4] Joseph Hillebrand, Die deutsche Nationalliteratur im XVIII. und XIX. Jahrhundert, revised by Karl Hillebrand, 3rd ed. (Gotha: Friedrich Andreas Perthes, 1875) 3: 439.

[5] Louise von François und Conrad Ferdinand Meyer. Ein Briefwechsel, ed. Anton Bettleheim (Berlin: Walter de Gruyter, 1920) 32.

[6] Richard M. Meyer, Die deutsche Literatur des neunzehnten Jahrhunderts (Berlin: Georg Bondi, 1900) 406.

[7] Eduard Engel, Geschichte der deutschen Literatur, 2nd ed. (Leipzig: Gustav Freytag, 1907) 2: 977.

[8] Paul Fechter, Dichtung der Deutschen (Berlin: Deutsche Buch-Gemeinschaft, 1932) 674.

[9] Arthur Eloesser, Die deutsche Literatur (Berlin: Bruno Cassirer, 1931) 318.

[10] Emil Staiger, Vorwort, Frau Erdmuthens Zwillingssöhne by Louise von François (Zurich: Manesse, n.d.) 28.

[11] Sigrid Meinecke, "Louise von François," Diss. Hamburg 1948, p. 1. Walter Reichle, "Studien zu den Erzählungen der Louise von François," Diss. Freiburg 1952, 1.

[12] Lionel Thomas, "Louise von François: 'Dichterin von Gottes Gnaden,'" Proceedings of the Leeds Philosophical and Historical Society, 11 (1964) 23.

[13] Fritz Martini, Deutsche Literatur im bürgerlichen Realismus. 1848-1898., 3rd ed. (Stuttgart: Metzler, 1974) 457.

[14] Jeffrey L. Sammons, "The Mystery of the Missing Bildungsroman, or: What Happened to Wilhelm Meister's Legacy," Genre 14 (1981): 238-39.

[15] Otto Lange, Literaturgeschichtliche Lebensbilder und Charakteristiken, 2nd ed. (Berlin: Rudolph Gaertner, 1875) 65. Robert Koenig, Deutsche Literaturgeschichte, 4th ed. (Bielefeld: Velhagen und Klasing, 1879) 631. Koenig incorrectly states her year of birth as 1825.

[16] Karl Barthel, Vorlesungen über die deutsche Nationalliteratur der Neuzeit (Gütersloh: C. Bertelsmann, 1879). Christian Oeser, Geschichte der deutschen Poesie, 4th ed. (Leipzig: Friedrich Brandstetter, 1879). Wilhelm Pütz, Übersicht der Geschichte der dt. Litt. für höhere Lehranstalten, 8th ed. (Leipzig: Karl Baedeker, 1881).

[17] Franz Hirsch, Geschichte der deutschen Literatur (Leipzig: Wilhelm Friedrich, 1883).

[18] Hermann Kluge, Geschichte der deutschen National-Literatur (Altenburg: Oskar Bonde, 1892).

[19] Adolf Stern, Die deutsche Nationalliteratur vom Tode Goethes bis zur Gegenwart, 3rd ed. (Leipzig: N.G. Elwert, 1894). Friedrich Kirchner, Die deutsche National-Literatur des 19. Jahrhunderts (Heidelberg: Georg Weiss, 1894).

[20] Max Koch and Friedrich Vogt, Geschichte der deutschen Literatur, 2nd ed. (Leipzig: Verlag des bibliographischen Instituts, 1904).

[21] Bruno Golz, Vorwort, Die letzte Reckenburgerin by Louise von François (Hamburg: Hanseatische Verlagsanstalt, 1925), n. pag.

[22] Elisabeth Lorentzen, "Ein deutsches Frauenbuch," Neue Christoterpe (Halle: E. Ed. Müller, 1902) 126-27. Georg Ellinger, "Louise von François," Die Nation 11.4 (Oct. 1893): 60. Else Fuchs-Hes, "Die letzte Reckenburgerin," Die Frau 24 (1917): 407. Walter Heynen, "Louise von François," Die Hilfe 26 (1917): 429.

[23] Ernst Alker, Geschichte der deutschen Literatur (Stuttgart: J.G. Cotta, 1950) 2: 29-30.

[24] Franz Deibel, "Louise von François und Conrad Ferdinand Meyer," Die Frau 13 (1906): 359. Eugen Lerch, "Die Dichterin der 'letzten Reckenburgerin,'" Münchner Neueste Nachrichten, 27 June 1917: 2. Lorentzen 136. Enz 131, 136. Meinecke 181. Till Urech, Louise von François, Diss. Zurich 1955 (Zurich: Juris, 1957) 13.

[25] Roquette cited in Fritz Oeding, Bibliographie der Louise von François (Weißenfels: Leopold Kell, 1937) 10. Grosse cited in Die Akte Louise von François, ed. Helmut Motekat (Weimar: Aufbau, n.d.) 11.

[26] Reinhard Buchwald, "Die Dichterin der Befreiungskriege," Bonner Zeitung 17 November 1913: 3.

[27] Paul Ernst, Nachwort, Die letzte Reckenburgerin by Louise von François (Leipzip: Insel [1919]) 383.

[28] Helena Szépe, "The Term Frauendichtung," Unterrichtspraxis 9 (1976): 11-15.

[29] Arthur Eloesser, "Louise von François und Conrad Ferdinand Meyer. Ein Briefwechsel," Das literarische Echo 9 (1907): 866.

[30] Helmut Langenbucher, Nachwort, Die letzte Reckenburgerin by Louise von François (Bayreuth: Gauverlag, 1943).

[31] Max Zollinger, "Louise von François," Neue Zürcher Zeitung, 7 March 1919, Feuilleton.

[32] Paul Szczepanski, "Louise von François," Daheim 30.6 (Nov. 1893): 94.

LA MUJER Y LA HISTORIA EN MAS ALLA DE LAS MASCARAS DE LUCIA GUERRA

Elías Miguel Muñoz
The Wichita State University

>Marginadas estamos desde que el hombre Neanderthal nos prohibía hacer dibujitos en las paredes de las mejores cavernas. (Ana Lydia Vega, "De bípeda desplumada a escritora puertorriqueña con E y P machúsculas: Textimonios autocensurados.")

La novela Más allá de las máscaras[1] de Lucía Guerra surge dentro del contexto de la crítica literaria y cultural que la autora ha producido.[2] Como ensayista, Guerra se propone mostrar aquellos elementos que han caracterizado la literatura escrita por la mujer, subrayando con éstos un discurso que en apariencia sigue las modas y los movimientos literarios establecidos por el discurso dominante, pero que también logra subvertir este discurso. Guerra examina, por ejemplo, el tipo de compromiso político que la mujer latinoamericana ha asumido en la historia, y analiza numerosos textos producidos por mujeres como si fueran obras palimpsésticas, es decir, viendo bajo la explicitez niveles de significados menos aceptados y visibles para el receptor de la época dada.[3] La primera novela de Guerra se inserta dentro de este marco de desmitificación, proponiendo la necesidad de una toma de conciencia femenina y la apropiación de la mujer, como voz literaria y como ente social, de una labor histórica importante que el hombre--escritor de la historia--le ha negado.

En este trabajo veremos en qué medida y de qué manera esta obra de Guerra sitúa a la mujer dentro de un discurso histórico que la ha excluído represivamente. Para ello explicaremos la función de la lectora explícita en el texto y examinaremos la experiencia femenina que el lenguaje representa. Esta experiencia, concluiremos, se alza como llamado a una toma de conciencia política de la mujer, ubicándose dentro de un sistema de relaciones más amplio, la lucha de clases. Para la protagonista de Más allá de las máscaras--escritora como lo es Lucía Guerra--el último y más eficaz instrumento de combate será la palabra.

"Mi historia," dice la narradora, "no tiene nada que ver con las historias escritas por los hombres," y termina este pasaje inicial con la siguiente confesión: "No. No sé cómo ni cuándo empezó verdaderamente mi historia . . . " (13). Desde el comienzo la narradora--que en esta primera parte de la novela se asemeja mucho a la narradora de los ensayos y artículos de Guerra--intenta definirse fuera de la historia tal como ésta ha sido escrita por los hombres. Su discurso encuentra una primera pauta en las sociedades matriarcales, cuando las mujeres "eran dueñas de un mundo sencillo y hermoso" (26) y no había surgido el concepto de "propiedad privada." La fuerza física del hombre tuvo en aquellos tiempos un papel decisivo en la división del trabajo, relegando en la mujer las tareas de la vivienda mientras él se encargaba de la caza. El hombre se apoderó luego de la palabra y fijó, como explica Guerra en su estudio de la narrativa de María Luisa Bombal,

> los códigos legales, eligió sistemas de gobierno, luchó en las guerras, exploró la naturaleza con un afán de lucro e incursionó en las esferas del arte. Estas actividades motivaron la creencia de que el hombre era, por definición, un ser activo, intelectual y agresivo, mientras que a la mujer, generalmente ausente en cada una de estas manifestaciones de la cultura, se la concibió con características innatas opuestas a las ya recién mencionadas.[4]

Al tomar conciencia la protagonista Cristina del fraude que es su vida, se propone subvertir todas las leyes sociales que la han mantenido subyugada y buscar por medio del rechazo su liberación. Esta liberación implica, a nivel de vivencia, separarse de su esposo, arriesgándose a sufrir "horca en la plaza pública portando en el pecho una letra escarlata" (48). Liberarse es también, ya en un plano ideológico, "borrar, de un zarpazo, todos los mitos falsos sobre la espiritualidad del sexo en la mujer" (60). Cristina cree apropiarse de la voz del poder en el discurso de la sexualidad, entendiendo el poder como lo entienden los hombres, un placer desligado de lo espiritual y la utilización del Otro en el acto sexual: "La idea de acostarse por acostarse la fascinaba . . . " (60).

Cristina, sin embargo, transgrede las reglas sin conseguir la satisfacción esperada. Esto se debe, piensa ella en un principio, a su concepción romántica del amor, a su "sentimentalidad femenina" que la hace esperar una reafirmación en "el cuerpo de un hombre amado" (64). Luego comprende que "la verdadera respuesta no estaba en esa burda imitación de la conducta de los hombres" (63). La razón implícita en el texto es que al invadir Cristina--la Mujer--el territorio de los hombres y atribuirse los derechos que ellos gozan, troncha el proceso que ha iniciado de redefinición fuera de las categorías filosóficas masculinas, ignorando su potencialidad para construir un nuevo discurso al margen de las leyes de los hombres. Las categorías filosóficas en lo que a los roles sexuales respecta, dice Jonathan Culler, han sido creadas para relegar lo femenino a una posición subordinada y para reducir la alteridad radical de la mujer a una relación especular. "La mujer," afirma Culler, "o es ignorada o es vista como lo opuesto del hombre".[5] El Dios Padre, por ejemplo, es un concepto ligado a la constitución biológica del hombre, al carácter invisible, hipotético, de la paternalidad.

Culler cita a Freud en Moses and Monotheism y apunta, a propósito de la conexión entre el patriarcado y el predominio de lo racional en nuestra sociedad, que para Freud la sustitución de un orden matriarcal por uno patriarcal implica una victoria de lo intelectual sobre lo sensual, es decir, un "avance" de la civilización, ya que la maternidad se prueba con la evidencia de los sentidos mientras que la paternidad es una hipótesis, una premisa. Pero Culler utiliza este mismo argumento para explicar que se trata de una imposición y no de un avance "natural" de la civilización. Recordemos, dice Culler, que el Dios omnipotente, invisible, es Dios el Padre, Dios de los Patriarcas (Culler 59).

Más allá de las máscaras denuncia esta imposición del orden patriarcal en la historia de la humanidad. El texto alude, además, al argumento que presenta Dorothy Dinnerstein en su libro La sirena y el minotauro, en el cual la escritora discute la obsesión del padre por afirmar su relación con sus hijos, dándoles a éstos su nombre y estableciendo "rituales de iniciación por medio de los cuales afirman simbólica y apasionadamente que son ellos quienes crearon a los seres humanos."[6] El concepto de paternalidad es sólo uno de los muchos que podríamos presentar como ejemplos de la imposición represiva del orden patriarcal en la historia. El texto de Guerra ofrece sucintamente muchos otros:

> . . . el padre, la autoridad máxima, dueño y señor de la casa, la madre (señora de) pariendo hijos que no llevarían su apellido, laborando silenciosamente en la cocina para servir el alimento al pequeño dictador que gana el dinero y el sustento diario. El hombre, amo de todo lo creado, Jehová, Padre, Hijo y Espíritu Santo sentados en el trono celestial, el hombre, inventor de códigos legales, líder de grandes empresas, especulador de sistemas filosóficos, poseedor de la Palabra. (27)

En la novela de Guerra se presenta la búsqueda y subversión del mito femenino de la "espiritualidad" no sólo con la denuncia explícita que hace la protagonista Cristina, sino también por medio de la relación dialógica de dos lenguajes: uno romántico, sentimental, que parodia la mitología amorosa del folletín, de la novela rosa y de los boleros; otro que desmitifica e interroga violentamente al primero. Con el lenguaje paródico se describe una naturaleza pura que confirma la imagen tradicional de la mujer: "Como un suave pétalo de rosa su recuerdo me rozaba el alma" (50). En el segundo lenguaje la naturaleza es representada por la sangre, uno más de los obstáculos que debe confrontar la mujer en su lucha por situarse en el devenir histórico: la "mofa ancestral hacia las mujeres que pretenden ser modernas" (71). Esta sangre es también, paradójicamente, el elemento primordial que caracteriza la experiencia femenina: "Mujeres íntimamente unidas a la luna por el ciclo de veintiocho días que en forma simétrica se reflejaba en la sangre menstrual" (26).

Los dos lenguajes se adecúan a experiencias radicalmente opuestas. Una es la experiencia de la mujer que lucha en el mundo de los hombres y que descubre las trampas de ese mundo; otra es la experiencia de la mujer manipulada por el discurso masculino, es decir, la mujer que aún busca el "amor verdadero." Ambas experiencias se manifiestan en la protagonista Cristina:

> Mientras la otra, como autómata, escribía párrafos y dictaba listas para las compras de la semana, ella se encerraba en una esfera luminosa para tejer sueños y reconstruir los detalles de cada encuentro. (41)

La que escribe párrafos y dicta listas es la esposa que no ha tenido nunca el "derecho a elegir su vida" (48). La "otra" es la que todavía se empeña en vivir "los románticos abandonos imaginados por ella cuando niña" (50), la que sigue creyendo en la mitología del amor. Cristina-la-esposa, al intentar liberarse por medio del sexo, se desconocerá: "Esa mujer desnuda que absurdamente traía una cartera bajo el brazo para fumar un cigarrillo en la cama deshecha no era yo . . . " (56). Cristina-la-romántica será rechazada por su amante y fracasará en todos sus intentos de encontrar el amor verdadero. Y entre estos dos tipos femeninos emerge Cristina-la-escritora, mujer concientizada que vislumbra una primera posibilidad de lucha:

> La mujer que se tragaba la ira y oía fantasmas aullando entre los cristales de un hogar decente había quedado atrás, también daba la espalda a la heroína romanticona que derrama lágrimas y suspiros sobre un tocador lleno de frascos multicolores y figurillas de loza. (81)

En la oración con que abre <u>Más allá de las máscaras</u> aparece un personaje, la "señora," hacia quien se proyecta toda la narración. Lectora explícita del texto y también imagen del espejo en que se mira Cristina, esta señora es el estereotipo femenino de una clase social. De cierto modo este personaje-receptor es una reformulación del lector sobre-codificado que aparece en las obras realistas, "mi querido lector."[7] Pero en <u>Más allá de las máscaras</u> la fórmula, como veremos, se ha alterado. En la novela de Guerra el lector sobre-determinado del realismo se convierte en receptor de una denuncia y de una toma de conciencia. Esta "señora" aparece en los pasajes narrados en primera persona. Por ejemplo:

> Porque yo, señora, era igual a usted, creía ciegamente en la moralidad, las buenas costumbres, la virginidad, la monogamia e implícitamente aceptaba la superioridad de los hombres. (25-26)
>
> Roles estáticos que marginaron a nuestra raza, señora, a ser cuerpo reproductor de futuros hijos de la patria. . . . (27)
>
> Usted bien sabe, señora, que se supone como verdad irrefutable que el hombre debe ser siempre superior a nosotras. . . . (57)
>
> . . . esa temible depresión que usted tan bien conoce, señora, esa depresión que nos anuncia con señales de humo fastidioso que estamos a punto de tener nuestra menstruación. (67)
>
> Cómo podría intentar siquiera describir ese mundo misterioso y heróico de la pobreza. No, señora . . . porque usted y yo estamos detrás de un muro que nos separa de Aurora. . . . (86-87)

La narración establece así un diálogo entre una mujer que era--que sigue siendo en la "señora"--y una mujer-en-potencia. La narradora en primera persona, o el "yo," como apunta Mercedes Valdivieso en su prólogo a la novela, "persiste aunque se desplace, se distancie a un tú y a un ella pero referidos siempre a esa receptora invisible" (7). Este "yo," efectivamente, predomina aún en los pasajes narrados en tercera persona, constituyéndose, como el mismo discurso, en relación a otra voz silenciada. Por eso las convenciones o "máscaras" que aparecen descritas en el texto (la juventud, la ropa, la moralidad), como los clichés[8] que estudia Myrna Solotorevsky en dos novelas de Manuel Puig, tienen una función <u>desocultante</u>: revelan a la otra mujer un mundo femenino que ha sido definido por los hombres, aquellas cosas "que nos han hecho creer" (14).

Al despreciarse a sí misma, Cristina desprecia a todas las "señoras" que no han descubierto la "galaxia de fraudes" (87). La experiencia femenina que la narradora describe a su señora lectora es un "vodevil en tono menor" (57) en el cual no se le ha permitido a la mujer descubrir su ser esencial. El matrimonio, por ejemplo, es un circo "donde un reflector único ilumina la profesión del marido, las camisas del marido, las manías del marido, el mismísimo culo del marido" (58). La mujer, según la narradora, ha sido excluída de los sitios discursivos del poder: " . . . ellas no pertenecen al clan, no son miembros del ebullente contexto de la política, la economía, la cultura . . ." (24). La experiencia auténtica del amor ha sido suplantada por la mitología prevalente en la sociedad (femenina) de consumo: ". . . me casé pensando que las parejas felices del cine, las novelas románticas y los cuentos de hadas representaban una verdad irrefutable" (29). En la realidad, sin embargo, ha sido víctima del doble standard y de la violencia física: "Su otra vida se quedaba siempre en la puerta de la casa porque ´su hogar era sagrado´ y su mujer debía ser una santa . . . " (29); "Ella estóicamente aguantaba el dolor en las nalgas . . . pensó en todas aquellas mujeres que frente a la violencia del marido deben bajar la cabeza . . . " (47). El hombre, en esta sociedad denunciada, es el único que puede controlar y definir las relaciones humanas: "Antonio, podríamos ser tan felices juntos. Levantándose muy serio repuso secamente. Esas son decisiones que únicamente me corresponden a mí" (49).

En el texto dialógico, como ha dicho Mikhail Bakhtin, el autor entabla un diálogo metatextual con sus personajes, y los personajes entablan un diálogo entre sí. Este dialogismo, según Bakhtin, es característico de la novela polifónica.[9] Partiendo de Bakhtin, Christine Brooke-Rose agrega que en la novela polifónica el personaje tiene un diálogo consigo mismo como si apelara a un Otro imaginado.[10] El Diálogo implícito que hemos detectado en <u>Más allá de las máscaras</u>, entre dos tipos de lenguajes femeninos, se encuentra potenciado por otro mucho más explícito: el diálogo que entabla el personaje Cristina con un Otro imaginado. Este Otro en la novela de Guerra aparece en la figura de Ariadna, una muñeca que funciona como confidente de la protagonista: "ella fue la hija que debía proteger y, luego, . . . la confidente que escuchaba mis pueriles historias de amor . . ." (17). Ariadna es presencia constante de la infancia de Cristina, o sea, de la etapa de adoctrinamiento. Lo que apunta Guerra sobre el motivo de la muñeca en <u>Papeles de pandora</u>, de Rosario Ferré, podría también aplicarse a su novela: "La muñeca (es un) motivo que funciona como símbolo de la pasividad, la ornamentación artificial y la enajenación de la realidad histórica. . . . "[11]

Como es de esperarse, al tomar conciencia de los fraudes sufridos, Cristina destruirá su muñeca; rompe así la última máscara--una parte de sí misma--que la ataba al pasado:

> . . . la arrojé violentamente contra la muralla, su rostro se hizo añicos. . . . Me incliné a recogerlo, detrás del frío cristal estriado de verde había una pieza de yeso cóncava y opaca transpasada por un alambre negro. (86)

Mostrar este alambre negro significa mostrar--citando la última frase del texto--"aquel alambre carcomido que nos fijaba en una galaxia de fraudes" (86). Con la destrucción de Ariadna (el Otro femenino), Cristina abandona definitivamente el "Reino de las Mujeres Decentes" (57) y emprende la tarea de redefinición adueñándose del "poder de las palabras" (87).

La novela ("mi historia") comienza ahora, en la última página, después de conocer Cristina a Aurora Espinosa, mujer de clase obrera quien le muestra "una verdad en tazas trizadas, ropa de tela áspera y cuartos fríos" (87) y quien muere en manos de los militares. Esta verdad implica "hablar y denunciar lo que está malo" (80), denunciar la explotación del pobre y de los oprimidos, "pelear hasta que este sistema se acabe . . . " (80). De este modo la lucha de la mujer se incorpora a la lucha de clases. Se sugiere así en el texto, citando el mismo comentario que hace Guerra al estudiar la obra de Mercedes Valdivieso, que "la verdadera liberación de la mujer sólo se logrará con un cambio radical de la estructura capitalista".[12] Sólo entonces la mujer dejaría de ser "propiedad privada" del hombre y podría emprender la escritura de una historia en la cual ella, como el proletariado, fuera sujeto y no objeto de la clase en poder; la construcción de una sociedad más justa, libre de guerras y de explotaciones.

NOTES

[1] Lucía Guerra, Más allá de las máscaras (México: Premiá Editora de Libros, S.A., 1984). Todas las citas de la novela aparecerán como un número de página entre paréntesis.

[2] Véase de Lucía Guerra, "Desentrañando la polifonía de la marginalidad: Hacia un análisis de la narrativa femenina hispanoamericana," artículo que se publicará en Crítica Feminista Latinoamericana, ed. Susana Hernández-Araico; "Función y sentido de la muerte en La amortajada, de María Luisa Bombal," Explicación de Textos Literarios 7.2 (1978-1979): 123-128; "Cuento maravilloso y tragedia en 'La historia de María Griselda´ de María Luisa Bombal," en Mujer y sociedad en América Latina, ed. Lucía Guerra (México: Editorial del Pacífico, 1980) 233-241; "Algunas reflexiones teóricas sobre la novela femenina," Hispamérica 28 (1981): 30-39; "Feminismo y subversión en la novela chilena," Literatura Chilena 21 (1982): 4-9; "Tensiones paradójicas de la femineidad en la narrativa de Rosario Ferré," Chasqui, 13, núms. 2, 3 (febrero-mayo 1984); también, el libro de Guerra, La narrativa de María Luisa Bombal: Una visión de la existencia femenina (Madrid: Editorial Playor, 1980), y su "Introducción" al libro Mujer y sociedad en América Latina, en la cual presenta un panorama histórico de la mujer desde las culturas indígenas hasta el presente.

[3] Por ejemplo, dice Guerra en su artículo "Desentrañando la polifonía de la marginalidad," p. 13, refiriéndose a la novela Sab de Gertrudis Gómez de Avellaneda: ". . . a la historia romántica del buen salvaje que se sacrifica y muere por amor, sentimiento que impide una acción a nivel del devenir histórico, se añade la historia de Carlota y Teresa que en el típico formato romántico resulta ser una adición marginal no obstante ella plasma en su totalidad la visión del mundo de la autora. En este sentido, entonces habría que calificar Sab como una obra palimpséstica, ya que bajo su diseño explícito se esconden niveles de significado menos visibles y menos aceptables para el receptor de la época."

[4] Guerra, La narrativa de María Luisa Bombal 32-33.

[5] Jonathan Culler, On Deconstruction, Theory and Criticism after Structuralism (New York: Cornell University Press, 1982) 58.

[6] Dorothy Dinnerstein, The Mermaid and the Minotaur: Sexual Arrangements and Human Malaise (New York: Harper, 1976) 80. La traducción es nuestra.

[7] Dice Christine Brooke-Rose de este tipo de lector: "A code is over-determined when its information . . . is too clear, over-encoded, recurring beyond purely informational need. The reader is then in one sense also over-encoded, and does in fact sometimes appear in the text, dramatised, like an extra character: the 'Dear Reader.'" A Rhetoric of the Unreal: Studies in Narrative and Structure, Especially of the Fantastic (Cambridge: Cambridge University Press, 1981) 106.

[8] Myrna Solotorevsky, "El cliché en Pubis angelical, y Boquitas pintadas: desgaste y creatividad," Hispamérica, 13.38 (agosto 1984): 3-18.

[9] Mikhail Bakhtin, Problems of Dostoevsky's Poetics, ed. y trad. Caryl Emerson (Minneapolis: The University of Minnesota Press, 1984) 6-7, 47-75.

[10] Brooke-Rose 123.

[11] Guerra, "Desentrañando la polifonía de la marginalidad" 19.

[12] Ibid. 19.

GENDER AND EXILE IN CRISTINA PERI ROSSI

Amy Kaminsky
University of Minnesota

According to Angel Rama, "literary production in forced or voluntary exile is almost a continental standard from Alaska to Tierra del Fuego" (17).[1] Though Rama may have overstated his case, it is certainly true that exile is a condition of literary production in much of Spanish America, and that it is not simply idiosyncratic to individual writers but is, significantly, a result of the communal experience of political repression and economic suffering.

The exile writer's responsibility is expressed by the Chilean novelist, Antonio Skármeta, who calls writing in exile "an emergency operation to recuperate the land that is its desired destination" (64). The state of exile, he says, "breaks the ceremony of cultural identity. The exile faces the break and tries to repair it" (64). The fact that the project of repairing the break takes place, by necessity, somewhere other than home means that the writer must function within the framework of international culture, and that having departed from a closed and hostile atmosphere the writer gains a certain clarification of vision (Rama 18). As outsiders, exile writers are not immediately constrained by the cultural norms of their adopted lands and are thus further freed into a perspective of universality from which to contemplate their now distant homes. The freedom of a universal perspective is accompanied by a sense of dislocation, however. The place of exile may be perceived as a non-country, not as a different country, defined by what is missing, not by what it contains.

Skármeta, in his insistence on the continuing participation of the exile writer in the political and cultural process, presupposes that the repression which precipitates the state of exile is an aberration disrupting a beneficent culture. The writer's task is the preservation and continuation of the national culture elsewhere, while the disruptive power remains in control at home. What this construct does not take into account is the pernicious effect of androcentric culture on women living in virtually all modern societies. While women can and do act against the repression of, say, a military junta, for them the culture being strangled by such repression is by no means unproblematically benign. The ceremony of cultural identity Skármeta seeks to make whole may well include such rituals of female degradation as the repression of women's sexuality, the exclusion of women from public discourse, and the economic disempowerment of women.[2] The experience of living within any modern nation state is informed by gender, and so is the experience of being cast out of a nation state. This paper examines the ways in which gender and exile interact in the poetry and short narrative written by Cristina Peri Rossi in the ten years following the 1972 military coup in Uruguay. Exile is a condition of Peri Rossi's writing; it is as well theme and metaphor through which issues of gender and sexuality are played out in the literary texts.

Among the striking images Cristina Peri Rossi uses to evoke certain states of consciousness in her work are those which call forth the multiform experience of exile.[3] The cold vacant-eyed figures of her mini-narrative, "Las estatuas, o la condición del extranjero" ("Statues, or The Foreigner's Condition"), which appears in the 1983 collection, El museo de los esfuerzos inútiles (The Museum of Futile Efforts), are tangible figures of absence. In this piece, which is virtually devoid of anecdote, the land of exile is represented by the town square, i.e., the center of community for the occupants of the place. Yet, for the foreigner, the square is recognizable as such only by its shape. All the human and social institutions which normally frame and mark it-- buildings, church, houses, jail--are missing. Even nature barely survives: "The trees were almost dry, their leaves were gray and the trunks on the point of disintegration" (Museo, 132). This null space, first described as "empty," is in fact densely populated with people whom the speaker sees as statues, since they are, to him, lifeless. Like statues, they do not see him, do not admit him to what for them must be life but for him has none of the color and warmth of life. To them the foreigner/exile is simply invisible. His sense of causing disturbance is directed inward since statues cannot be aware of it. The only one disturbed is himself:

> No one looked at me, but it was precisely that absence of contemplation which made me feel strange. I discovered then that the foreigner's condition is the void: not to be recognized by those who occupy a place simply because they are there. (Museo 132)

Rendered invisible by those around him, the speaker experiences less his own emptiness than the emptiness that surrounds him. Here the familiar items of home are displaced but not replaced, and the land of exile becomes a spectral land of absence.

But to the exile the homeland can be a hallucinatory space as well. Peri Rossi's "La ciudad" ("The City"), also from El museo de los esfuerzos inútiles, contains an exile's recurrent dream of the native city he left sixteen years before. The dream combines reassuringly familiar details: a courtyard filled with flowers and mosaics, the window of a friend's house; with disconcerting ones: spinning mountains, blue leaves on the trees, an uncharacteristically empty urban landscape, and an enigmatic presence which most disturbs the protagonist because he cannot ascertain its sex. As a result, the protagonist feels he simultaneously belongs to and is excluded from the city. Statues are once again part of the scene, this time with their backs turned to the dreamer to suggest the inhabitants' refusal to acknowledge his presence. In the second half of the story, the protagonist tries unsuccessfully to elicit information from a friend who has recently returned from a visit to their native city. Like the dream, the friend is unable to provide him with what he wants--namely, a vital connection with home. In the final scene, he achieves that connection by merging dream with waking life, converting his friend's vague description together with his dream into a sort of phenomenal reality. Caught between dream of home and the increasing alienation of exile, between desire and fear, the character, accompanied by the androgynous presence, enters this third city. It is this intermediate place which traps him in the end. Sucked into a sink of mud which announced itself as a street--a road to somewhere--accompanied by the now oppressive and annihilating presence, the protagonist is consigned to his own nightmare city. Obsessed by it, he is consumed.

Simply going home, in the sense of returning to a (politically) prelapsarian space, is not possible for the exile who is therefore constrained to live in a state of spiritual and physical displacement. The father in Peri Rossi's "La influencia de Edgar Allan Poe en la poesía de Raimundo Arias," from La tarde del dinosaurio ("The Influence of Edgar Allen Poe on the Poetry of Raimundo Arias," The Afternoon of the Dinosaur) is uprooted, dislocated, and ineffectual. Living outside his own country he is unable to fulfill his primary function--earning money to support himself and his young daughter. In "Las estatuas" the foreigner is unacknowledged, invisible, while in "La ciudad" the exile's experience of alienation is denied. He is told that he has had sufficient time to adjust to life in Europe, which, it is suggested, is far superior to his own continent. For his homeland has become the repository of all the dangers and attributes Europeans wish to deny in their own lives. His ex-wife Luisa

> had never been with him in his native city. She experienced a strong feeling of rejection toward any non-European country, convinced, in an obscure and uncontrollable way, that beyond the ocean a different world began, filled with

> malignant diseases, poisoned food, grotesque
> creatures, wild animals, choleric volcanoes,
> raging rivers and a general dirtiness. The
> long conversations that he had had to convince
> her that things weren't quite like that clashed
> with a resistance that much more than rational
> was instinctive: as if Luisa wanted to defend
> herself against a great danger, which she
> placed across the ocean, in order to live
> comfortably and in peace on this other side.
> (<u>Museo</u> 179)

Invisibility, denial of one's experience by the dominant group, economic impotence, displacement of unwanted characteristics onto one, marginality--all these phenomena of exile have a familiar sound. The condition of the exile in all of these stories and that of women in male-dominated culture are remarkably alike. It is not at all surprising that Peri Rossi uses male characters to tell these three tales of exile, since the suffering of each of the protagonists is predicated on his unself-reflexive experience as a gendered subject. The male exile is feminized by his displacement into a foreign culture. He experiences there the alienation and disempowerment that women "at home" have learned to consider normal.

As a man, the protagonist of "La ciudad" suffers the anguish of the displaced citizen--by definition male--, whose vital connection with his country has been severed by the condition of exile. He feels split off from a part of himself, and that part is "home". At one with his culture before political circumstances forced his departure, he yearns for return, not only to a beloved place but to an earlier time. It is no coincidence that the reassuring elements of the dream city in Peri Rossi's story are associated with the character's childhood, when the nurturance of the culture was embodied in and magnified by the nurturance of the mother. Antonio Skármeta's project of repairing the break with a cultural identity is perfectly congruent with Peri Rossi's male exile's yearning for home, and both take for granted a culture that nourishes the individual. But Peri Rossi refuses her exiles that solution. Her male exiles remain lost and confused. In "La ciudad" the character who attempts to go back is annihilated.

Happily, the condition of exile can produce more than a desperate and fruitless desire to return. Exile can be, as perhaps the first exile was, a fortunate fall offering possibilities for growth and transcendence. In Peri Rossi these possibilities are figured in female characters. Less nurtured and protected by the national culture which they are constrained to leave, women are perhaps less likely than men to experience exile as a division within the self that can be healed only through reunion with the homeland. While the pain of being torn from a familiar place, from family and friends, often from one's own language, is as intense for women as for men, this pain is accompanied by a potential for emancipation from that in their culture which oppresses them as women. Even during the time of intense shock and grief of the initial moment of exile, there is, in Peri Rossi's work, a recognition of a woman's empowerment when she discovers in herself the capacity to survive.

Descripción de un naufragio (Description of a Shipwreck) is Peri Rossi's cycle of poems concerned with the aftermath of the military takeover of Uruguay in 1972, and especially with the effects of the coup on the politically progressive groups to which the poet and many of her compatriots belonged. The shipwreck is an extended metaphor for the lost revolution; the sailors are political activists who are advised by their captain to save themselves at the moment it becomes clear that their cause is lost. One woman, observed by the captain and by her husband, follows that advice. Three of the four poems dealing with the shipwreck itself and of the woman's escape into exile are spoken by the husband who is surprised to discover that his wife is strong, brave and magnificent in her decisiveness, even as he condemns her as despicable and selfish for abandoning him and their comrades. The fourth--which is actually the third in the series, allowing the husband to have the last word--is spoken by the woman, who discovers that the catastrophe has given her the opportunity to act for herself, to survive, to be, in fact, reborn. What appears to her husband to be coldness and strength (her not looking back as she rows away) is, in truth, an admission of sentiment. The woman reports that only by suppressing the desire to look back could she be sure of maintaining her determination to escape and survive.

> If I had looked
> if I had looked back
> like Eurydice
> I could not have leaped
> I would belong to the past
> anchored among the nets of the ship, your captain, the
>   mold on the chairs
> the poems we consumed on the nights we sat watch
> your laziness in leaping
> your shame of running
> trapped in the lovely vines of our favorite poems,
> I might not again have breathed the salty air
> nor seen the sun appear;
> it was a case of life or death
> "Every man for himself"

>   the captain shouted,
>   life was a sudden hypothesis
>   remaining, a certain death. (Descripción 88)

Once the courageous leap into an unknowable future has been taken, the woman finds the physical strength to save herself. Survival, however, must constantly be won, and in other pieces by Peri Rossi it is again the female character who is competent to do so. Alicia, the little girl in "La influencia de Edgar Allen Poe en la poesía de Raimundo Arias," assumes the role of parent when she and her father are in exile in Spain. It is she who, in the improbable disguise of a South American Indian, begs enough money for them to live on. Here, the child turns the Europeans´ massive ignorance of America to her advantage. Her invisibility allows her, a fair blue-eyed girl, to "be" Indian. Unlike the male protagonists of "La ciudad" and "Las estatuas," for whom the unfamiliar experience of being rendered invisible means only an eviscerating alienation and an inability to cope with their surroundings, Alicia, accustomed to being doubly insignificant as female and child, makes use of what Brazilian educator Paulo Freire calls manhas, a mixture of cunning and canniness the underclass must cultivate in order to survive.[4]

Descripción de un naufragio is Peri Rossi's homage to the lost revolution and especially to its heroes and victims, some of whom she names in the final poem. The work fulfills one of the tasks of Spanish-American exile literature, the obligation to offer testimony to political repression. It is not surprising, (and not to be condemned but certainly to be noted) that the revolutionary content of the poems unquestioningly embraces the terms of androcentric politics. While the expressions of loss, confusion, grief, and anger which pervade the poems are not marked for gender, the poetic voice (with the exception of the single poem noted above) is male; and the language reinscribes male dominance and female subordination. The speaker of one of the early poems of the collection evokes a female sexuality marked by extreme passivity:

>   As if all the calm of the world
>   had taken residence in her body, upon her skin,
>   to hold her so,
>   mute
>   white
> still
>   freed from time
>   from appointments and from cities
>   Sleek. Smooth and impervious as a statue,
>   with no more hair on her body than a gentle tuft on
>   her pubis,

>   like a breeze,
>   where lips wind afternoon heat and tears
>   are trapped
>   --Salt water I drank between her legs--.
> Impenetrable.
>   Rocked by the air
>   that rises and falls from her body
>   making her sway like a reed,
>   without her feeling it,
>   without her breathing it,
>   without her moaning or responding.
>   Soaked by the rain
>   that dripped once and again on her skin
>   opening her pores like portal
>   --where all the sea entered--. (Descripción 17-18)

The marmoreal repose of this figure makes her invulnerable, but it is the invulnerability of death:

> Immobile,
>   fixed in time,
>   like a statue
>   so quiet that she seems dead,
>   solid,
>   unbreakable,
>   resistant to all assaults,
>   indestructible,
>   she gazes indifferently at the couples loving,
>   I cannot possess her
>   cannot dislodge her from me,
> and   so alone that sometimes I feel sorry for her.
>   (Descripción 19-20)

In another poem, Peri Rossi superimposes the rape--or at best the seduction--of a woman on the image of a defeated, sinking ship. The identification between the two is not complete, however, since the woman may experience pleasure:

>   Conquest of the boat, of the woman
>   from the effects of a strong wind, seasickness
>   or the current.
>   The boat falls leeward,
>   the woman on her back
>   whose humbling is measured by degrees.
>   A large audience gathers.
>   The boat tilts.
>   The woman moans
>   and sometimes enjoys it. (Descripción 62)

Perhaps the most extreme example of the appropriation of female sexuality by patriarchal language in these poems is Peri Rossi's use of the archetypal figure of the Whore of Babylon. In the three final poems but one, history is personified as a bikini-clad harlot, whose obscene body entices men to imperialist destruction:

> And in a bikini we saw
> history in synthesis go by,
> with great spongy breasts
> from which hung, openmouthed,
> three ministers and five generals. . . .
> (Descripción 92)

This monumental figure seduces men through dance and devours them sexually. Her power, tied to her sexuality, is undeniable, but it is also reprehensible.

Descripción de un naufragio takes seriously the task of personal and political testimony, and it does so by heeding Skármeta's injunction to keep intact the ceremony of cultural identity. In this case, ironically, the culturally sanctioned linguistic appropriation of female sexuality serves to disempower women. The single woman actor in the shipwreck, the one who rows away and saves herself, is undermined not only by the comments of her husband and her captain, but by the symbolic use to which woman has been put in the surrounding poems. Of course, it is also quite legitimate to claim that the heroic figure of the woman who survives calls into question the assumptions concerning female sexuality that inform the poems in which men are speakers. It is also possible, perhaps, to read a certain covert power in the passive impregnability of the figure in the early poem, or a vengeful majesty in the whore of the later ones. One curious poem in the collection appears to be an acknowledgement of the work of Olga Broumas, whose celebration of lesbian sexuality, Beginning with O, may have encouraged Peri Rossi to reconsider the ways in which women's sexuality could and should be represented, if not in these poems in later ones.[5]

Written not long after the military takeover of Uruguay, Descripción de un naufragio concentrates on the loss and pain of seeing the failure of the left to prevent the fall of the poet's country. Under these circumstances of mourning, even mere survival is an almost unthinkable gift. The guilt of the survivor is evident in the sailor who, after the shipwreck, finds himself lured by the whore of history, and that guilt is projected onto the woman and other anonymous survivors who forsake heroism and community in favor of staying alive. It is only much later that the survivors of the lost revolution can experience, no less recognize and celebrate, any positive outcome of the catastrophe. The poems of *Lingüística general* (*General Linguistics*), which Peri Rossi published in 1980, continue to rely on the maritime language that infuses *Descripción de un naufragio*. They reaffirm the implication of *Descripción* that the shipwreck is at least partially redeemed by the will to navigate--to choose a course, to act morally and ethically:

> To navigate is necessary,
> to live is not. (*Lingüística* 17)

In *Lingüística general*, however, the emphasis shifts from the disaster to the recovery of the course. The erotic poems of the section of the book entitled "Cuadernos de navegación" ("Navegation Notebooks") indicate that sexuality and language are its essential components:

> In the nostalgic distance that travels
> from dream to reality
> the alchemy of the poem
> and of love
> is installed. (*Lingüística* 31)

In this collection, the talk is of love and eroticism rather than rape and prostitution, and sexuality is healing, often playful. It is also freed of the male voice. An early poem in the collection, "Te conocí en septiembre" ("I met you in September"), specifically connects the damaging experience of exile to the healing encounter with the beloved. In this poem, the nightmare image of blue-leaved trees which haunted the protagonist of "La ciudad" becomes a symbol of transformation, a promise of hope and love. Exile becomes rebirth:

> I met you in September
> and it was autumn in the hemisphere of the
>   great marine fossils,
> and it was spring in the country whose war we
>   had lost
> --beautiful and naive as children--
> and violently it sent us off
> whose wounds we call
> second birth, exile
>   --bitter meditation or disillusion.
>   (*Lingüística* 10)

The rebirth is not easy, but it means that the speaker, fully embracing her status as outsider not only as political exile but as a lesbian as well, turns toward the new world that exile offers her. The final section of Lingüística general chronicles the travels of the speaker and her lover through Europe. Now, movement from place to place is wholly voluntary and joyful. The lovers, as lesbians, know they can never belong to the places they visit; their relationship is a "subversion/of the status quo." Yet they are far from invisible, and take a playful enjoyment from

> scandalizing the fish and the good citizens of
> this and all other parties. (Lingüística 74)

The speaker identifies her lover as "my double, my equal, my likeness," and later as "my sister." They become each other by wearing each other's clothes and by claiming as their own the other's body and her history:

> I love you this and other nights
> with our signs of identity
> exchanged
> as joyfully as we trade clothes
> and your dress is mine
> and my sandals are yours
> As my breast
> is your breast
> and your ancient mothers are my own. (Lingüística 74)

This unfolding of self through a shared history and shared identity, the annihilation of dominance and submission as terms of interaction between the lovers, marks an enormous change from the notion of female sexuality that pervades Peri Rossi's earlier work. In an 1978 interview, in which she comments on new ways to represent sexuality, Peri Rossi suggests that erotic poetry in contemporary Western culture objectifies women almost of necessity (Deredita 136-138); and in Descripción de un naufragio, her attention focused on the recent political catastrophe, Peri Rossi seems content to use the disempowering erotic language already in place. Surviving exile, I believe, gave Peri Rossi the freedom to explore lesbian sexuality in Lingüística general, and to proclaim it as a valid continuation of the political struggle in which she has been engaged as a writer and activist.

NOTES

[1] This and all other translations from the Spanish are my own.

[2] For the phrase, "rituals of female degradation," I am indebted to sociologist Barbara Laslett.

[3] To my knowledge, the critic who first wrote about "states of consciousness" in Peri Rossi's narrative was Hugo Verani.

[4] The word mañas also exists in Spanish, of course. I refer to the Portuguese because it is Freire who brings to the surface the political content of the term latent in both languages.

[5] Although Beginning with O was published a year after Descripción de un naufragio, it is possible that Peri Rossi was familiar with the individual poems Broumas published in small magazines.

WORKS CONSULTED

Broumas, Olga. Beginning with O. New Haven, Conn.: Yale University Press, 1977.

Deredita, John F. "Desde la diáspora: entrevista con Cristina Peri Rossi." Texto Crítico 9 (1978): 131-142.

Peri Rossi, Cristina. Descripción de un naufragio. Barcelona: Lumen, 1976.

_____. Lingüística general. Editorial Prometeo, 1979.

_____. El museo de los esfuerzos inútiles. Barcelona: Seix Barral, 1983.

_____. La tarde del dinosaurio. Barcelona: Planeta, 1976.

Rama, Angel. "Los contestarios del poder." Novísimos narradores hispanoamericanos en marcha, 1964-1980. Ed. Angel Rama. Mexico: Marcha Editores, 1981.

Skármeta, Antonio. "Perspectiva de 'los novisimos.'" Hispamérica 10 (1981): 28.

Verani, Hugo. "Una experiencia de límites: La narrativa de Cristina Peri Rossi." Revista Iberoamericana 48 (1982): 118-119.

TRES ESCRITORAS DE COSTA RICA Y SU APORTE
A LAS LETRAS NACIONALES

Rodrigo Solera
Millersville University of Pennsylvania

La novela y el cuento en Costa Rica son realmente productos del siglo XX puesto que su origen data de 1900, cuando Joaquín García Monge publicó la primera novela nacional: El moto.[1] Desde entonces, la participación femenina ha significado numerosas e importantes contribuciones al desarrollo de la prosa narrativa costarricense, estableciendo pautas y creando primicias en el proceso evolutivo de la novela y el cuento.

La importancia de la mujer para las letras costarricenses puede ilustrarse con tres escritoras que, en diversas épocas y bajo distinta inspiración, aportaron rico y relevante caudal a la literatura del país. Ellas son María Fernández de Tinoco (1877-1961), Carmen Lyra (1888-1951) y Yolanda Oreamuno (1916-1956).

Entre 1900 y 1920, siguiendo el ejemplo de García Monge, la novela y el cuento costarricenses se encauzaron por la rica vertiente del costumbrismo, concediéndole prioridad a los ambientes y los personajes típicos y dándole mucha importancia al lenguaje popular. Contrastando con lo anterior, Fernández de Tinoco, la primera mujer costarricense que publicó novelas, introduce al género nacional una técnica y una perspectiva nuevas en sus dos novelas publicadas en 1909: Zulai y Yontá.[2] Ambas obras, que aparecieron juntas en un mismo tomo, están unidas por el tema y la orientación ideológica. Zulai trata el amor entre Ivo y Zulai, jóvenes indios, el cual termina trágicamente por la mala voluntad y celos del cacique Kaurki y de su sucesor Irzuma. La novela Yontá relata acontecimientos anteriores a Zulai, pero fue escrita después. En ella se descubre el origen de Ivo, hijo de Yontá y de un ser misterioso venido a la América precolombina desde la India. La novela desarrolla los amoríos entre Yontá y el místico forastero y presenta las enseñanzas morales y religiosas que él imparte a los indios y cuyo contenido ético se basa sobre el credo teosófico de la autora.

Zulai y Yontá no son novelas históricas porque no se basan en hechos de tal carácter ni siquiera como motivo de fondo. El asunto es romántico pero rodeado de un ambiente arqueológico realista, cuyas descripciones de la vida precolombina en Costa Rica evidencian el interés de Fernández de Tinoco por la arqueología americana. Los protagonistas con quienes simpatiza la autora son típicos del "noble salvaje." En este respecto, ella es quien introduce en la novela costarricense un tema que ya gozaba de larga tradición en la novela continental romántica en obras como Guatimozín (1846), de Gertrudis Gómez de Avellaneda, Los mártires del Anahuac (1870), de Eligio Ancona y Cumandá (1871), de Juan León Mera. Después de Fernández de Tinoco, el tema indígena no se manifestará en la novela costarricense durante casi veinte años hasta que vuelve a surgir en las obras de autores como Anastasio Alfaro, Carlos Salazar Herrera y Euclides Chacón Méndez.

María Isabel Carvajal, que desde un principio adoptó el nombre de pluma de Carmen Lyra, fue la segunda mujer en contribuir a las letras costarricenses. Mujer de ideas sociales avanzadas, participó activamente en la vida política del país durante treinta años. Ella fue uno de los primeros miembros del Partido Aprista, que Haya de la Torre fundó en Costa Rica y, a partir de 1931, militó en las filas del socialismo, siendo ella la inspiradora y organizadora del movimiento durante sus primeros años. Dirigió la revista Ariel, cuya orientación intelectual se basó en el ideario de José Enrique Rodó, y el periódico Trabajo, donde sacó a luz numerosos artículos de carácter socio-político y varios cuentos de protesta social. En 1948 se marchó a México y allí murió tres años después.

Carmen Lyra se inició a la vida literaria en 1918, con la publicación de su única novela: En una silla de ruedas,[3] obra realista pero en la cual el costumbrismo, que todavía campeaba por la prosa narrativa nacional, queda relegado a segundo plano. En el estilo de la novela, el lenguaje popular es muy escaso y sólo lo usa Canducha, la vieja criada. Aspecto sobresaliente de la obra es su temple sicológico, que Carmen Lyra maneja admirablemente y que hasta entonces había tenido exigua representación en la novela y el cuento costarricenses.

En una silla de ruedas se desarrolla en la ciudad de San José, cuyo ambiente contemporáneo la autora recrea fielmente. La trama abarca veinte años de la vida aciaga de Sergio, joven paralítico de ambas piernas. Las lecciones de violín que le enseña un inmigrante italiano convierten a Sergio en virtuoso y obtiene gran éxito con su primer concierto público. Al final, Sergio está viviendo de nuevo en la casa de su niñez, rodeado de sus amigos más queridos, y ganándose la vida como profesor de música.

La trama de la obra está bien manejada y es muy extensa, pues la autora ejercita gran maestría para incorporar el detalle pequeño que en sus hábiles manos se vuelve rico en poder sugestivo. El alma de la novela es la devoción que une a Sergio, a la vieja criada y al músico italiano, y el estoicismo que los tres muestran ante la adversidad. Los personajes resultan ricos en observación sicológica y la narración se interrumpe, en ocasiones, para que ellos se expresen en la primera persona mediante recuerdos, cartas y confidencias de diario. En la novela predominan el detalle sentimental y la emoción, que en este caso son capaces de conmover por la habilidad de la autora para manejar el sentimiento y por su sinceridad emotiva.

No obstante los méritos de En una silla de ruedas, Carmen Lyra goza de mayor fama literaria como autora de Los cuentos de mi tía Panchita, publicados por primera vez en 1920 y que se han convertido en obra clásica de la literatura costarricense. Ya son varias las generaciones infantiles que se han iniciado en el mundo de la fantasía literaria con la lectura de estos cuentos, considerados por largo tiempo de suma importancia en la tradición nacional literaria.

Con la publicación de Los cuentos de mi tía Panchita,[4] Carmen Lyra le dio gran categoría al folklore nacional como motivo artístico e impulsó su cultivo de forma definitiva, como lo atestigua la obra posterior de folkloristas costarricenses tan destacados como Carlos Luís Saénz y Víctor Manuel Elizondo.

Los personajes de los cuentos son animales con sicología humana y el nexo común a todas las narraciones es la presencia de tío Conejo, que en cada episodio tiene que sobrevivir siendo más listo que adversarios físicamente más fuertes como tío Coyote, tío Tigre y tía Zorra. En estos protagonistas animales, especialmente en tío Conejo, Carmen Lyra ha sabido incorporar los perfiles anímicos más característicos del costarricense medio: la socarronería, el espíritu conservador, la religiosidad y la tacañería. En el estilo de los cuentos, contrario a lo que sucede en su novela, la autora refleja hábilmente la rica gama del lenguaje del pueblo y del refranero costarricense.

En el devenir del tiempo, Yolanda Oreamuno es la tercera autora costarricense de importancia, cuya obra se proyecta más lejos en el tratamiento del tema sicológico, resultando ella su mayor exponente entre los escritores de Costa Rica. El talento precoz de Yolanda Oreamuno se manifestó cuando muy joven empezó a publicar cuentos en el Repertorio Americano; luego vino una vida angustiada y errabunda que la obligó a viajar por Chile, los Estados Unidos, Guatemala y México, donde la sorprendió la muerte prematura.

La primera novela de Oreamuno, Tierra firme, ganó el tercer premio en el concurso patrocinado por la editorial Reinhart y Farrar en 1941, pero nunca fue publicada y el manuscrito se perdió. Su segunda novela: La ruta de su evasión, obtuvo el primer premio en el concurso de novela centroamericana celebrado en Guatemala, en 1949, y se publicó el mismo año.

La ruta de su evasión[5] narra la desintegración de una familia trágica, víctima de un padre egoísta, tiránico y arrogante. La cortina que cuelga en la sala de la casa representa el abismo que existe entre el ambiente sofocante y enfermizo de la familia y la vida libre de afuera que invita a la evasión. La madre, Teresa, agoniza en su lecho durante toda la narrativa y muere al final. Es una mujer totalmente dominada por el esposo, cuyos abusos inauditos ha soportado durante años con estoicismo, tratando de levantar y mantener una casa que, al fin de cuentas, nunca logra categoría de hogar. Lo único amable en la vida de Teresa es la memoria de Esteban, antiguo socio de su marido, y enamorado secreto de ella. Esteban sacrificó su futuro cuando aceptó la culpa de un desfalco financiero, ingeniado por el marido, para salvar a la familia de la desgracia pública. El odio de Teresa por su esposo y su sometimiento a él la empujan a una obsesión por el cuidado físico de la casa, olvidando la formación moral de los hijos. De ellos, Roberto resulta egoísta y cruel, Gabriel es víctima de una sensibilidad enfermiza y Alvaro es un degenerado. Tres miembros de la familia descubren la ruta de la evasión propia del infierno doméstico desprovisto de afecto. Teresa se deja morir, Roberto se marcha y Gabriel se suicida, después de que los dos últimos han tenido amores fracasados con distintas mujeres.

En la novela resalta el gran contraste entre la condición de los sexos. Los hombres, exceptuando a Esteban, son egoístas y dominantes, actúan con más aplomo y se consideran superiores. Las mujeres resultan víctimas dóciles, llenas de incertidumbre e inferiores. Lo único que las redime es su capacidad para darse en el amor y su estoicismo. La autora no manifiesta ni admiración ni repudio a tal actitud femenina. Por otra parte, la gran tensión de la novela radica en el hecho de que los protagonistas, a pesar de ser muy cerebrales, no encuentran las palabras justas para la comunicación íntima, haciendo estéril cualquier intento de solidaridad humana.

La trama de la novela salta de uno a otro personaje al pasar de un capítulo al siguiente pero sin fragmentar la unidad narrativa porque la autora mantiene la cohesión temática mediante nexos sutiles que apuntalan la totalidad estructural. El tiempo no es cronológico sino que consiste en saltos atrás de la memoria. Al lector le corresponde ir colocando las piezas del rompecabezas en el sitio adecuado hasta lograr el cuadro total.

La forma y el contenido de La ruta de su evasión, su estilo deliberado, atrevido y rico en matices sicológicos, la apartan del grueso de la novelística costarricense y la señalan como primicia de las letras nacionales.

Con Yolanda Oreamuno se cierra el ciclo de novelistas femeninas costarricenses cuyas obras señalaron rumbos nuevos y dieron impulso decisivo a la novela y el cuento nacionales durante su primer medio siglo de vida.

NOTES

[1] Joaquín García Monge, El moto (San José: Imprenta Parón y Pujol, 1900). El título de esta novela, en el lenguaje campesino de Costa Rica, significa "ternero huérfano." Por extensión, el vocablo "moto" se aplica a todo joven huérfano.

[2] María Fernández de Tinoco, Zulai, Yontá (San José: Imprenta Alsina, 1909).

[3] Carmen Lyra, En una silla de ruedas (San José: Imprenta Lines, 1918).

[4] Carmen Lyra, Los cuentos de mi tía Panchita (San José: Editorial El Convivio, 1920).

[5] Yolanda Oreamuno, La ruta de su evasión (Guatemala: Editorial del Ministerio de Educación Pública, 1949).

HACIA UNA NARRATIVA FEMENINA EN LA LITERATURA DOMINICANA

Emelda Ramos
Universidad Nordestana, República Dominicana

(Edited by Elías Miguel Muñoz)

En su valioso volumen, Mujeres en espejo: Narradoras latinoamericanas siglo XX,[1] Sara Sechojovich antologa en un recorrido por todo el continente lo que escriben actualmente las mujeres, y al llegar a la República Dominicana acota que sabemos poco de lo que sucede hoy en este país, ya que no hay un Max Henríquez Ureña que lo comunique. Y del fértil diálogo autor-lector, la laboriosa ensayista del Instituto de Investigaciones Sociales de la UNAM, logra convencerme de la necesidad de una labor, primero: de catálogo y segundo: de examen. De ese diálogo resulta esta comunicación que asumo como renuevo de narradora y como representante de la última generación discipular de don Max Henríquez Ureña.

Nombrarlas primero, como decía Carpentier, para saber que existen. Estamos frente a un universo virgen y por ende, es imprescindible rescatar nombres y prestablecer que no obstante ser en nuestro país donde se inicia la literatura femenina del Nuevo Mundo, cuando en 1610 Leonor de Ovando, monja dominica escribe en el Monasterio de Regina cinco sonetos y versos blancos, simultáneamente con Elvira de Mendoza, empero es precaria, cónsona con las vicisitudes del discurrir histórico-social, político-económico, la participación de la mujer en el quehacer literario a través de su desarrollo en el Continente. Y a pesar de que en el nacimiento de la República una mujer estuvo presente como testigo y narradora: Rosa Duarte, cuyos providenciales apuntes aportaron pasajes sobre la vida de Juan Pablo Duarte, nuestro Padre de la Patria y de la de "Los Trinitarios," movimiento clandestino que gestó nuestra Independencia, reitero, no se ha prodigado cuantitativa ni cualitativamente la mano femenina en la prosa de ficción. Veamos las que intentaron crear un mundo fabulado por ellas, sin sucumbir al impulso fatal que parece llevar a tantas a confinar esos mundos una vez creados, a la oscura nada de armario familiar.

En 1894 Manuela Rodríguez "La Deana," que en su propia pequeña imprenta hacía labor literaria y política, escribe una especie de autobiografía titulada Historia de una mujer, pero fue en 1850 (año en que nace nuestra luminar poetisa Salomé Ureña de Henríquez) cuando nace Amelia Francisca de Marchena, quien oculta bajo el seudónimo de Amelia Francasci se convertiría en nuestra primera novelista. Publica en 1893 Madre culpable y en 1901 Francisca Martinoff pero ya había logrado éxito desde 1892 con las entregas de sus novelas, paradigma de la literatura de folletín en boga en Europa durante todo el siglo XIX. También en 1901, Virginia Elena Ortea (1889-1903) publicó Risas y lágrimas en la que recopila cuentos, artículos y crónicas, siendo autora de una zarzuela que fue presentada en el teatro a fines de siglo. Francisca A. Vallejo García (1859-1909) publicó La mano de la providencia y Rosa Smester (1859-1945), educadora y destacada luchadora durante la ocupación norteamericana, escribió sus Juveniles: Cuentos de color de rosa. En 1925 una de nuestras más prolíficas escritoras, Abigaíl Mejía (1895-1941), publica su novela Sueña Pilarín y su contemporánea Jesusa Alfau escribe Los débiles y Teletusa. Feminista como las que anteceden, Delia Weber, que nació en 1900 y además de descollar como pintora, publica poesía y en 1952, Dora y otros cuentos. Mas nuestra primera cuentista es Hilma Contreras que nació en 1902. Aunque su primer volumen Cuatro cuentos sale a la luz pública en 1953, prueba su primacía el hecho de que ya en 1937, Juan Bosch escribe una carta crítica donde a propósito de su cuento "La desjabada" dice: "al país le nace una escritora cabal, no una principiante, ni siquiera una aficionada feliz. Un fruto sazonado." Y añade, refiriéndose a quien hasta entonces se seudonominaba "Silvia Hilcom," "con esta página saluda Hilma Contreras al país. Recibámosla como una compañera excepcional." Otra escritora dominicana, Virginia Bordas, publica Toeya en 1949, pero no se trata de un cuento, sino una fantasía indígena, un relato donde la figura central es la cacica cuyo nombre recibió la isla que hoy se llama Catalina.

Retornemos a 1945, cuando Beatriz Roldán edita su novela A través de los años y en 1947 María Antonia Sagredo publica en La Información su novela Ercilia. Insistiendo en el 1945, Carmen Natalia Bonilla, nuestra militante poeta, participa con su novela La Victoria, escogida para represenatr a la República Dominicana en el Concurso Literario Hispano-Americano en Estados Unidos. Melba Marrero, que alcanzó nombradía como poetisa, da a conocer su novela Caña dulce, seguida en 1955 por Postales sin estampillas (libro de viajes) y de su novela El voto, permaneciendo lo mejor de su producción, inédita. En 1953 publica un ensayo bibliográfico, "Sor Juana Inés de la Cruz," quien era reconocida como cuentista a través del Listín Diario: Milady de L'Official. En 1955 se publica El destino manda de Marta Polanco Castro. En 1964 da a conocer su novela Los depravados Eurídice Canaán, que en 1969 publica Los monstruos sagrados y en 1980 Morir por última vez; tiene en su haber diecisiete manuscritos de novelas inéditos.

En 1967 publica su novela Sueño ideal Altagracia Vargas de Toyos, y en 1969 Carmita Henríquez de Castro, Cuentos para niños, siendo pionera de este género, en el cual, a posteriori, se ha labrado un lugar Lucía Amelia Cabral con Hay cuentos para contar (1977), Gabino, separata del mismo en 1979 y Sorprendido el plátano (1984). La secundan María Cristina de Farías con Cuentos en versos para Maricris y Eleanor Grimaldi con Cuentos infantiles y juveniles.

En 1969 Aída Cartagena Portalatín llega al final en el Premio Biblioteca Breve de Seix Barral con su novela Escalera para Electra; en 1978 publica Tablero, libro de cuentos, y en 1984 con La tarde en que murió Estefanía (novela) se consagra, quien inicialmente fue la única figura femenina del movimiento literario "la Poesía Sorprendida." En 1972 Jeannette Miller publica su Fórmulas para combatir el miedo, libro de poemas, y Suplementos culturales, una colección de modernos relatos. Al concentrarse Miller más en la crítica de arte y el ensayo recopilado que fructifica en Historia de la pintura dominicana, tal vez la narrativa dominicana ha perdido en ella una posibilidad. En 1979 obtiene una mención de honor en el concurso de Casa de Teatro Mary Rosa Jiménez con su cuento "Tan sólo unos lirios." En 1983 Emelda Ramos obtiene un premio regional de narrativa con El despojo o por los trillos de la leyenda. En 1984 Aida Bonnelly de Díaz publica su libro Variaciones, exquisita sorpresa para la crítica literaria dominicana.

Es precisamente asistidos de la crítica literaria actual, que podemos abordar el siguiente ítem. Hasta aquí ha sido sólo el nombrar, la historia, el rescate, el catálogo. Para esto seguimos las huellas en los archivos, antologías y por supuesto, el canal de información más usual: el mercado editorial. Ahora trataremos de escrutar lo que escriben hoy las mujeres que tributan su energía en la labor creadora, hacia una narrativa femenina en la literatura dominicana. Es preciso advertir las temáticas, las tendencias, los códigos, las propuestas estéticas, el uso de los arquetipos femeninos universales, la rebeldía subyacente, en fin, la inscripción de estas narradoras en el movimiento latinoamericano en general.

La narrativa dominicana de los últimos veinte años se ha remozado y la escogencia de su temática se ha ampliado de lo rural a lo urbano, pero a pesar de que recibe un nuevo aliento particularmente en su género corto, sigue siendo escasa y limitada en su calidad, considerándose la novela dominicana como un proyecto a alcanzar. Un vistazo por las obras nos revela que los escritores del año '60 hasta hoy están absortos en estas preocupaciones: 1) la dictadura y sus efectos sobre el pueblo; 2) la guerrilla de '63, intento de retorno a la constitucionalidad; 3) la guerra de abril del '65 y la segunda ocupación norteamericana; 4) resquebrajar las viejas formas narrativas; 5) búsqueda de formas de expresión que se ajusten a la realidad social. ¿Corresponden nuestras narradoras de hoy a este esquema? Examinemos lo que escriben.

El hecho de que un país posea viva a su primera cuentista, da cuenta de cuán joven es su narrativa. Según Pedro Peix esa pionera, Hilma Contreras, es "cuentista de sorprendente e inusitada resonancia poética."[2] Contreras publica Cuatro cuentos en 1953, El Ojo de Dios--cuentos de la clandestinidad publicados en 1962--, así como el ensayo Doña Endrina de Calatayud. Además, ella guardaba en insospechados escondites varios cuentos impublicables por la persecucioñn literaria omnipenetrante. Estos cuentos son realmente miniaturas donde se enmarcan hechos y escenas de la vida del dominicano, en su ámbito familiar, bajo la dictadura. Para pintarlos esta mujer echa mano de una prosa fuerte y contenida para denunciar varios temas. Se ve el poder militar en "Biografía de una hora":

> Un Jeep cruzó por la "Rosa Duarte", un maldito jeep militar. En seguida me llené de voces. Arriba pasó el zumbido aullante de uno de los helicópteros a chorro que fueron vendidos por un voto en las Naciones Unidas. Vivimos en un cochino mundo. Tanto por tanto. El ideal --que es como decir el coraje de la dignidad-- ¡al diablo!

Otro tema, la persecución represiva, tiene importancia en "El Ojo de Dios":

> ¡Hora Abel!... te advierto que insisto en que aceptes la sindicatura. ¿quién mató a ese hombre? -preguntó a quemarropa. Entornando los ojos de agudo mirar, el gobernador inquirió a su vez ¿qué hombre? -El que has dado orden de exhibir al público. El cuento concluye: Al verlo pasar, el "Ojo de Dios" abandonó a Caín, para darse por entero a la persecución de Abel.

Y, por fin, se examinan el terror y el crimen en "Los rebeldes":

> ¿Vive aquí Marcelino Torres? preguntó el chofer a tiempo que paraba en seco la ambulancia. -Sí- contestó interrumpiendo apenas la dulce faena de chupar su pipa. -¿Qué se le ofrece? El chofer hizo señas al hombre sentado junto a él. Abrían ya la puerta de la ambulancia, cuando el segundo individuo se dignó explicar: -Entonces este muerto es suyo.- Sorprendido don Marcelino retiró su pipa de los labios golosos. -Eso es

un error- protestó. Nosotros no tenemos a nadie enfermo en el Hospital. -Pero éste es suyo... Sacaron un bulto del vehículo, echaron a un lado a don Marcelino y sin más miramientos arrojaron el paquete en medio del zaguán. Dentro de la casa gritó una mujer. El viejo la miraba sin atreverse a bajar los ojos horrorizados antes de ver...

Escalera para Electra, de Aída Cartagena, "es no sólo uno de los primeros experimentos novelescos válidos que propone la actualización de la narrativa dominicana sino posiblemente el único que posee un alto grado de coherencia, es decir, de adecuación temático-formal que hace que los recursos técnicos no sean gratuitos ni forzados," dice Alcántara Almanzar.[3] En efecto, esta obra --harto escarceada en antologías, escuelas y universidades-- resulta una verdadera provocación al análisis metatextual, porque en ella la autora nos conduce a través de una escalera de planos superpuestos y alternos hasta la conformación del texto, monologando en un momentum de su narración:

¡Ah las cosas de Helene! ¿En qué laberinto ha caído? no es que sea novelera de veleidades ajenas porque hay muchas que son de su ocurrencia. Luego de escribir: "La Tierra," se desdobla el libro de Swain en desconcertantes planos. Se le antoja que ya inició una mecánica que debe continuarla en esta escalera. Esa mecánica corresponde en una interrelación casual, con los llamados "estilos modernos" que se mofan de Aristóteles, Nebrija, Cervantes y de todo cuanto hijo de puta que trató de encarcelar la escribanía. (33)

Se nos revelan aspectos importantes y muy definidos en el discurso de Cartagena, que podemos aprovechar, en vista de que este espacio no nos permite ni aún sucintamente abarcar cabalmente el metatexto. Primero, Helene es la biógrafa de Swain, la Electra Dominicana del pueblo natal de la autora, por ende Helene es Aída Cartagena, desdoblada en una tercera persona, es la "ella" del "yo." Segundo, el propósito de ruptura de los cánones del novelar, habrá de ser brújula del viaje hacia la modernidad de esta arqueóloga-antropóloga, estudiosa del arte, viajando por la Grecia de Eurípides. Tercero, el descubrimiento de su "técnica de los planos" nos irá dejando ser coparticipantes de su propio hallazgo, cuando avanza: "veo que esta escalera, se alarga en altitud, que a veces siento vértigos ¿se caerá mi escalera? ¿quién derribará mi escalera?" Se construye la novela sobre trozos memoriosos, testimonios epocales, cables dirigidos a sus amigos dominicanos, comentarios ilustrativos sobre el arte de la antigua Grecia, la situación política del país, contradicciones y dubitaciones existenciales, mensajes a París, mientras va desenrollando el pergamino del viejo asunto, del amor incestuoso y la tragedia. Cuarto, la angustia inherente al proceso de producción y recepción de la obra, referente nuevo en nuestra narrativa femenina, que se hará patente y patético de un plano a otro, a través del texto: "¿qué tengo yo para ganar o perder con este libro que no encontrará editores, porque dirán que no es una novela ni nada que sirve para anuncio. Que Helene no es retórica..." La angustia la llevará hasta la duda y casi total negación ya arribando al desenlace de la tragedia, y más allá del coro griego: "Señora Helene: ¿Insiste usted en hacer creer que esto es una novela?" (159). Cartagena encarna la realidad de los literatos dominicanos que hizo a F. García Godoy decir: "a todo lo dicho adiciónese lo reducido y pobre de nuestro medio literario, que no permite al autor vislumbrar la más leve esperanza de legítimo lucro." Sin caer en un pesimismo momentáneo en el que parecen hundirla las consideraciones de Robbe Grillet, ella dice:

> Ahora sí que estoy segura de que dejo esto y tiro los papeles de Swain y organizo los cartones de un Bingo que dejó una sueca en esta habitación. Juego, hago Bingo. Me digo: Mujer, usted no es sueca, anímese e imponga su criterio, el propio, el suyo, termine su novela. Tiro las fichas y los cartones. Me comprometo conmigo a liquidar el caso Swain. (136)

El compromiso sigue la toma de conciencia, producto de una búsqueda de su identidad: Mujer, que ya en un plano retrospectivo anterior confesionalmente vierte: "me obligó un poco más de lucha, porque nací mujer: control del desarrollo de yo, tendencia obligada al dominio propio: propósito sin resultado positivo de todo cuanto molesta al sexo opuesto: obligación del desarrollo en grandes dimensiones del potencial humano o intelectual" (26). Nos bastan estos peldaños para asumir que esta <u>Escalera para Electra</u> es una novela feminista por excelencia, dentro de la literatura construída por las mujeres.

Mientras la prosa de Aída Cartagena ha sido calificada de culta y la de Hilma Contreras de viril, la de Aída Bonnelly nos permite abordar el tópico actual: ¿Hay una literatura femenina? ¿O sólo hay una literatura? Y es que con la prosa de esta pianista y profesora de música armonizan adjetivaciones que oscilan entre elegante, cuidada, de sintaxis regular, maravillosa economía de palabras, "femenina" exquisitez, contenida en una artística edición de lujo y gusto excepcionales. Soslayando el debate urticante, debo confirmar el uso de materiales de la cotidianidad, como referentes predominantes en el texto, en cuya estructuración la autora se ha servido de un artificio: el de traspasar a la forma narrativa el patrón estructural de la variación musical, composición per sé femenina y maternal, de la cual se desprenden la melodía, el ritmo, la armonía, el tipo de lengua y sobre todo el carácter contenido. En estas variaciones la sonoridad de las palabras es importante, pero creo que los silencios aún más, así como el tiempo y su persistencia, y su manejo dentro del tema "El Baño." En el tema "El Amor," una figura aparece en todas y cada una de sus variaciones: el perro, que como personaje simbólico, habrá de jugar un rol muy singular en cada narración. Porque esto es precisamente lo que son estas facturas de Bonnelly de Díaz: no son cuentos, no es una novela, no es un relato, son narraciones (¿narravariaciones?). Persisten las dudas frente al género, como es el caso de mi libro El despejo, o por los trillos de la leyenda, calificado ora de novela corta, ora de relato largo, rescate de una leyenda de mi región, donde los personajes hablan la variante dialectal, objeto de la preocupación investigativa de Pedro Henríquez Ureña. Finalmente Variaciones de Aída Bonnelly, contiene de principio a fin: 1) La intención didáctica, 2) El mensaje de amor, y 3) Una convocatoria a la belleza.

Y ahora, a modo de conclusión, se incluye un conversatorio en el que participan las narradoras discutidas en este ensayo.

E. Ramos: El hecho de ser mujer, ¿las ha condicionado en su oficio y desarrollo?

H. Contreras: No, no creo que ser mujer condicione, más bien creo que el obstáculo está en el temperamento individual.

A. Cartagena: Piensas en esa mujer, cuyos escritos leí desde niña y que es una de las figuras centrales de la Literatura Universal: Teresa de Avila: combatida, combativa y combatiente...

A. Bonnelly: Sí, el hecho de ser mujer en Latinoamérica condiciona a la escritora, porque todavía no estamos desprendidos de la alienación de la cultura, cumplir con deberes preestablecidos, observar conductas que son patrones arcaicos y que terminan por estrechar la visión de la mujer de la realidad.

E. Ramos: Hay un rasgo común entre las narradoras dominicanas: han viajado todas al continente; ¿será esto un factor determinante de la dirección narrativa de nuestra imaginación insular?

H. Contreras: Sí, hice mis estudios secundarios en Europa, regresé al país y realicé mi carrera universitaria y luego a

Sorbona para tomar cursos de Antropología, de Civilización y de la Cultura. Sí, en Europa una entra en contacto con el movimiento intelectual y artístico del mundo; aunque siempre escribía y relataba un Diario, fue a mi regreso, 1935, cuando tuve la necesidad de escribir cuentos.

A. Cartagena: Es que en los Continentes una se pone en contacto con otras culturas, se amplía, se nutre. Viajando se gana más, que todo que se lee y se estudia. Escalera para Electra la escribí mientras viajaba por Grecia y recogía un reportaje que me había encargado la revista Mundo Nuevo, en París.

A. Bonnelly: La distancia nos da la perspectiva de lo pequeño y grande, lo cotidiano y lo transcendente. Estuve desde 1945 al 50 en New York para mi maestría en piano; en París estudié del 54 al 55, y viví diez años en Washington.

E. Ramos: Finalmente, ¿a qué atribuyen que haya una recurrencia de la mujer en la poesía, también un buen número de prosistas de ensayo periodístico o histórico y sin embargo, tan pocas narradoras de ficción en el país?

H. Contreras: Creo que el fenómeno es mundial, pero puedo decir, y esto se relaciona con tu primera pregunta: el medio es estrecho y no admite que los hechos que narramos sean imaginarios, y te achacan las acciones que cuentas, así las de temperamento tímido se cohiben, no se arriesgan al choque y a la hostilidad social.

A. Cartagena: Es más fácil la poesía aún hoy, que es una cosa muy seria, precisa cultura, ya no es sólo inspiracional: mirar una luna que ya no está ni brilla. Narrar es otra cosa: hay que investigar hasta los mismos hechos que se presencian. Y hay hechos: la explotación, el hambre, la represión, el artista está obligado a narrarlos, a estar al lado del otro hombre, el que sufre.

A. Bonnelly: Creo que la mujer novelista escasea, hay más poetas porque al fin y al cabo el mundo imaginado sí cabe dentro de la vida, de las restricciones de la mujer latina, ahora bien, con la liberación de las costumbres, el acceso a la producción y al trabajo, a terciar en los foros junto al hombre, con el tiempo va a cosechar mujeres de un intelecto comparable e igual al de los hombres de talento.

Esbozadas más claramente las trabajadoras de la ficción, se ve que las mujeres narradoras dominicanas comparten las mismas preocupaciones temático-formales que su otredad. Carecen, como los hombres, de una tradición narrativa fuerte y definida, pero buscan también nuevas formas de expresión ajustables, representativas de nuestra realidad social, que conduzcan nuestra narrativa hacia un espacio importante dentro de la actual Narrativa Latinoamericana.

NOTES

[1] Sara Sechojovich, *Mujeres en espejo: Narradoras latinoamericanas siglo XX* (Folios Ediciones, 1981).

[2] Pedro Peix, *La narrativa yugulada* (Santo Domingo: Editora Alfa y Omega, 1981).

[3] José Alcántara Almanzar, *Narrativa y sociedad en Hispanoamérica* (Santo Domingo: Instituto Tecnológico de Santo Domingo, 1984).

NOTES ON HANS CHRISTIAN ANDERSEN TALES
IN ANA MARIA MATUTE´S PRIMERA MEMORIA

Suzanne Gross Reed
The Wichita State University

Five tales of Hans Christian Andersen are alluded to in Ana María Matute´s novel Primera memoria. These are: "The Snow Queen," "The Little Mermaid," "The Wild Swans," "The King of the Elves," and "Inchelina."[1] References to these tales, and images derived from them, occur throughout the recollections of the protagonist, Matia. In every instance, whether only referred to by name, as "Los Once Príncipes Cisnes" (Matute 16); or by comparison of characters like that of Sanamo and the troll king (Matute 191), the allusion to the Andersen tale serves two functions. The first of these is to emphasize Matia´s juvenility. By consistently relating the circumstances, events, and persons around her to the frame of reference of the tales, she demonstrates her failure to advance beyond the emotional parameters of her childhood. The first mention of the tales establishes this function, forming as it does a part of the catalogue of lost treasures: the Atlas, which defines her perception of the physical world (Matute 15); the toy theatre, which defines her perception of alienation; and the tales, which define her perceptions of human relationships and behavior (Matute 16). Repeated references to the tales reinforces the theme of Matia´s fear of growing up, by showing that she consistently relates the events and people affecting her life to those of the tales, which are familiar to her and therefore understandable. It is by this means that she is able to overcome in some degree the disorientation of her removal to the house of Doña Práxedes; and to establish affective relationships with strangers. By assigning to each roles analogous to those in the familiar tales, which are for her models of human life, she is able to place each in a context that makes sense to her, and allows her to define her own roles in relation to each.

It is not enough, however, to note that Matia refers from time to time to characters or situations in the Andersen stories (Matute 163, 208 passim). The relevance of such allusions is to be discovered only by taking them as allusions to the whole tale in every instance. Each tale, taken as a whole, is a model of Matia´s perception of the events she recollects, taken as a whole. Moreover, this frame of reference used by the child Matia is not repudiated by the woman Matia in recalling this period of her life. As Matia the child relies on the tales to provide a familiar context in a strange environment, Matia the woman reinforces this reliance and extends its function to that of ironic commentary which illuminates the novel as a whole. Because the tales are alluded to simultaneously by the Matia remembered and the Matia remembering, both functions reveal a nonliteral dimension of what is happening in the novel.

The first direct allusion to an Andersen tale is that to "The Snow Queen," in which Matia describes herself in terms of the boy Kay, after his eyes and heart have been pierced by fragments of the trolls' mirror (Matute 17); which cause him to "see the world distorted . . . since even the tiniest fragment contained all the evil qualities of the whole mirror. If a splinter should enter someone's heart . . . that heart would turn to ice" (Andersen 235). In the tale, this passage is immediately followed by that which describes the mirror fragments as being "so large that windowpanes could be made of them, although through such a window it was no pleasure to contemplate your friends"; or of such a size that they could be made into spectacles (Andersen 235). Knowing this, it is possible to recall the opening of the novel, in which Doña Práxedes is described in terms which suggest the Snow Queen herself: her wave of white hair, pale face, and glittering diamonds (Matute 9; Andersen 237, 239); her habit of looking from the window of her room to scrutinize the dwellings of her tenants below through the lenses of her opera glasses (Matute 9,10).

Borja, too, before the first overt allusion to "The Snow Queen," has been presented in terms which suggest Kay in the Snow Queen's power. If Borja knows very well the meaning of the words inheritance, money, and lands (Matute 12); so Kay, abducted by the Snow Queen, wants to pray but can only remember arithmetic drills and geography statistics (Andersen 239, 240). Matia refers three more times to Kay and Gerda, the devoted children of "The Snow Queen" (Matute 163, 195, 196); in each case with reference to Borja and herself. But many details demonstrate the presence of the tale as an ironic mirror in the background. In the Andersen tale, Kay and Gerda are not brother and sister, but love one another as if they had been (Andersen 235-236). They meet to play on an upper balcony formed by adjoining flower boxes (Andersen 236); there is a Grandmother who tells them stories and reads the Bible to them (Andersen 236-237, 362). Just so, Borja and Matia develop a sibling relationship (Matute 55, passim); meet to talk and play on the loggia (Matute 19, passim); and live with a Grandmother who prays and tells stories (Matute 12, passim).

The correspondences of <u>Primera memoria</u> and "The Snow Queen" are bitterly ironic. The kind Grandmother of the tale is the evil Snow Queen herself in the novel; the sunny homes of the children in the tale become the Snow Queen's palace in the novel, full of mirrors, marble, and cold (Matute 18, 72-73, passim; Andersen 236,

258-259). The irony is perhaps bitterest in the correspondences of the two stories' conclusions. The Andersen tale ends with the devoted Gerda at last finding her Kay and embracing him with tears of loving joy which, falling on his breast, melt the ice of his heart; so that his own responding tears wash the evil splinters from his perceptions (Andersen 260). The two children return home to find the sun shining, the flowers blooming, and the smiling Grandmother reading aloud the Bible passage about little children and the Kingdom of Heaven. They discover that they have become grown-ups, and yet are children still (Andersen 262). At the end of the novel Matia and Borja meet on the loggia under a cloudy, pre-dawn sky. They embrace, but it is Borja who weeps while Matia remains rigid and frozen, holding him against her while his tears fall upon her neck. The garden below them appears all white, and the Biblical passage alluded to by the crowing white cock is of love denied and trust betrayed (Matute 244-245).

Like "The Snow Queen," "The Wild Swans" ("Los Once Príncipes Cisnes," Matute 16) is a story of brothers transformed by an evil female power and rescued by the faithful love and courage of a sister, or infant lover, who assumes a sister's role. In "The Wild Swans" the enchantment of the boys by their step-mother and their rescue by their sister, after long searching and suffering, links the story as a whole with that of the Snow Queen and Kay and Gerda. The circumstance that indefinite self-imposed muteness is one of the sufferings the sister must bear to save her brothers (Andersen 125) links this story with that of "The Little Mermaid." Here, the little mermaid must give up her voice forever in order to acquire the human shape that will enable her to seek a human soul. Her speechlessness, though chosen by her, is not effected by self-control; she allows the witch to cut out her tongue in exchange for the magic drink that will transform the mermaid into a woman (Andersen 69). As the tale of "The Snow Queen" serves Matia as a model, in terms of which she can order her perceptions of Doña Práxedes' household, "The Little Mermaid" is the model of her relationship with Manuel Toronjí.

Just as she always alludes to "The Snow Queen" by the emblem of Kay and Gerda in their garden on the roof, so she always alludes to "The Little Mermaid" by a reference to her desire for an immortal soul (Matute 21, 82, 243, passim). In the Andersen story, the mermaid can acquire a human soul only by marriage with a human man, through which she will share in his immortal soul. To make it possible for a man to love her enough to marry her, however, she must renounce her mermaid body and take on human legs (Andersen 66). These requirements are expounded in the Andersen tale by her grandmother; precisely as the analogous physical requirements for marriage and a share in the local society are expounded to Matia by her own grandmother, Doña Práxedes; whose veterinary scrutiny is so embarrassing to Matia (Matute 120-121). The prince, whom the mermaid has already seen and loved, and for whose sake she desires an immortal soul, marries another girl in error (Andersen 73-74). The mermaid's sisters sacrifice all their long hair to purchase a knife with which the mermaid may kill the prince as he lies asleep and so regain her mermaid nature in the touch of his blood. This she refuses to do and so dies and is transformed into sea-foam among the spirits of the air. These inform her that her selfless act has gained her the right to try to earn an immortal soul through three hundred years of good deeds (Andersen 75-76). This story, however, is not quite the story that Matia remembers (Matute 243). For her, the story is one of irremediable longing, loss, and dissolution. It is at once the model of her change from child to woman and of her relationship with Manuel Toronjí.

The first reference to "The Little Mermaid" occurs early in the novel, when Matia likens the butterflies in the woods of the ravine to the gorgeous ships in which sailed the strange young man with black eyes who could not give a soul to the little mermaid (Matute 21). Shortly after this, Matia encounters Manuel Toronjí, not sailing in a splendid silken ship but standing with the body of his murdered foster father beside the rotting hulk of a fishing boat (Matute 36-37). Manuel is described in terms that may amount to "strange young man" (Matute 21, 38, 41, 43, passim). He has the memorable brilliant black eyes of the prince (Matute 42; Andersen 62, 70) and, like the prince, he is sixteen years old (Matute 43; Andersen 62).

As the little mermaid's desire for an immortal soul is an image of her desire for love (Andersen 66; Matute 243) so the transformation of fish's tail into woman's legs is an image of sexual maturity, feared and desired. In the tale, their possession is attended by unremitting pain and effusion of blood (Andersen 68, 70, 71). It is when she discovers the prince looking steadily down at her that the little mermaid finds her new legs, and is aware of a nakedness she is now impelled to cover with her hair (Andersen 70). In church during the singing of the Te Deum, Matia, remembering a moment of sexual awareness and hostility occasioned by Juan Antonio's caressing her knee and casting doubts upon her parentage, remembers also the words which describe the pain of walking on two legs when one is a mermaid. The quotation from Andersen (70) is immediately followed by the verse of the Te Deum which is being sung: "whom by precious blood thou didst redeem" (Matute 82).

That the tale of "The Little Mermaid" is associated in Matia's mind with Manuel is strongly reinforced by the circumstances that he also knows the story; that she talks to him of her childhood memories and treasures which she hides from everyone else; and that she asks him more than once why the little mermaid would want an immortal soul, to which his answer is only to stroke her hair (Matute 218). At the end of her belated and futile attempts to undo the treachery she has silently permitted Borja to work upon Manuel, she remembers (or comments) that the little mermaid did not gain an immortal soul because men and women do not love; that she was left with useless legs --that is to say, crippled and denatured --and became sea-foam. The stories, Matia suddenly thinks, were horrible (Matute 243).

As in the case of "The Snow Queen," correspondences with "The Little Mermaid" are one of the textual and textural threads of Primera memoria. Though the overwhelming presence of the sea as both pleasure-ground and death-bringer in both stories is surely fortuitous, that of the red sun is not (Andersen 63; Matute 35, 37, 43, passim). Both the yacht and the house of the semi-royal, semi-mythical Don Jorge de Son Major, Manuel's natural father, are described in language which relates them to the ship and palace of the prince in the tale (Andersen 62, 65; Matute 101, 102, 189). Both stories have in common an exceptionally rich, lurid, and intrusive flora.

Though only two of the Andersen stories mentioned in Primera memoria have been discussed, and none of the other classics of children's literature which appear as allusions in the novel, these two are the paradigm of the uses of them all. Each tale, in its entirety and seen as a whole, is both a mirror and model of the novel itself; creating resonances significantly different than those which would be produced by similar allusions to literature less firmly associated with children and less directly intended for their enjoyment and instruction. All of the children's stories are stories about the growth from child to adult; stories about the naturalization of the child in the country of alien grown-ups. The stories are also models of this vital process of transformation, itself a vital element in each of them. As well as being models of experience for Matia the child and mirrors of experience for Matia the woman, the stories are also the clues of thread which serve to guide the reader through the verbal and chronological labyrinths of Matia's recollections, along the true path of an essentially simple plot-line; a tale as straight-forward as "The Snow Queen" or "The Little Mermaid" in spite of the rich and complex glamour of events and adventures. Primera memoria, seen in the mirror-model of the tales, becomes just such another tale.

NOTES

[1] Ana María Matute, *Primera memoria* (Barcelona: Ediciones Destino, 1960) 16, 191, 208, passim. English titles of the Hans Christian Andersen stories are those in Hans Christian Andersen, *The Complete Fairy Tales and Stories*, translated from the Danish by Erik Christian Haugaard (Garden City, New York: Doubleday & Company, 1974) xi, xii. All references in the text are to these two editions.

"CUANDO LAS MUJERES QUIEREN A LOS HOMBRES"
MANIFIESTO TEXTUAL DE UNA GENERACION

Carmen Vega Carney
Missouri Southern State College

Entre las diferentes tendencias de la crítica feminista reciente, me interesa lo que Elizabeth Abel en su volumen Writing and Sexual Difference considera la corriente hermenéutica de mayor importancia: la interpretación de textos escritos por mujeres desde una perspectiva femenina.[1] Dentro de este esquema exegético la experiencia de ser mujer se convierte en el eje central tanto de la obra como del análisis literario. Como resumiera Abel, "feminist critical attention has shifted from recovering a lost tradition to discovering the terms of confrontation with the dominant tradition" (Abel 179).

El cuento "Cuando las mujeres quieren a los hombres," de Rosario Ferré, ejemplifica un tipo de narrativa en que una escritora se acerca a situaciones tradicionales en un microcosmo definido, Puerto Rico, desde la perspectiva de un personaje femenino y su doble también femenino.[2] Si tomamos como punto de partida de nuestro estudio la manera en que la autora a través de su texto se enfrenta y desafía una tradición social y literaria, este trabajo representa un estudio crítico feminista dentro de la definición que Abel propone.[3]

Al acercarnos a la nueva narrativa puertorriqueña, a la que pertenece Rosario Ferré, nos encontramos de inmediato con una innovación de alcance mayor: la presencia de la mujer como forjadora de pautas literarias. Las mujeres, al tomar la iniciativa en la formación de arquetipos literarios, han ido más allá de la creación de una tradición paralela a la establecida por los escritores masculinos.[4] Nos hallamos ahora ante voces femeninas que le imparten autenticidad y fijación en la historia literaria no sólo a expresiones femeninas, sino a la literatura boricua en general.[5] Esto lo logran precisamente mediante la confrontación con las corrientes que imperan en todos los frentes de la sociedad en que se mueven. Esta nueva narrativa puertorriqueña surge a partir de los años setenta con los cuentos escritos por varias mujeres, entre ellas: Magali García Ramis, Ana Lydia Vega, Carmen Lugo Filippi y Rosario Ferré.[6] Durante los mismos años Rosario Ferré se destaca como la voz principal de la vanguardia feminista y publica en 1976 una colección de narraciones de primer orden: Papeles de Pandora.[7] Los nuevos narradores, tanto mujeres como hombres, exploran a través del lenguaje regiones prohibidas de la cultura puertorriqueña. De esta experimentación surge una variedad lingüística, ecléctica y subversiva que pretende descubrir la profunda y fundamental identidad del puertorriqueño.[8] Como resumiera Ivette López, "uno de los rasgos más contundentes de esta nueva narrativa es la doble búsqueda [mediante] la recopilación de elementos de nuestra identidad que provienen tanto de la realidad observable como de las estructuras ocultas" (2). La narrativa femenina reciente presenta una pluralidad de personajes femeninos que carecen de la perspectiva abstracta tan característica de la cuentística anterior.[9] Estas mujeres revelan "conflictos de clases sociales, choques culturales e ideológicos, imágenes de la psicología del colonizado, la mitología femenina y la relación amo sirviente" desde situaciones específicas (López 2). Ellas hablan de sí mismas desde sí mismas. La interpretación y concepción masculina del ente femenino que es otro apartado y separado, diferente pero arquetípico, queda destruido mediante un autorretrato del objeto imaginado. La respuesta de estas escritoras, "nuevas Pandoras literarias," como las llamara Ivette López, inicia un mundo narrativo en que se enlazan "la pasión por revelar, afirmar y denunciar los signos sociales de la vida puertorriqueña" (López 2). A esto habría que añadir el deseo por destruir y desacralizar altares sagrados de la cultura femenina y de la sociedad en general. El acto de subversión comienza por el lenguaje y se desborda e incluye las reglas que ordenan no sólo la relación hombre-mujer, social y sexual, sino también los ritos establecidos considerados falsos y por lo tanto inútiles. Esta tendencia aparentemente destructiva, contiene en sí la potencialidad de la construcción de modelos de expresión más afines al dialecto social puertorriqueño. La retórica de la subversión define un estilo literario.

Rosario Ferré en su colección Papeles de Pandora, impone un sistema literario que se aleja de la tradición narrativa anterior. No es nada extraño que en contraste a la dogmática y artificial manera de arreglar el mundo femenino por parte de los escritores de esa época, aparezca la prosa de Rosario Ferré y sus secuaces que comienzan a desarreglar el universo narrativo puertorriqueño a partir de los años setenta. La nueva prosa de Rosario Ferré crea una erosión de los significantes, o como ha dicho Diana Vélez en referencia a Papeles de Pandora, esa nueva prosa "points to the decentering of signifiers."[10] Esa descentralización a la que se refiere Vélez expresa la erosión de los tabúes masculinos concernientes al sexo y a la lengua. La lengua al desenmascararse, desviste también al ser y deja al desnudo la humanidad reprimida.[11] La autora agrupa en su colección, crónicas sociales de periódicos conocidos en la isla, cartas, letras de canciones populares, y citas y fragmentos de otros textos. Esta serie diversa permite examinar los mitos femeninos desde variados ángulos. El lector, presagio si es lectora, comparte con la escritora el enfado que produce la lectura de esos recortes que presentan imágenes femeninas arquetípicas. Al estar fuera de su medio, la crónica social, las cartas y las canciones, conspiran para denunciar un orden social anticuado e injusto. En Papeles de Pandora, con el ciclo narrativo titulado La bella durmiente, la trayectoria del desvestir a la humanidad la recorre una mujer. A través del cambio de niña protegida y reprimida emocional y sexualmente, a mujer que pretende crear su propio destino, Rosario Ferré denuncia la burguesía puertorriqueña y pone al descubierto un mundo que se concibe enfermo precisamente porque se rige por un orden, o sistema de mitos, inventado por los hombres.

El cuento "Cuando las mujeres quieren a los hombres," incluido en Papeles de Pandora, ejemplifica la determinación de la autora por transgredir una tradición literaria. Este cuento además de ser el más evocador y mejor construido de la colección, representa un tipo de manifiesto que recoge las preocupaciones estéticas e íntimas que se revelarán en otra parte de la obra de Rosario Ferré. En este marco interpretativo de la estética de la confrontación, observamos con claridad la necesidad de la autora de invertir el orden social que distinguiera la narrativa que precedió su grupo generacional. En el cuento la autora nos introduce un mundo femenino desde el punto de vista femenino, y mediante un discurso doble presenta la herencia social y cultural de dos mujeres de clases sociales distintas y opuestas, convertidas en víctimas de un mismo hombre. El conflicto no se reduce a un triángulo amoroso, como superficialmente podríamos suponer, sino que explora la psicología de estas dos mujeres a la luz de conflictos sociales de mayor profundidad. A lo largo de la narración el texto aduce a los aspectos sociales y raciales que separan y confunden a las mujeres y sus discursos dramáticos:

> Nosotras, tu querida y tu mujer, siempre hemos sabido que debajo de cada dama de sociedad se oculta una prostituta. . . . Porque nosotras siempre hemos sabido que cada prostituta es una dama en potencia, anegada en la nostalgia de una casa blanca como una paloma que nunca tendrá. . . . Porque nosotras, Isabel Luberza e Isabel la Negra, en nuestra pasión por ti, Ambrosio, desde el comienzo de los siglos, nos habíamos estado acercando, nos habíamos estado santificando la una a la otra sin darnos cuenta, purificándonos de todo aquello que nos definía, a una como prostituta y a otra como dama de sociedad. . . . Isabel Luberza recogiendo dinero para restaurar los leones de yeso de la plaza que habían dejado de echar agua de colores por la boca, o Isabel la Negra,

> preparando su cuerpo para recibir el semen de
> los niños ricos, de los hijos de los patrones
> amigos tuyos. . . . (27-28)

El título del cuento se deriva de una forma popular musical, la plena, cuya posición de honor en el folklore puertorriqueño no quita que la identifiquemos como música de origen obscuro. La letra de la plena recoge y celebra eventos locales e internacionales, y su ritmo alegre y repetitivo se presta para el baile. Durante sus comienzos en la ciudad de Ponce en Puerto Rico, se bailaba en el barrio pobre y en los arrabales urbanos y más tarde pasó a ser parte del folklore isleño. Aunque las mujeres del relato pertenecen a clases sociales distintas, clases marcadas además por el elemento racial ya que una es blanca y la otra es negra, la plena rompe con la diferencia esencial: la plena las nivela: "Cuando las mujeres quieren a los hombres/ Cogen cuatro velas y se las prenden/ por los rincones." Esa versión, una de las más conocidas, viene a la mente de inmediato al leer el título del cuento. En el complejo dramático las mujeres quedan niveladas e igualadas por el testamento de Ambrosio: "Fue cuando tú te moriste, Ambrosio, y nos dejaste a cada una la mitad de toda tu herencia" (26). El poder de Ambrosio sobre las dos mujeres borra las diferencias culturales. El acto de prender velas, o cualquier otro truco parecido para atraer y mantener la atención de un hombre, tiene su contrapartida en el rito refinado de la esposa. El culto al hombre las iguala:

> Comencé a colocar diariamente la servilleta
> dentro del aro de plata, junto a tu plato, a
> echarle gotas de limón al agua de tu copa, a
> asolear yo misma tu ropa sobre planchas
> ardientes de zinc. Colocaba sobre tu cama las
> sábanas todavía tibias de sol bebido, blancas y
> suaves bajo la palma de la mano como un muro de
> cal, esparciéndolas siempre al revés para luego
> doblarlas al derecho y desplegar así, para
> deleitarte cuando te acostabas . . . (41)

La letra de la plena no sólo aparece como intertexto implícito, sino que la autora la incorpora en la narración: "Cualquiera diría que hiciste lo que hiciste Ambrosio a propósito, por el placer de vernos prenderte cuatro velas y ponértelas por los rincones para ver quién ganaba" (26).

La acción del relato se concentra en dos mujeres cuyos discursos se alternan y se funden en uno. Las dos mujeres, la amante y la esposa, viven supeditadas a la voluntad de un hombre. El discurso acusatorio y de desate, al desarrollarse presenta al desnudo la interioridad de esas mujeres. Los nombres de las mujeres, Isabel Luberza e Isabel la Negra son tomados de la vida real. Isabel Luberza, alias Isabel la Negra, fue un personaje muy conocido en la isla cuyo nombre sugiere el prostíbulo por haber sido propietaria de uno durante largos años. La autora toma este personaje, ahora como la plena parte del folklore popular, y lo convierte en el eje central del relato. En el cuento Isabel Luberza es la esposa blanca, y su rival lo encarna la mapriora y prostituta, Isabel la Negra. El tomar a Isabel la Negra y su famoso y cachendoso "Elizabeth Dancing Hall" como objetos del relato representa en sí un acto subversivo. De ahí en adelante los altares se vienen abajo. La mujer, una en la historia, dos en la ficción del cuento, personifica dos caras de unas realidades que convergen. Esta doble dimensión o doble interpretación recoge una de las ideas principales que fluyen a lo largo de este cuento. El emblema del doble nos entrega la lucha íntima por liberar la identidad propia de la mujer, de tal forma que se integren los aspectos sexuales con los espirituales. La Isabel Luberza "bizcochera, tejedora de frisitas y botines de perlé color de nube," se contrasta con una imagen palesiana, divisa retórica de la poesía negrista: "Isabel la tembandumba de la Quimbamba, contoneando su carne de guingambó por la encendida calle antillana . . . " (29). La antilogía continúa entre la imagen blanca, pura y burguesa de la esposa, y la de la mujer erótica de piel obscura: "Isabel Segunda, la reina de España . . . Isabel, la Perla negra del Sur, la Reina de Saba, the Queen of Chiva, la Chivas Regal, la Tongolele, la Salomé . . . descalabradas por todas las paredes, por todas las calles, esta confusión entre ella y ella, o entre ella y yo, o entre yo y yo . . . " (29). Los intertextos bíblicos, culturales y populares, reanudan la referencia a la integración de los opuestos. La culminación de la técnica dramática de la confluencia y fusión de las dos mujeres se logra cuando la mujer blanca, la esposa, quiere ser negra para satisfacer sus fantasías y de esa manera poder poseer a Ambrosio completamente:

> Empecé . . . a cerrar la sombrilla cuando salía a pasear por la calle para que la piel se me abrasara del sol. Esa piel que yo siempre he protegido con manga larga y cuello alto para poder exhibirla en los bailes porque es prueba fidedigna de mi pedigree, de que en mi familia somos blancos por los cuatro costados. . . .
> Exponiéndome así por ella al que dirán de las gentes, al has visto lo amercochadita que se está poniendo sutanita con la edad, la pobre, dicen que eso requinta, que al que tiene raja siempre le sale al final. (42)

Isabel la Negra quería poseer la casa de Ambrosio, añoraba "sentarse detrás de aquél balcón de balaustres plateados . . ." (33). Se imaginaba blanca y rubia, como las señoritas que podían amar a Ambrosio:

> Pero el ansia de poseer aquella casa, . . . respondía a una nostalgia profunda que se le recrudecía con los años, al deseo de sustituir, [sic] aunque fuera en su vejez, el recuerdo de aquella visión que había tenido de niña, . . . la visión de un hombre vestido de hilo blanco, de pie en aquel balcón, junto a una mujer rubia, increíblemente bella, vestida con traje de lamé plateado. (33)

Las dos secuencias narrativas en que se alternan los discursos de las mujeres convergen hacia el final en una tirada uniforme, en la que la esposa anuncia la final reunificación de los dos entes femeninos. El pelo de la prostituta no es "una nube de humo rebelde encrespado alrededor de la cabeza, sino delgado y dúctil, . . . la piel ya no negra, sino blanca, derramada sobre sus hombros como leche de cal ardiente . . ." (44). La transformación con la que cierra el cuento utiliza el esmalte de uñas que ambas mujeres usan, Cherries Jubilee, como una ecuación patética de la igualdad. A la esposa, al efectuarse la evolución hacia la otra, se le revela su íntimo ser:

> [T]ongoneándome yo ahora para atrás y para alante sobre mis tacones rojos, por los cuales baja, lenta y silenciosa como una marea, esa sangre que había comenzado a subirme por la base de las uñas desde hace tanto tiempo, mi sangre esmaltada de Cherries Jubilee. (44)

Al nivel textual podemos alegar que la búsqueda de la armonía de los opuestos surge paralela a la búsqueda de la armonía, en la sociedad y en las formas lingüísticas de ese medio:

> Isabel Luberza la Dama Auxiliar de la Cruz Roja o Elizabeth the Black, la presidenta de los Young Lords, afirmando desde su tribuna que ella era la prueba en cuerpo y sangre de que no existía diferencia entre los de Puerto Rico y los de Nueva York puesto que en su carne todos se habían unido. . . . Isabel la Negra, la única novia de Brincaicógelo Maruca, la única que besó sus pies deformes y se los lavó con su llanto, la única que bailó junto a los niños al son de su pregón Heshybarskissesmilkyweys . . . (28-29)

El texto inicia, o augura, la confrontación al "asedio del idioma" mediante la creación desde la lengua popular "viva." La lengua "viva," tanto oral como escrita que prevalece en el Puerto Rico de hoy, se nutre de una pluralidad de modelos locales y extranjeros:

> De ahora en adelante nada de fukinato de malamuerte, del mete y saca por diez pesos, los reyes que van y vuelven y nosotras siempre pobres. Porque mientras el Dancing Hall esté en el arrabal, por más maravilloso que sea, nadie me va a querer pagar más de diez pesos la noche. . . . Alquilaré unas cuantas gebas jóvenes que me ayuden y a cincuenta pesos el foqueo o nacarile del oriente. Se acabaron en esta casa las putas viejas, se acabó la marota seca, los clítores arrugados como pepitas de china o irritados como vertederos de sal, se acabaron los coitos en catres de cucarachas, se acabó el tienes hambre alza la pata y lambe, esta va a ser una casa de sún sún doble nada más. (37-38)

Este texto, al igual que muchas otras narraciones contemporáneas en la isla, funciona como un archivo cultural y lingüístico en donde se recoge una multiplicidad de variados aspectos de la lengua y la cultura.

La intención de la autora de crear desde la lengua "viva" se evidencia en el catálogo lingüístico que presenta. La lengua popular, pese a su insistencia en imágenes que se inspiran en los órganos sexuales se incorpora a fórmulas literarias de primer orden: la esposa se considera "tabernáculo tranquilo de tu pene rosado que . . . siempre [lleva] adentro, un roto cosido y bien apretado con hilo cien para los demás . . ." (42). El orgasmo del marido en la esposa se describe como "casi puro, tan limpio como el de una mariposa, tan diferente a los que tienes con ella . . . un orgasmo fértil, que depositó en mi vientre la semilla sagrada que llevará tu nombre . . ." (41).

Vocablos populares y crudos, considerados obscenos o de mal gusto, tales como, "la crica multitudinaria," "su culo monumental," o el acto sexual oral, se usan de manera explícita y en gran número:

> [A]rrodillándomeles al frente como una sacerdotisa oficiando un rito sagrado, el pelo enceguecíéndome los ojos, bajando la cabeza hasta sentir el pene estuchado como un lirio dentro de mi garganta, teniendo cuidado de no

apretar demasiado mis piernas podadoras de hombres, un cuidado infinito de no apretar demasiado los labios, la boca devoradora insaciable de pistilos de loto. (35-36)

En este cuento el conflicto de las dos mujeres sirve de vehículo para confrontar una situación insostenible: al nivel del complejo dramático la "unidad familiar" en donde el hombre ejerce su prerrogativa de la infidelidad que ocurre impune; al nivel del texto es insostenible continuar la creación asediada por un legado cultural que resulta inútil para exponer la realidad isleña de hoy. La autora elimina el triángulo amoroso al fundir a las dos mujeres en una, y abandona el desenlace en que la prostituta se redime. La autora, aunque concibe la prostitución como una forma de liberación, expone y sostiene que la total soberanía se encuentra en la fusión final de los opuestos: "esta confusión entre ella y ella, o entre ella y yo, o entre yo y yo . . ." (29). En el texto se descartan los modelos en donde la lengua pura y correctiva pretendía compensar y reparar la lengua contaminada por corrientes extranjeras o vocablos propios del elemento popular. "Era cierto que ahora ella era una self made woman," "mariconcitos," "santoletitos con el culo astillado de porcelana," "San Jierro y Santa Daga," representan un mínimo de las muchas expresiones propias de un léxico enriquecido con discursos provenientes de varias tradiciones culturales. La fuerza que atrae a las mujeres es el amor por el mismo hombre; ellas le dan la bienvenida a la confrontación y de rivales se convierten en aliadas. La lengua confronta las formas establecidas por las generaciones anteriores mediante la destrucción de los tabúes verbales. El uso explícito del vocabulario de la prostituta, sacarle "los quesos a los niñitos ricos," "el pene estuchado . . . dentro de mi garganta," "metiendo tu lengua dentro de mi vulva sudorosa," "coitos de coitre," rechaza los eufemismos poéticos y anquilosados de la retórica de rescate característica de épocas más conservadoras.

La subversión lingüística y cultural que brota de la obra de Rosario Ferré, como consecuencia de la experiencia femenina en la isla, rompe con una invención literaria y cultural iniciada por los escritores masculinos. El sentido de misión de Isabel la Negra, liberadora de la sexualidad, explica la intención de ruptura total que la autora manifiesta en su narración: "el hombre más macho no es el que enloquece a la mujer sino el que tiene el valor de dejarse enloquecer, . . . no está bien que las niñas bien se monten encima y galopen por su propio gusto . . ." (36). Rosario Ferré al salir en defensa de la mujer que monta, nos entrega una opción en cuanto a estilos y temas literarios específicos de su género sexual y rechaza abiertamente una forma de vida en la isla en que la mujer se redujo al archi-discutido objeto del placer masculino. Pero las crisis, tanto lingüísticas como sociales, han dejado una huella indeleble en los escritores que como Rosario Ferré inician su obra literaria en los años setenta.

"Cuando las mujeres quieren a los hombres" encarna un cuento que simboliza el derrotero estético de una tradición literaria, por su tema, el tratamiento poético, la estructura y principalmente, la lengua. El "escándalo" que podría producir un cuento como éste no resulta sólo del texto en sí, sino de que Rosario Ferré, procedente de un contexto social y cultural típico de la burguesía más empedernida, declarara su independencia psíquica y personal por medio de un acto revolucionario: la escritura. Tal vez la mayor contribución de "Cuando las mujeres quieren a los hombres" a la renovación de la fuerza creadora de una generación, sea, calcando a Enrico Mario Santí, "la dramatización del cuestionamiento de la identidad misma como fuente de autoridad, sea ésta textual o política."[12] Este cuestionamiento se logra mediante la confrontación con el sistema de mitos que ha regido hasta el presente la vida de la mujer.

NOTES

[1] Elizabeth Abel, "Editor's Introduction," *Critical Inquiry* 8.2 (1981): 179.

[2] El cuento "Cuando las mujeres quieren a los hombres," de Rosario Ferré apareció en *Papeles de Pandora* (México: Joaquín Mortiz, 1976). Las citas del texto serán tomadas de esta edición.

[3] Joel Hancock resume los diferentes acercamientos de crítica feminista reciente en su artículo "Woman's Image in Poniatowska's *Hasta no verte Jesús mío*: The Remaking of the Image of Woman," *Hispania* 66 (September 1983): 353-358. Según él "among the most prominent methods are the sociological, particularly Marxist; structuralist, with all its ramifications; formalist; psychological; and thematic"(353). En sus notas refiere al lector a dos trabajos importantes: "Some Notes on Defining a 'Feminist Poetics,'" *Critical Inquiry* 2.1 (Autumn 1975), escrito por Annette Kolodny; y el artículo de Elaine Showalter, "Towards a Feminist Poetics" que se encuentra en la colección editada por Mary Jacobus, *Women Writing and Writing About Men* (New York: Barnes and Noble, 1979). Sin embargo no incluye los trabajos del excelente volumen editado por Elizabeth Abel del cual hago mención en este ensayo.

[4] Edna Acosta Belén resume la caracterización femenina en la literatura puertorriqueña de las generaciones anteriores, especialmente entre los escritores de los años cincuenta, en la siguiente manera: "La presencia de una imagen negativa de la mujer no es el resultado de un esfuerzo conciente [sic] de parte de los escritores de la Generación del 50, sino que esta es expresión de una particular visión del mundo en que la mujer se acomoda, o no, a ciertos patrones y valores tradicionales. Cuando lo hace, es que generalmente representa algunas formas del deterioro moral o social, especialmente cuando se le presenta en el contexto de la sociedad moderna. Las imágenes de la mujer que se encuentran en la literatura de los escritores de la Generación del 50 son generalmente estereotipadas o desfavorables; imágenes que reflejan valores ideológicos de dominación masculina y subyugación femenina." Acosta Belén, *La mujer en la sociedad puertorriqueña* 155-156.

[5] Una discusión bastante completa sobre el tema de las narradoras recientes de la isla se encuentra en la tesis doctoral de Ivette López, "Puerto Rico y las narradoras del 70," Yale, 1977.

[6]Efraín Barradas simplifica la contribución de las nuevas narradoras de la siguiente manera: "En nuestros días, en cambio, es imposible descartar y, menos aún ignorar, la corriente femenina-feminista en nuestro cuento. Rosario Ferré, Ana Lydia Vega, Mayra Montero, Carmen Lugo Filippi, Magali García Ramis, entre otras, comienzan a utilizar incidentes de la vida de la mujer boricua de distintas clases sociales para denunciar a través de sus cuentos la opresión machista que sufre la mujer en nuestra cultura. Esta corriente anti-machista también les sirve a algunos cuentistas--pienso especialmente en Manuel Ramos Otero--para presentar otra variante o perspectiva de esa misma opresión sexista. En general, una de las contribuciones mayores de los nuevos narradores--especialmente de las narradoras--es esta denuncia de nuestro machismo." "Palabras Apalabradas: Prólogo para una antología de cuentistas puertorriqueños de hoy," Apalabramiento: Cuentos puertorriqueños de hoy (Hanover: Ediciones del Norte, 1983) xix. Véase también, Edna Acosta Belén, "Ideología e imágenes de la mujer en la literatura puertorriqueña contemporánea," La mujer en la sociedad puertorriqueña (Río Piedras: Ediciones Huracán, 1980) 136-139, y Juan Angel Silén, La generación de escritores del setenta (Río Piedras: Editorial Cultural, 1977). Para una reciente discusión sobre la narrativa contemporánea en oposición a la narrativa de los escritores de la generación del 50, véase el artículo de Juan Gelpí, "Desorden frente a purismo: La nueva narrativa frente a René Marqués," Literatures in Transition: The Many Voices of the Caribbean Area/A Symposium, ed. Rose Minc (College Park: Hispamérica and Montclair State College, 1982) 177-178.

[7]Véase nota número tres.

[8]Ivette López, "Puerto Rico: las nuevas narradoras y la identidad cultural," ponencia leída en Twentieth Century Literature Conference, Louisville, 1979, p. 13.

[9]Véase el estudio de Acosta Belén.

[10]Diana Vélez, "Power and the Text: Rebellion in Rosario Ferré's Papeles de Pandora," MMLA 17.1 (Spring 1984).

[11]Vicente Urbistondo, "Sobre el machismo en la narrativa hispanoamericana," Papeles de Son Armadans Año XXIII, 90.268: 10.

[12]Enrico Mario Santí, "El sexo de la escritura," Revista de la Universidad de México 23 (Marzo 1983).

EROTICISM IN OLGA SAVARY´S REPERTORIO SELVAGEM:
THE STRUGGLE FOR FULL FREEDOM

Joyce Carlson-Leavitt
University of New Mexico

With the publication of Repertório Selvagem: Poesia Erótica[1] this year Olga Savary celebrates her thirty-fifth year of marriage to poetry.[2] As an adolescent she began publishing poetry in newspapers and magazines, and she continued throughout her years of marriage and childbearing. Many of these poems were collected in her first published book of poetry, Espelho Provisório.[3] Since then she has brought out three other books of poetry and an anthology of what she considers her best poems: Sumidouro,[4] Altaonda,[5] Magma,[6] and Natureza Viva: Seleta dos Melhores Poemas de Olga Savary.[7] Savary startled the literary world with the 1984 publication of Magma, the first book of erotic poetry written by a woman in Brazil.[8] Repertório continues development of this theme, for it too is almost completely devoted to an exploration of sexuality from the point of view of its female author.

Repertório is divided into several sections ("Zôo," "A Bela e a Fera," "Ah King Kong," "Hora do Recreio," "O Dia da Caça," "Berço Espléndido," "O Coração do Fruto," "Carne Viva," and "Magma") in which the reader senses a progression in the poet´s treatment of eroticism, culminating in "Magma," now the final section of the larger work. Here a picture of utter sexuality unfolds, full embrace replaces a certain earlier tentativeness, and a gradual release from conflicts leads to an uninhibited expression of the total enjoyment of female sexuality. This is not a lock-step progression, with each section portraying only a certain theme in the movement toward full erotic expression, but rather a presentation of certain tendencies: Bestiality, Androgyny, Mythical Sex, Telluric Sex, and Geminine (conflicted) Character. In the earlier sections such as "Zôo" erotic love [9] is not generally portrayed as freely and fully as in "Magma." The poems in earlier sections contain more analytical explorations of the nature of love than expression of the enjoyment of it; the portrayal of love is rather abstract, as opposed to the intense erotic images of "Magma." In the "A bela e a Fera" and "Ah King Kong" sections the poet explores the role of bestiality in erotic love, with all its concomittant horror-versus-ecstasy tensions. "Hora do Recreio" moves away from savage imagery to descriptions of sex in terms of nature, water, and ripe fruits. The poems of the "O Dia de Caça" section emphasize the conflicting quality of the lyric speaker´s love, her indecision and ambivalence concerning the aerial and the telluric in her nature. While

"Berço Espléndido" (Splendid Cradle) tends toward a fuller expression of erotic love, varying tensions are portrayed, such as that between the woman of the past and the present, between the woman arising from the land or from the water. "O Coração do Fruto" is closer to "Magma" with more descriptions of sexual union. Fruit and water images abound, and a feeling of the archetypal nature of erotic love is more prevalent. In the penultimate section, "Carne Viva," the poet moves to more self-examination, to an exploration of what it means to be a woman in conflict, to a comparison of the old and new sexual woman.

Careful reading of Repertório reveals that "Magma" is the culmination of the lyric speaker's struggle to become a new, totally sexual woman, free from the strictures of the past, able to follow her instincts and participate actively in erotic pleasure. In "Magma" and in some poems from the earlier parts of Repertório the speaker is a female at one with the universe, enjoying her sensuality and natural eroticism:

> Assim para ti me faço: primeiro musa.
> Depois, votiva caça e caçadora, fetichista,
> e até--por que não? já que sou também cruel--
> sádica e masoquista, ogra lúdica,
> saltimbanco, acrobata, ousada feiticeira tímida,
> luxuria insolente, alquimista, poeta,
> menina de novo, adolescente,
> fêmea, animal espléndido, mulher.
> ("Neputira, Paem [tua amada, tudo] "[10] Polivalência 110)

> [Thus for you I make myself: first, muse. /
> Then, votive prey or hunter, fetishist, / and
> even--and why not? since I am also cruel-- /
> sadist and masochist, playful ogress, / jug-
> gler, acrobat, daring timid sorceress, / inso-
> lent lasciviousness, alchemist, poet / a girl
> again, adolescent, / female, splendid animal,
> woman.][11]

> Pelos braços da manhã é que escorro
> tendo no corpo o cantar do dia.
> De branco chegas como um noivo, estou
> também de branco ritualizando a espera.
> O que de mim fica é o procurar-me
> e o encontrar de baixo do teus flancos.
> ("Nome," M 49)

> [It is through the arms of morning that I trick-
> le / holding in my body the song of the day. /

In white you arrive like a bridegroom, I am /
also in white, ritualizing the wait. / What
remains of me is to search for myself / and
find myself underneath your flanks.]

She is able to become one with the land and the sea, to sense harmony with the universe:

> De posse da intimidade da água
> e da intimidade da terra,
> a animais vorazes é a que sabíamos.
>
> Amor é com quem me deito e deixo montar
> minhas coxas em forma de forquilha e onde
> amor abre caminho pelas minhas águas.
> ("Nome," M 37)

[From possession of the intimacy of water / and
from intimacy of land, / we tasted like voracious animals. / Love is with whom I lie down
and whom I let mount / my thighs in the shape
of a forked stick and where / love opens the
way through my waters.]

Although "Magma" contains only suggestions of the lyric speaker's struggle to arrive at the exuberant, fiery sexual union recreated in this final section of Repertório, parts of Savary's earlier works and the rest of Repertório reveal a lyric speaker who is exploring different aspects of her own sensuality, examining her own attitudes toward these, and attempting to reject societal limitations. It has not been easy for her to leave behind the stereotypical virgin, prostitute, and pure mother images of her culture and become a free sensual woman, close to her wild nature, in full possession of her sexual powers.

The conflicts with which the speaker must struggle to become sexually free are expressed in Repertório in several ways. Throughout the work, there are tensions between opposing forces, juxtapositions of opposite images, such as those of horror-versus-ecstasy in love, or those of aerial-versus-telluric tendencies within the speaker herself. At times the poetic "I" speaks of her own divided personality, her geminine character (reflecting her birth under the sign of the twins), comparing the new free woman with the old inhibited one. On other occasions she explores fully, and then partially rejects, the attractions of bestial love. Often the speaker is androgynous, the male and female parts of her nature sometimes being in conflict and other times blending into a sexual expression which is beyond the usual male/female distinctions.

The mythological view of the female as pursued and dominated by beasts is explored fully in the "Ah King Kong" and "O Dia da Caça" sections and only suggested in "Magma." It is as though the lyric speaker were trying out for herself this vision of sex and then later rejecting the extreme forms presented in these sections. In "Lavra" (Tilling--or mining--the Land) (M 32) and "E Permitido Jogar Comida aos Animais" (Throwing Food to the Animals is Permitted) and in her short stories, "Ah, King Kong" and "O Olho Dourado" (The Golden Eye) the speaker's lover is clearly a beast, "the beast who lies in wait for me" (147) or a human lover who has "muscles of wild beast," (150) and the erotic union takes place in a dark forest (M 25).

In these sections the lyric speaker pushes to the limit her animal nature. Not only does she want to be made love to, almost violated, by the bestial, yet attractive King Kong, but also in one poem she herself is King Kong, filled with his male sensual animal power ("Auá" quem , 47). She even becomes a vampire, drinking up her lover's blood of life ("Iraqui" [bebida inebriante] 70) or an animal clawing the back of her lover ("O Dia da Caça" 69). Even here where the speaker seems to be trying out a complete freeing of her animal nature, she only rarely accepts fully this part of her being. Usually she reveals intense conflict through the use of images of horror, cruelty, and danger in juxtaposition with those of ecstasy, pleasure, and sensuality ("Ah King Kong" 48).

In Repertório this theme of the tensions between pleasure and pain in bestial love takes on various forms. In "Profissão de Fé," in the section "A Bela e a Fera," the theme is portrayed in terms of images of smell and taste. The secret god of love within us is revealed by "a smell of bitter orange / the aroma of jasmin." The body, "machine of horror and happiness," eats the lover's flesh, tastes the salt of his saliva, and absorbs his smell of ripe figs and rotten "genipapo," finally becoming a tiger or a goat. Still, in spite of--or perhaps, because of--the threat of impending horror, the speaker convinces herself that becoming a beast/lover is worth the risk:

> De virar fera corre-se o risco
> mas antes abocanhar no salto,
> tigre ou bode, teu focinho
> do que o risco de virar pedra,
> perder os ossos, dobrar a espinha. (29)

> [Of turning into a wild beast one runs the risk/
> but rather seize in the jaws during the leap/
> tiger or goat, your muzzle / than to risk
> turning into stone, / losing bones, bending

over the spine.]

In several poems of the "Ah King Kong" section this conflict between joy and horror in bestiality is presented with an irony and humor often present in Repertório. Much of the work is tongue-in-cheek, as can be seen in the titles of these poems. For example, "King Kong" (40) recreates the lyric speaker's seduction by a laughing, whistling, grunting, and shaking King Kong who eyes his prey with a fixed, distant gaze--a humorous, exaggerated description of an animalistic Don Juan. In "Jaula Aberta no 77º Andar" (Open Cage on the 77th Floor) (41) the dream of union with King Kong, of exciting the animalistic sexuality, "the forbidden fear / of mysterious grapes stepped on in secret," takes place in a cage on the seventy-seventh floor of an impossibly tall (for Brazil) apartment building and culminates in King Kong's placing of a wedding band on the bitch lover's finger. "King Kong" (42) presents King Kong as a humanized beast who loses his power when he leaves the jungle and faces the public in the city. Clearly these are humorous juxtapositions which ironically mock the conventions of love.

In the sections of Repertório where the poet moves away from exploration of bestial love, the conflict abates as the lyric speaker comes to accept herself as a sexual being in a fuller sense than that of animals freely exercising their sexual instincts. Although the bestial part of love is present in "Magma" to a limited extent, almost as an accepted part of erotic love, the juxtaposition of horror and terror with ecstasy is rarely mentioned. For example, in "Acomodação do Desejo II" "ecstasy and terror of the gods" refers to the lovers' bodies and not to the thought of becoming an animal or having intercourse with an animal. Although they make love in the wild gardens, the lovers are also in "a bed close to the clouds." The love-making is more telluric and archetypal than bestial, with the magnitude of love and sex in the context of the whole universe inspiring the terror and ecstasy, not just fear of latent bestiality:

> Dos que se amam na cama rente às nuvens,
> nestas jardins ferozes, vê-se que amanhecem.
> Nela anca e espáduas eram como água.
> Nele tudo semelhante à terra. Seus corpos:
> êxtase e terror dos deuses.
> Que o comova o silêncio de seu corpo morno,
> o fragor mudo do seu corpo desabado.
> E que ela se abra como se abre uma urna
> que se abre não revelando o conteúdo. (M 46)

[Of those who make love in the close to the clouds, / in those feral gardens, one sees that they awaken. / On her, rump and shoulders were like water. / On him, all similar to the earth. Their bodies: / ecstasy and terror of the gods. / Let him be moved by the silence of his tepid body, / the mute crashing noise of his caved-in body. / And that she opens as if one opens an urn / which opens without revealing its content.]

The dominant tone of "Magma" is that of joyful giving of oneself to pleasure. Usually the lyric speaker allows herself to be seduced, happily opening up herself--her garden, her waters, her ripe fruit--to her lover. Only occasionally as in "Avesso" (Opposite, Reverse Side) (48) does she become the active pursuer, the one who dominates and wounds at the same time as she is dominated and wounded. In earlier sections of <u>Repertório</u> Savary presents more fully this option of being the active, pursuing female. In "Mulher Posta em Uso / Pronta para a Vida" (Woman Put in Use / Ready for Life), in the Berço Espléndido section, both the male and female lovers are desirous participants, while in "Caiçucáua" [amor, amado] the passionate, inflamed female thirstily drinks her lover's waters and calms his passion:

> Meu homem, por mulher que tomarias
> a romper-me os diques, trespassar-me o fosso,
> a conquistar-me as torres e as ameias,
>
> a tomar-me de assalto a fortaleza.
> E o frémito no interior da vulva
> era que nem o sangue a pulsar nas veias.
> ("Mulher Posta em Uso / Pronta para a Vida" 94)
>
> [My man, you would take me for a woman / on breaking my dikes, crossing over my trench, / conquering my towers and my battlements, / on taking my fortress by assault. / And the trembling in the interior of my vulva / just like blood pulsating in my veins.]

In reference to the lyric speaker as active, sometimes destructive pursuer of her prey, it is important to note that Savary uses "caçador" and "caçadora" interchangeably. This indicates a masculinization of the female lover or simply the belief that gender distinctions are unimportant. In either case, the poet is provocatively androgynous, free from the traditional gender separations.

Especially in "Magma," the poet expresses this androgynous point of view in another fashion. Her portrayal of sexual union through the joining of male and female waters is an image which goes beyond the usual representation of male penetration of the female:

> Mar é o nome do meu macho
> meu cavalo e cavaleiro
> que arremete, força, chicoteia
> a fêmea que ele chama de rainha,
> areia.
>
> Mar é um macho como não há nenhum.
> Mar é um macho como não há igual
> - e eu toda água. ("Mar II," M 31)
>
> [Ocean is the name of my male, / my horse and horseman / who incites, forces, whips / the female whom he calls queen, / sand. / Ocean is a male like no other. / Ocean is a male without equal / and I all water.]

The poet's use of the image of joined waters illustrates her general avoidance of explicit words describing male/female anatomy to portray sexual union. Rather, she prefers to create erotic scenes through the use of nature images. In doing this, although the poet usually selects images which clearly show the female lyric speaker opening up to the male, sometimes the poet presents the speaker as the male aggressor. "Vida I" and "Vida II" patently show this difference. In "Vida I" (M 20) the lyric speaker actively searches for the tree/lover (possibly a phallic symbol) so that she can savagely bite the tree's fruits--her usual images for her own sexuality--as if she were biting her lover's "purple flesh." On the other hand, in "Vida II" (M 21) she requests "a spike," "a hanging object," and "a naked dagger" which expand in "aerial foam gardens," "besieging the living form"--all obviously images of the female being penetrated by the male.

In "Lavra" (M 32) the lyric speaker swims in her lover's body against the current as if in a river. Then abruptly, as she is swimming she begins to burn and changes into lava, the poet's symbol for supreme female passion. At the same time, this "war of water" is peace, even though the lover (or burning lava) is a "dagger wounding the heart of the fruit."

Thus in Repertório the lyric speaker moves easily from femaleness to maleness, changes from the female prey into the male hunter, transforms herself from the female lover of King Kong into the male King Kong himself--all clear indications of the lyric speaker's androgyny.[12]

Throughout Repertório the images used in portraying erotic love suggest the poet's exploration of the mythic dimensions of sex. For example, passionate desire is "a secret god within us," ("Profissão de Fé" 29); the waters of lovemaking are archetypal and atemporal; the lover becomes a horse or a centaur ("Terminal," M 23) or a pterodactyl ("Personagem" M 34). Erotic love is often labyrinthian, taking place in deep forests or in secret submerged gardens, reminiscent of the Garden of Eden; the female lover occasionally is a serpent ("Insolencias" 43)--all images with mythic or prehistorical resonances. The mythic and bestial are combined in "Personagem" where the lyric speaker's lover was and is a prehistoric pterodactyl with savage wings. At the same time, the speaker was and is a wild beast who feeds on this birdlike reptile.

This use of the pterodactyl image suggests a vision of sexual love as a return to origins, to a primordial time. The poet reinforces this vision by her constant use of water images, since her use of water can easily represent the beginnings of life. As was seen previously in "Mar II," the speaker's lover is often the atemporal sea which continually washes up on the lover/shore:

> para ti queria estar
> sempre vestida de branco
> como convém a deuses
> tendo na boca o esperma
> de tu brava espuma.
> Violenta ou lentamente o mar
> no seu vai-e-vem pulsante
> ordena vagas me lamberem coxas,
> seu arremesso me cravando
> uma adaga roxa.   ("Mar I," M 30)

[for you I wanted / always to be dressed in white / as befits the gods / having in my mouth the sperm / of your untamed froth. / Violently or slowly the sea / in its pulsating to-and-fro motion / orders the waves to lick my thighs, / its hurling attack thrusting in me / a purple dagger.]

The sexually explicit water images of the "Mar" poems of "Magma" are not present throughout Savary's work. Rather, poems in previous works and earlier sections of Repertório often indicate a transitional use of water images. While they do not represent specifically the sexual union of male and female waters, water is usually associated with erotic love. For example, in "Signo," of the "Berço Espléndido" section, the lyric speaker leaves her natural elements of air and land to become "primitive water" because her lover is water:

> Se a outro pertencia, pertenço agora a este
> signo: da liquedez, do aguaceiro. E a ele
> me entrego, desaguada, sem medir margens,
> unindo a toda esta água do teu signo
> minha água primitiva e desatada. (93)
>
> [If I belonged to another, I belong now to this/
> sign: of liquidity, of the cloudburst. And to
> him / I give myself, drained, without measuring
> borders, / joining to all this water of your
> sign / my primitive and unbound water.]

In "Retrato" (Portrait) (107) of the "O Coração do Fruto" section, the lyric speaker accepts herself as part of the atemporal waters which encompass all life, but this time with clearly sexual connotations because she is the millenial all-encompassing water who has her lover/land on top of her.

Although in "Signo" the lyric speaker claims to have left the land behind, often the land, its forests and its fruits, represent the poet's union with nature, and are part of the rich erotic imagery associated with Savary's poetry.[13] In "Sem Escolha" (Without Choice), of the "Carne Viva" section, the poetic "I" perceives her lover's image in all the varied images of nature. She smells his odor in "the odor of the sea, of fruits and foliage / and of land." His "beautiful and modulated voice," more than being his, "is the perfection of the wind scattering sands." "She who hates [him] and adores [him] and scratches [his] belly, [is his] beloved formed by dance and the high tide." In addition to the nature images, this poem exemplifies Savary's rich portrayal of all the senses, for here almost all senses are represented: hearing, vision, touch, smell, and the kinetic sense of movement.

The sexually responsive female filled with burning lava, magma, ready to flow on full arousal by the male is one of the most intense of the poet's telluric images. In "Ygarapáua" [porto], of the "Carne Viva" section, the sexual source of this "magma in flight" is obvious. Here also are the personal conflicts which the lyric speaker needed to resolve before reaching the erotic plenitude of "Magma." She had to leave behind the societally-imposed false self to become the free female able to enjoy uninhibited sexuality in a way similar to that of a wild animal:

> Vivo embora tenha assassinado
> por graves razões aquela que eu não era.
> A nova mulher, magma em vôo,
> nela me resumo and me construo: fera. (133)
>
> [I live even though I have assassinated / for serious reasons that one which I was not. / The new woman, magma in flight, / in her I sum up myself and I construct myself: wild beast.]

The burning magma of sexual passion which comes from the depths of both the lover and the earth is related to the previously-mentioned images of violence and life. It is associated as well with ripe fruit images which represent sexual passions and satisfactions, as when the purple grapes which the female lover eats become the female ripe fruit which opens up to receive the love:

> É das uvas roxas que abocanho
> em tua boca e em fruto exposto
> que faço meu vinho, meu sangue,
> minha paixão, muso do meu canto
> vindo do fundo da terra,
>
> de fundas furnas e de grutas
> e das fendas submersas
> de onde atocaiado me espias. . . .
> ("Vida," M 50)
>
> [It is from the purple grapes that I devour / in your mouth and in exposed fruit / that I make my wine, my blood, my passion, muse[14] of my song / coming from the depth of the earth, / from deep caverns and grottos / and submerged fissures from which, in ambush, you lie in wait for me.]

In this poem the magma also becomes the lyric speaker's "purple song, / howling from the depths," a song dedicated to her lover, carried in his teeth like a knife. Thus, the poet reinforces the association of erotic love with poetic creation implicit in Savary's statement about her thirty years of marriage to poetry.

That this plenitude of erotic expression did not come easily to the poet is shown in several poems of Repertório where the lyric speaker portrays directly her indecision and conflicts. Besides the aforementioned repulsion/attraction to bestiality, the speaker has other conflicts, many stemming from what she sees as her geminine character. For the poetic "I" her being geminine means that she is indecisive and multifaceted, pulled in different directions at once.[15] "Geminiana" (114) shows the evolution of the speaker from a fugitive from love to an active lover who enjoys being both the pursuer and the pursued. The woman who always ran away from the snare of love discovers the pleasure of being captured by her lover. On other occasions, the geminine poetic voice is so torn by opposites that she does not even know who she is. "Geminiana," (126) which is based upon the piling up of opposing images, shows this clearly. Heaven and Hell, day and night, heart and mind, are simultaneously present in the speaker's soul. Still, through all the confusion, burns the clear fact of love. Gradually the speaker comes to accept a love which brings unity to her divided soul:

> Certeza alguma nunca tive.
> Sei tudo do inferno,
> alguma coisa do paraíso.
>
> Desconhecida de mim, sou
> não dupla mas múltipla
> e uma.
> ....
> O muro crescendo
> todo ao redor, não sei
> se sou noite ou dia.
>
> Mas o amor ardia. (126)

[I never had any certainty. / I know all about hell, / and something about paradise. / I am unknown to myself / I am not double but multiple / and one. / ... / The wall growing all around, I do not know / if I am night or day. / But Love was burning.]

Geminine indecisiveness is shown by other deep conflicts, conflicts which are present in Savary's previous works. As we have seen, the lyric speaker is deeply telluric, pulled strongly by the terrestial forces of the land and the sea. At the same time, she wants to fly off into the air, soaring freely with her poetic imagination. "Sumidouro" (Sinkhole), the first poem of "Magma" and the final poem of <u>Sumidouro</u>, shows this geminine tension:

> Talhe da audácia
> e da covardia, meu rei e vassalo,
> engolir de asa,
> fartura de água
> na árvore da vida,

205

> na terra me tens
> com os pés bem plantados.
> Aqui nado, aqui vôo,
> telúrica e alada. (M 15)
>
> [Form of audacity / and of cowardice, my king and vassal, / swallowing of wing, / satiety with water / in the tree of life, / on land you have me / with my feet well implanted. / Here I swim, here I fly, / terrestial and winged.]

Other conflicts appear in "Retrato"--where the winged woman, who is also a woman of the water, cannot decide if she wants a certain lover or not--and in the "Geminiana" poems where the poet's aerial quality is associated with a lightness of heart conducive to brevity in love.

The geminine character of the poet is shown not only by specific poems in Repertório which reveal a poetic voice in conflict; Olga Savary's whole poetic work is permeated by tensions between opposite forces which pull the lyric speaker in different directions. The conflicts between the terrestrial and the aerial, between acceptance or rejection of bestiality, between full freedom of erotic expression and hesitancy in acknowledging the desire for erotic love are all emphasized by the poet's technique of juxtaposing opposite images. This tension between opposites reinforces the suggestion found in the poetry that the plenitude of erotic expression in Repertório Selvagem was not obtained without conflict and struggle. The sexually free and fulfilled woman of today needs to rise from the ashes of the past.

NOTES

[1] To be published in Rio de Janeiro by Nova Fronteira in 1987. Single numbers in the text after quotations refer to pages of the unpublished manuscript. M refers to the already published Magma which is now the last section of Repertório Selvagem.

[2] Savary's own term. "Entre Erótica e Mística" reveals the close connection between eroticism and poetic creation: "Antes que me esqueça, poesia, / as palavras não só combato:/durmo com elas." (Before I forget it, poetry, / I not only struggle with the words / I sleep with them (84). [Translation mine.]

[3] Espelho Provisório (Provisional Mirror) (Rio de Janeiro: Livraria José Olympio Editora, 1970). (Referred to in the text as EP).

[4] Sumidouro (Sinkhole) (São Paulo: Massao Ohno/João Farkas Editores, 1977). (Referred to in the text as SD).

[5] Altaonda (Highwave) (São Paulo/Salvador: Massao Ohno Editor/Edições Macunaíma, 1979).

[6] Magma (São Paulo: Massao Ohno/Roswitha Kempf Editores, 1984).

[7] Natureza Viva: Seleta dos Melhores Poemas de Olga Savary (Recife: Edições Pirata, 1983).

[8] Gilka Machado (1893-1980) was the first Brazilian woman to write erotic poetry. Writing poems with an intense sensuality which was daring for her time, Machado's poetry is considered a pioneering forerunner of modern female erotic poetry. Although none of her books were completely devoted to this theme, as is Olga Savary's Magma, her daring caused almost complete ostracism from Brazilian literary circles. (Fernando Py, ed., Gilka Machado: Poemas Completas: [Rio de Janeiro: Livraria Editora Cátedra, 1978]).

[9] In RS "love" and "sex" are used interchangeably, with both being expressed by the word "amor."

[10] The translations in brackets are the author's own versions of Tupi words. These are included in the texts of the poems, set apart by asterisks.

[11] The literal translations of the poems are mine.

[12] Note that Savary's portrayal of androgyny is not of an asexual being, nor of a person with both male and female characteristics existing concurrently, but rather a complex portrayal of shifting of gender roles.

[13] In some poems such as "Cantiga para Folha e Agua" (Song for Leaves and Water) (EP 95) the nature images of sun, water, and clouds become regional, referring to an earthy vision of a telluric, magical, and wild Brazil. This poem, in combination with her own testimony at the end of RS, reveals that Savary's sense of being Brazilian is intimately bound up with the Brazilian land in all its aspects, even its wild people. Hence her frequent use of the "selvagem" image and the use of Tupi, a Brazilian native language glorified by romantic writers in search of their native Indian roots. In this the "Russian-Amazonian" poet, as she calls herself in her testimony, is in step with so many Brazilians, from the romantics and modernists on, who living in

highly civilized urban centers, have felt the need to search for their Brazilian origins in the land and the native people.

[14] Note the poet's masculinization--"muso"--of the usually female muse.

[15] In interviews Savary often refers to herself as "geminiana," multifaceted and in conflict, since she was born under the astrological sign of the twins.